T0295666

Success on the Spectrum

Success on the Spectrum

Practical Strategies for Engaging Neurodiverse Audiences in Arts and Cultural Organizations

Emily Wiskera, Anna Smith,
Tina Sue Fletcher, Lynda Wilbur,
and Francis Yong Chen

ROWMAN & LITTLEFIELD
Lanham • Boulder • New York • London

Published by Rowman & Littlefield
An imprint of The Rowman & Littlefield Publishing Group, Inc.
4501 Forbes Boulevard, Suite 200, Lanham, Maryland 20706
www.rowman.com

86-90 Paul Street, London EC2A 4NE

British Library Cataloguing in Publication Information Available

Library of Congress Cataloging-in-Publication Data

Names: Wiskera, Emily, author.
Title: Success on the spectrum : practical strategies for engaging neurodiverse audiences in arts and cultural organizations / Emily Wiskera [and four others].
Other titles: Practical strategies for engaging neurodiverse audiences in arts and cultural organizations
Description: Lanham : Rowman & Littlefield, [2023] | Includes bibliographical references and index.
Identifiers: LCCN 2023041274 (print) | LCCN 2023041275 (ebook) | ISBN 9781538171011 (cloth) | ISBN 9781538171028 (paperback) | ISBN 9781538171035 (ebook)
Subjects: LCSH: Museums and people with disabilities—United States—Handbooks, manuals, etc. | Neurodiversity—United States. | Museums—Activity programs—United States—Handbooks, manuals, etc.
Classification: LCC AM160 .W57 2023 (print) | LCC AM160 (ebook) | DDC 069/.1087—dc23/eng/20230912
LC record available at https://lccn.loc.gov/2023041274
LC ebook record available at https://lccn.loc.gov/2023041275

To my family for encouraging a lifelong love of museums.
—Emily Wiskera

*To my mother, for her work with neurodiverse learners,
and to my Nasher team, who never ceases to amaze me.*
—Anna Smith

Here's one for the team: Rick, Rose, Lily, Austin, and Colt.
—Tina Fletcher

For my husband, Jeff, who shares in my joy for art and teaching.
—Lynda Wilbur

*I am forever grateful for the support of Masako, who always
believes in me, and my daughter, Maia, who always cheers for
me. I'm grateful to musicians and artists Chris Gates and Tim
Kerr of the Big Boys for telling me, "Start your own band!"*
—Francis Yong Chen

Contents

Acknowledgments

The authors would like to thank the many individuals and entities that helped this book take form. Edgar Pizarro and Alicia Chen, doctoral students in occupational therapy, offered research assistance, grant management, budget development, and—as seen throughout these pages—photo modeling. We are grateful to James Jillson, Vanessa Hadox, and Cale Peterson for sharing their depth of knowledge in the field of fundraising for education and access programs, and for their work in bringing these programs to fruition at the Nasher Sculpture Center. Amanda Zerangue advised on issues of intellectual property and copyright, John Humphrey provided insight into existing literature in the field of health sciences, and Taylor Woods contributed the perspective of a cultural educator at a performing arts venue. Thanks to Charles Harmon and Erinn Slanina for editorial support and advice.

We appreciate the Dallas Museum of Art and Nasher Sculpture Center for giving permission to use images of signage and sensory events, and the members of the Dallas Sensory Consortium for their shared desire to provide rich cultural experiences for neurodiverse learners and their families in North Texas. Thanks to Amanda Blake and Danielle Schulz for recognizing the need for access programs and paving the way with hard work and compassion, and to Dennis Schulze and his mom, Rachel, for improving the DMA's access programs with their thoughtful feedback and years of dedication. Thanks also to students, faculty, and staff at the Texas Woman's University School of Occupational Therapy for developing and implementing sensory-friendly programs with cultural partners.

Finally, we are immensely grateful to the many anonymous neurodiverse research participants and program attendees who have shared their unique and important perspectives.

Preface

Embracing Neurodiverse Audiences in Cultural Institutions

The role of arts and cultural institutions is changing. Once primarily viewed as stewards of objects, these institutions are increasingly being upheld as stewards of people—spaces where the diversity of human experience is asserted, explored, and celebrated. As such, they function as a type of community resource and should be equally accessible to all members of the diverse community. Individuals with autism spectrum disorder (ASD) account for a significant portion of the community, with an estimated one in thirty-six children in the United States diagnosed with autism.[1] Gradually, cultural institutions are putting forth more effort into creating tailored programs and resources to welcome neurodivergent visitors, including those with autism, who have historically been excluded from these spaces.

At a minimum, all cultural institutions must adhere to the accessibility standards set by the Americans with Disabilities Act (ADA), a civil rights law that prohibits discrimination against individuals with disabilities.[2] Now, beyond developing accommodations that support people with vision, hearing, and speech disabilities, cultural institutions are challenged to provide resources for people on the autism spectrum. Autism-focused programs and resources are tailored to reach beyond what the ADA requires of institutions to provide for visitors. The needle on the dial has shifted, and institutions are now tasked with providing programs that are not just accessible, but truly equitable. While there is great interest across the cultural sector to create more inclusive spaces for neurodivergent visitors, many fear that they lack the expertise or resources needed or simply don't know where to start.

The authors of the following chapters are all founding members of the Dallas Sensory Consortium, a growing collaboration between educators of our city's arts and cultural institutions and experts in the field of autism and occupational therapy. The consortium currently consists of two fine art museums, a transportation museum, a zoological park, and the city's public library system, guided by experts in the field of occupational therapy (OT) and autism. The Dallas Sensory Consortium was officially formed in 2017, but the founders had been working together for many years before that, with the shared goal of increasing equitable access to our institutions for visitors on the autism spectrum. Through this partnership, we have developed a set of best-practice guidelines and strategies for removing barriers to participation and promoting engagement within our community.

The team who created this book represents a variety of perspectives that may inform cultural educators with differing needs and experience levels. Three co-authors hail from the Dallas Museum of Art (DMA) and Nasher Sculpture Center, which are neighboring institutions in downtown Dallas, Texas. While similar in location, these museums are quite different in scope and capacity. The DMA is an encyclopedic museum that employs around two hundred fifty professional staff members including one dedicated to access programming. The Nasher is a much smaller institution focused on modern and contemporary sculpture with around forty professional staff and one team member who splits time between access and outreach programming. In this book, co-authors share strategies that have been effective in both environments.

The other two members of the team are an occupational therapy professor with a research doctorate in curriculum design and instruction and a licensed school psychologist. Occupational therapists work in educational, clinical, and natural settings where autistic people engage in various activities of daily living. Because neurodivergent people face different challenges across their lives, OTs focus on helping them develop the skills they need to successfully transition from school settings into community life. Professors of occupational therapy can create and use data-based research evidence for clinical and educational practice. School psychologists are trained to work at the individual and systemic levels to conduct evaluations and offer counseling or consultation. They use data-based research evidence about neurodivergent people to create appropriate programming that extends to the family and community systems.

Through *Success on the Spectrum: Practical Strategies for Engaging Neurodiverse Audiences in Arts and Cultural Institutions*, we offer advice based on what has worked for us and share the sometimes-difficult lessons we have learned along the way. However, this advice comes with the caution that there is no one-size-fits-all solution. To be truly successful, cultural institutions must respond to their unique community, and work within the resources and limitations of their institution.

We hope this book will be a helpful guide for anyone who wants to create effective programs and resources for neurodiverse visitors, such as those with autism, and echo the initiatives of the American Alliance of Museums as they focus on developing new standards for diversity, equity, accessibility, and inclusion.³ Content is specifically geared toward educators, administrators, and frontline staff at cultural institutions such as museums and galleries, performing arts venues, zoological and botanical parks, and libraries. Our practical goals for the reader are threefold:

- to understand the value of programming for neurodivergent visitors and be able to effectively communicate this to others;
- to build a toolkit of strategies and resources for neurodivergent visitors to have a successful visit to your institution, no matter your staff size, budget, or current stage of accessibility; and
- to develop evaluation strategies to gauge the impact of your offerings for neurodivergent visitors with resulting information that will help you improve, grow, and refine for the future.

Within *Success on the Spectrum,* we include a host of practical ideas and strategies designed to support cultural educators who are just beginning to engage with neurodiverse audiences as well as more seasoned practitioners looking to enhance existing programs. Content in this book is laid out roughly in order of the steps a cultural educator might take when developing, preparing for, implementing, and evaluating a program. The first section lays out a foundation: what are autism and neurodiversity and how do they shape someone's experience, how should cultural institution staff define and address the people they hope to connect with, and how should cultural educators co-create programs with neurodivergent stakeholders? The second section focuses on creating a vision for programming, including recommendations for achieving institutional buy-in and building a framework for long-term program success, an overview of common program models, and strategies for goal setting. In the third section, we offer tools to prepare your space and train your staff to welcome neurodivergent visitors, such as best practices in communicating with images and words, guidelines for developing resources such as success stories and schedules to help visitors prepare for and structure their experience, and techniques for training and educating institutional staff. The fourth section presents an overview of sensory processing along with field-tested ways to evaluate potential pitfalls in your environment, make changes or accommodations for the benefit of neurodiverse visitors, and create practical sensory spaces. The fifth section shares how the ideas and tools laid out in this book work in practice, and how they have been put to use in Dallas Sensory Consortium partner institutions with a healthy dose of lessons learned and suggestions for building an audience for programs. In the sixth and final section of this book, we offer strategies for fundraising, evaluation, and critical information for community researchers hoping to share findings with the wider field. Two appendixes round out our toolkit, with a glossary of helpful terms and annotated bibliography to direct further study.

While tailored programs and resources do require at least a minimal commitment of time and intention, the authors of *Success on the Spectrum* have been consistently surprised by the impact that even the simplest of solutions can offer. Cultural institutions exist for the benefit of all, and as we have discovered during our past decade of autism programming, what is good for *some* benefits *all*. Just as wheelchair ramps are used by those with carts or baby carriages, examples of disability accommodations benefitting a wider public are numerous and adaptive resources for autism are no different. We hope that the work we share in this book will be of use to you, our reader, in your efforts to make your own institution a more welcoming place for all visitors, and that the work that you do will be part of a ripple effect reaching across the cultural landscape and creating new connections and opportunities for those who have faced barriers to participation.

AUTHORS' NOTE: A WORD ABOUT TERMINOLOGY

In writing *Success on the Spectrum*, the authors were immediately faced with a decision—*neurodivergent, neuroatypical, pervasive developmental disorder (PDD), autism spectrum disorder (ASD), sensory processing disorder (SPD)*—what terminology should be used? Language is nuanced and context is important when selecting the right word to capture your intent. The members of the Dallas Sensory Consortium initially developed programming and resources that were specifically targeted to visitors with autism. In fact, the DMA originally had the word *autism* in the name of their family day event and summer camp. However, staff at participating venues soon noticed that the attendees of their events were not just those on the autism spectrum. Visitors with specific sensory needs were self-selecting to attend the programs, and the cultural institutions—who view themselves as a community resource and not a medical center—were happy for them to participate. Furthermore, staff realized that many of the participants who have autism also have concurrent cognitive disabilities or conditions such as ADHD, dyslexia, epilepsy, learning difficulties, and anxiety that fall under a wider umbrella of neurodiversity.

The term *neurodiversity* was coined by Australian sociologist Judy Singer to reflect the natural differences in thinking related to learning, mood, attention, sociability, and other mental functions.[4] Unlike autism, it is not a medical diagnosis, and because it embodies a changing number of conditions, including giftedness, it is often self-diagnosed by people during their school years. The authors of this book gravitate toward the term neurodiversity, as it frames specific needs and preferences as differences, not deficits. By creating tailored programs for neurodiverse communities (and in writing this book), the authors hope to promote spaces and experiences that can be enjoyed by a full spectrum of visitors.

For the purpose of this book, the authors agreed to use the term *neurodiverse* and *neurodivergent* generally, and *autism* or *autism spectrum disorder* when speaking more specifically about strategies or data that pertain to that community. The authors use the word *neurodivergent* when describing an individual, and *neurodiverse* when describing a community, network of people, or the strategies that apply to that broader audience.

For more on terminology related to neurodiversity and autism, you will find a full glossary of terms at the end of this book and a chapter about preferred nomenclature to help you select the words to describe your audiences intentionally and respectfully. With the understanding that what is good for some is beneficial to many, the authors of this book have shared tips and strategies to create positive experiences for a full spectrum of visitors who have a spectrum of sensory needs.

NOTES

1. M. J. Maenner, Z. Warren, A. R. Williams, et al. "Prevalence and Characteristics of Autism Spectrum Disorder among Children Aged 8 Years—Autism and Developmental Disabilities Monitoring Network, 11 Sites, United States, 2020," *Morbidity and Mortality Weekly Report* Surveill Summ 72, no. 2 (2023):1–14, DOI: http://dx.doi.org/10.15585/mmwr.ss7202a1.

2. A helpful primer to the Americans with Disability Act can be found via the US Department of Justice Civil Rights Division at https://www.ada.gov/topics/intro-to-ada/.

3. For more information see the American Alliance of Museum's October 2022 press release on embedding diversity and equity into museum accreditation standards: https://www.aam-us.org/2022/10/17/diversity-equity-to-become-required-for-museum-accreditation-standards/.

4. Judy Singer, *Neurodiversity: The Birth of an Idea*, 2017.

Part 1

UNDERSTANDING AND CONNECTING WITH NEURODIVERSE PEOPLE

Chapter One

Know Your Audience

*Characteristics of
Autism and Neurodiversity*

Why is it important for staff at cultural institutions to be knowledgeable about autism and neurodiversity? During a sensory-friendly program at the Dallas Museum of Art (DMA), a younger sister of a boy with autism independently approached a museum staff member. The sister tapped the staff member's shoulder and made a short, yet profound statement: "I like coming here because no one stares at my brother." Her words were simple, and her message was clear. The sister was feeling a sense of acceptance for her brother that wasn't typical when the family ventured out into the community. When the event attendees and facilitators saw children walking on tiptoe, repeatedly snapping their fingers, or flapping their arms, they did not react with stares and whispers. Instead, they reacted with acceptance because they, too, loved someone with autism. At the core of acceptance is understanding. The staff and visitors at the museum that day understood the characteristics and behavior associated with autism and simply accepted the children as they were. For that reason, we open *Success on the Spectrum* with a chapter designed to offer a foundational knowledge of the people your programming will serve.

Although this book, as a whole, is geared toward the concept of *neurodiversity*, and how people with a range of conditions may benefit from programming in cultural institutions, this chapter focuses specifically on understanding *autism*. Unlike neurodiversity, autism is a medical diagnosis, and many strategies for sensory-friendly or neuro-friendly programming have people with autism in mind as a core audience. With one out of every thirty-six American children being identified with autism spectrum disorder (ASD) in 2020, inclusive programs at cultural institutions are a welcome tool for meeting their needs. In their characteristics and prevalence report, the Centers for Disease Control (CDC) also reported that nearly 40 percent of children classified as being autistic also have an intellectual or developmental disability (IDD), which limits their ability to learn and function at an expected level for their age. At present, children with both ASD and IDD receive their diagnoses around the age of forty-three months, and those without intellectual disability learn of their ASD at about fifty-three months. This implies that as the number of cultural institution visitors with autism grows, their skill sets reflect increasing intellectual diversity, and many preschool children, in particular, will need a wide range of supports during their visits.[1]

In this chapter, we present a broad overview of autism through the lens of what a cultural educator might find helpful. This includes

- common behaviors or characteristics that contribute to an autism diagnosis;
- how these characteristics affect the experiences and perceptions of a person with autism; and
- general strategies that may improve the quality of a visit to a cultural institution for people with autism.

COMMON CHARACTERISTICS

There are many paths to an official autism diagnosis in the United States. According to the CDC, most children typically have met the definition of autism by age eight, and either have a written ASD diagnostic statement completed by a licensed healthcare provider or have a special education diagnosis of autism by this point.[2] For the 40 percent of these children who are also diagnosed with the co-occurring condition of intellectual and developmental disability (IDD), this means they have an IQ score of 70 or less. For reference purposes, an average intelligence IQ score is considered to be between 85 and 115, and an eight-year-old child with IDD who has an IQ of 70 will have a mental age of between five and six years.

The federal government began putting laws into place starting in 1975 to mandate that local education agencies identify, locate, and evaluate children with disabilities.[3] An understanding of the characteristics that often accompany ASD and the types of support or resources provided by school systems and healthcare providers can help cultural educators form a better understanding of whom their programs are serving and what these individuals may be accustomed to in school and home settings. Generally speaking, people with ASD or similar conditions meet diagnostic criteria that include difficulties interacting with others, having restricted patterns of behavior or interests, and exhibiting unusual sensitivities or reactions to sensory input.[4] The Centers for Disease Control and Prevention offers helpful resources on diagnostic criteria for those who want to learn more. [5]

Difficulties Interacting with Others

Social interaction and language skills are a significant factor in a diagnosis of ASD. When working to identify ASD in youth, a healthcare or educational diagnostic team evaluates a child's ability to use language, with particular focus on *pragmatic language* (basic conversational skills) as well as *expressive* and *receptive language* (the words someone uses to express themself and how well they understand others). People with autism have difficulty with nonverbal language, which includes the use of gestures, facial expressions, and body postures to communicate or add to the verbal communication being made by others. They may also face challenges when using language to communicate wants and needs or to show reciprocity in social communications. In cultural arts environments, this can create challenges when a young visitor with ASD is unable to communicate their questions and wonderings about exhibits, along with being able to self-advocate for their basic needs such as needing a break from crowds or locating bathrooms.

Evaluators may also look for difficulties relating to others, such as being unable to have a topical back-and-forth conversation. People with autism may be unable to see the perspective of others, such as discerning that another person is feeling sad through a combination of statements and facial expressions. These qualities may make it difficult to form friendships and share enjoyment from others' points of view. A person with autism might experience challenges with nonverbal communication, such as the use of eye contact and gesturing. Some individuals also face barriers to understanding relationships, such as problems shifting expectations as a situation changes, and difficulty maintaining a connection that is not concretely based. For example, these individuals may not respond to invitations to play or could have difficulty working on group projects.

Restricted Patterns of Behavior or Interests

People with autism may exhibit rigidity in their thinking or actions. This means that when their expectations are unmet for short-term outcomes or a set routine, they could experience anxiety. They may show rigidity in food preferences, what they wear, and how they schedule their day. Someone with autism may strongly prefer having tasks or activities only done in a specific order or in a specific place. In a school setting, for example, a field trip, picture day, or fire drill that changes the typical schedule can be very disruptive. At a cultural institution, unexpected alarms, rearranged exhibits, or unfamiliar staff may trigger anxiety.

People with autism may also exhibit a tendency to move or interact with objects in repetitive ways. Examples include autistic children who show a strong interest in lining up toys, performing very specific or repeated movements such as finger twisting or snapping, and using art materials in nontraditional ways, such as flicking paintbrushes. They may have speech patterns that are idiosyncratic or with unusual vocal pitch—such as monotones, whispers, or shouts—or repeating verbatim what they hear, also known as *echolalia*. Many people with autism often have preferred and specific interests in certain topics, such as famous works of art, genus-species names for animals, famous people, and geographical locations. One example of this was reported by Bendor Grosvenor, a noted British art historian, writer, and broadcaster, who identifies as autistic. He shared the following in his monthly blog for the *Art Newspaper*:

> Without autism I wouldn't be an art historian. I didn't realise it at the time, but my fascination with historical portraiture grew out of the social awkwardness many people with autism encounter. As a teenager, a special place for me was the National Portrait Gallery in London. . . . In it I created a world of characters I could interact with on my own terms, who didn't judge, and who even seemed to enjoy my close study. They became the friends I struggled to make. And then further afield, in other galleries and especially auction houses, I began to notice mistakes in the way portraits were catalogued, and through the thrill of art-historical discovery began a consuming quest for "sleepers." I'm also lucky to have a good visual memory, another benefit of what is called neurodiversity.[6]

Unusual Sensitivities or Reactions to Sensory Input

People with autism may have sensory needs and behaviors that differ from their neurotypical counterparts and might rely on a single or group of senses to provide a feeling of calm alertness, also known as self-regulation. This can include seeking deep pressure, comforting movements like rocking, being squeezed in a hug, and smelling or tasting items. They may also use their senses in unusual ways, such as looking at objects from unusual angles, being attracted to lights or reflections, or focusing on a specific part of an item rather than what the object is or does as a whole. One example of this focus would be looking at a small detail in a kinetic sculpture rather than activating the movement mechanism.

In addition, people with autism may be hypersensitive or hyposensitive to temperatures or pain. Some may be *sensory avoiding*, and show an aversion to certain smells, sounds, and textures, while others may be *sensory seeking*, and seek out smells, sounds, and textures—sniffing, listening to, or touching anything new in their world. In a cultural setting, this can present challenges when children cautioned with the adage to "look with their eyes" may instead prefer to explore artworks and other objects with their hands, foreheads, or tongues. Regarding sensory-driven behaviors, Elise Freed-Brown, formerly of the Smithsonian Institutions, stated:

This means anything in the museum that is not part of the exhibit but is also stimulating—for example bright lights, loud sounds, big crowds—should be toned down, turned off or removed. Providing special hours is a common and effective method for cutting out lots of stimuli, as a crowd itself induces stress, along with all the unexpected noises it brings with it. Museums can also dim lights, lower volumes and be cognizant of other possible distractions.

Here, Freed-Brown identified environmental factors that can overwhelm the senses. You will find an in-depth discussion of the type of accommodations she mentions in chapter 14.

NURTURING A NEURODIVERSE POPULATION

While schools may be much better equipped to provide the kind of structure that helps a student with autism thrive, cultural institutions can benefit from understanding and, when possible, mirroring the strategies that are common to the everyday environment of these students. In school, support for children with autism often manifests in a structured routine that provides consistency in their day-to-day functioning. This may also be extended to home or community settings through consultation or support such as in-home and community-based training, which help children develop vital skills for functioning in settings beyond the classroom. For cultural institutions, some of these strategies include

• Helping visitors with autism cope with new situations through tools like *success stories*, which help them prepare for what to expect and what is expected of them in a given situation.
• Giving visitors a way to communicate their emotional state, such as a chart depicting different emotions, and sharing methods they might use to cope with any specific situation.
• In some cases, using a contingency-based reinforcement system—offering a tangible reward for completing a task—can help a person to agree to do something they otherwise might not.
• For some visitors, providing them with videos to model desired behavior prior to attending an event can provide opportunities to practice before they step out into the community.

Combining these tools can offer an even greater opportunity for success when asking a visitor to do something novel or engage in an unwanted activity such as quietly waiting in line or refraining from touching something. In school, students with autism receive social skills training as part of their educational support, and language supports such as assistive technology devices from speech and language pathologists and occupational therapists. In schools, this special program tailored to someone's unique skill set is called an individualized educational program/plan (IEP), which contains goals and strategies to support a student's success across settings, whether in school, at home, or in the community.

Beyond IEPs, schools may also provide support by developing and using an autism supplement.[7] This can include programming that extends beyond typical school hours, including community outings. Other considerations include modified schedules; parent, community-based or in-home training; behavior plans; vocational postsecondary academics; the availability of competent school staff for supporting students with autism; social skills instruction; communication interventions such as pictorial signage; and training sessions available to educational faculty and staff. These supports are designed to intervene when the child is at home or in public, including visiting community entities such as museums, zoos, libraries, performance halls, and other cultural venues. Parents often want their neurodivergent children to learn life skills and to participate in their community, and a cultural setting can be ideal for this.[8]

Translating these supports to an event at a cultural institution might include

- offering sensory-friendly programming outside of normal operating hours;
- modifying activities for different cognitive, skill, and focus levels;
- planning for communication supports such as multimodal signage and *communication cards* (a set of pictures or icons a visitor can use to show what they want, need, or have questions about);
- developing *success stories* to promote and reinforce desired behavior in both familiar and unfamiliar environments;
- extending age ranges for events to accommodate participants with differing abilities;
- collaborating with autism specialists on event planning and implementation; and
- training staff to ensure they can effectively and respectfully interact with neurodivergent visitors and their families.

STAYING CURRENT

Because the field of autism research is complex and quickly changing, proactively working to stay abreast of current findings and best practices is always a good idea. Co-author Francis Yong Chen shares the sources he finds useful:

To follow ongoing research on autism, I check the Autism Research Centre at the University of Cambridge.[9] Their site is easy to navigate and includes both research and advocacy resources. Another researcher in the area of autism that I follow is Simon Baron-Cohen.[10] Although there are many researchers around the world, Baron-Cohen's studies and publications are always interesting and innovative. The National Institute of Mental Health is a warehouse of current and past data and evidence-based research on autism.[11] Often the articles are free to download. Finally, Spectrum is a useful warehouse of current research and news related to autism.[12]

Your knowledge about visitors with autism and related forms of neurodiversity will grow as you develop and refine programs and resources to support them. A research-based awareness of what shapes the experiences of these audiences goes hand in hand with the first-person interactions that will help you build a nuanced understanding of their needs. In other words, learning can make you a better educator, and your real-world experiences can direct your future study.

NOTES

1. Matthew J. Maenner, Zachary Warren, Ashley Robinson Williams, et al., "Prevalence and Characteristics of Autism Spectrum Disorder among Children Aged 8 Years—Autism and Developmental Disabilities Monitoring Network, 11 Sites, United States, 2020," *Morbidity and Mortality Weekly Report* Surveill Summ 72, no. 2 (2023): 1, DOI: http://dx.doi.org/10.15585/mmwr.ss7202a1.

2. Maenner, "Prevalence and Characteristics of Autism Spectrum Disorder."

3. US Department of Education. "Sec. 300.111 Child Find." Individuals with Disabilities Education Act, May 3, 2017. https://sites.ed.gov/idea/regs/b/b/300.111.

4. American Psychiatric Association. *Diagnostic and Statistical Manual of Mental Disorders,* 5th ed., text rev. (Washington, DC: APA Publishing, 2022), https://doi .org/10.1176/appi.books.9780890425787.

5. Centers for Disease Control and Prevention, "Autism Spectrum Disorder (ASD): Diagnostic Criteria," https://www.cdc.gov/ncbddd/autism/hcp-dsm.html.

6. Bendor Grosvenor, "'Autism Made Me an Art Historian. But Museums Must Do More to Welcome Disabled and Neurodiverse Communities,'" *The Art Newspaper—International Art News and Events*, March 3, 2021, https://www.theartnewspa per.com/2021/03/03/autism-made-me-an-art-historian-but-museums-must-do-more -to-welcome-disabled-and-neurodiverse-communities.

7. An example of the Autism Supplement requirements for the state of Texas can be found at https://tea.texas.gov/academics/special-student-populations/special -education/programs-and-services/autism.

8. Jeffrey W. H. MacCormack, Ian A. Matheson, and Nancy L. Hutchinson, "An Exploration of a Community-Based LEGO Social-Skills Program for Youth

with Autism Spectrum Disorder," Western University, 2015, https://hdl.handle.net /10133/5135.

9. https://www.autismresearchcentre.com/.
10. https://www.autismresearchcentre.com/staff/simon-baron-cohen/.
11. https://www.nimh.nih.gov/health/trials/autism-spectrum-disorders-asd.
12. https://www.spectrumnews.org/.

Chapter Two

Responding to Culture Shifts
Identity and Terminology

Many cultural institutions have expressed legitimate concerns about the language they use in documentation and programming related to autism and other forms of neurodiversity. This chapter explores how people with autism and other neurodivergent individuals have taken on the challenge of labeling.

Our goal for this chapter is to offer readers a fuller understanding of how words can shape perceptions of autism and neurodiversity. With this in mind, we will explore

- the meaning and origin of the term *neurodiversity*;
- language used in legal and medical contexts to describe autism;
- the use of *person-first* and *identity-first* language; and
- terminology to use or avoid when discussing autism and neurodiversity.

NORMALIZING NEURODIVERSITY

The context of neurodiversity has become a call to social justice. Australian sociologist Judy Singer coined the term *neurodiversity* in the late 1990s. Singer, who identifies as neurodivergent, said,

> Neurodiversity refers to the virtually infinite neuro-cognitive variability within Earth's human population. It points to the fact that every human has a unique nervous system with a unique combination of abilities and needs. Neurodiversity is a subset of biodiversity, a term mostly used for the purpose of advocating for the conservation of species.[1]

As a reflection of its entrance into popular culture, the term *neurodiverse* is now defined in the online Oxford Dictionary, which notes the term's frequent use in conjunction with individuals on the autism spectrum, and describes neurodivergent people as, "Showing patterns of thought or behaviour that are different from those of most people, though still part of the normal range in humans."[2] In contrast to earlier thinking, the importance here is on situating behaviors and thoughts of neurodivergent people within a range of normalcy. Neurodiversity describes the natural differences in our brains related to learning, mood, socialization, attention, and other mental functions. It can also be used to describe people with attention deficit disorder, dyspraxia, dyslexia, and other neurological differences. Unlike earlier medical models, neurodiversity emphasizes difference, not deficiency, and argues that mental diversity is necessary within a flourishing community.[3] The terms *neurodiverse* and *neurodiversity* are used when describing a community or group of people, but *neurodivergent* is used to describe an individual. This line of thought follows that there is no such thing as a neurodiverse individual, as it describes a larger trend that requires looking at a group of people.

While terminology surrounding neurodiversity is still evolving, words associated with autism have been around for many years, and we will focus on tackling them. The term *autism* is also not capitalized in written documents because it is not someone's name. Start with a lowercase letter *a*, even when writing out autism or autism spectrum disorder.

DISORDER, DISEASE, DISABILITY

Some people might bristle when they hear the phrase *autism spectrum disorder* and wonder how the term *disorder* even found its way into the name of the condition. Occasionally, people unfamiliar with the term inadvertently slip the word disease or disability in there, too. The notion that having autism is a disorder can be offensive to people who identify as part of a neurodiverse population. Autism advocate Temple Grandin famously stated, "If I could snap my fingers and be nonautistic, I would not. Autism is part of what I am."

Understanding why autism is considered a disorder or developmental disability is helpful. The road to an autism diagnosis is not a straightforward path, and the time of diagnosis is often dependent on many factors, including access to healthcare services, cultural beliefs, and even birth order. Many families do not realize their child has atypical behavior or signs of autism until a neurotypical child comes along and provides a comparison. Examples include children who had not attended preschool or other childcare services before they entered school or who have no siblings or close contacts their age, such as neighbor children or siblings. Without a comparison, many families assume all is typical or that their child will grow out of unusual behaviors when they enter school. Regardless of these circumstances, many children with autism begin their lives without apparent differences. Still, by the age of two, difficulties in communication, social skills, and sensory behaviors, among other things, begin to manifest themselves, which is why autism is considered a developmental or neurodevelopmental disorder.

Autism is not considered a disease for many reasons. First, a disease is characterized by the body's response to either internal or external factors. These factors disrupt either body structure or functions. Typically, professionals can determine a cause. Medical professionals and educators have not yet identified these factors in autistic people, although the hunt is on. A current best practice is to avoid words implying autism is a medical condition and to use nonmedical words instead. An example is using the word *signs* rather than symptoms. Current practices also refer to co-existing or multiple disorders such as intellectual disability or speech delay as *associated conditions* instead of comorbidities.

The term *disability* refers to how a disorder or disease impacts a person's condition. For example, to have the legal right to receive special services through a public school, a child must have a legally recognized disability applied to them in some form, such as developmental delay or intellectual disability. Once educators identify the disability, they develop an individualized educational plan (IEP) for the student and provide specific selected services. A legal definition of disability differs from an unofficial definition of disability, which is rooted in personal beliefs and external realities. Universal design, a practice of providing environmental support to individuals so they can access and understand their surroundings, has removed many barriers that once disabled individuals. Famous examples of surmounted barriers that have reduced disability include curb cuts, ramps, grab bars, and appropriately sized toilets in public restrooms. Many individuals previously disabled by environmental barriers may no longer see themselves in this light because of universal design practices. These examples make it easier to see how disability is a fluid term compared to definitions of disorder and disease.

The gist of discussing the three Ds (disorder, disease, disability) associated with autism is to realize that while the words may evoke adverse reactions in present times, they are rooted in terminology that has social, cultural, and legal reasoning applied to their development and use. While some individuals may insist that they are not disabled, a designation of disability may allow them access to special services that improve their ability to function and optimize their independence.

Now, on to the challenge of person- or condition-first language. Many decisions on using person- or condition-first language are rooted in how people come of age and the terminology in vogue when they formed their identities. Times and attitudes change, but we offer some helpful guidelines to follow.

PERSON OR CONDITION FIRST?

Have you ever found yourself attempting to describe a person with autism—or an autistic person, or a neurodivergent person, or a person on the spectrum—and you feel like throwing in the towel? You want to say the right thing and not offend anyone. You want to be politically correct while being sensitive to individual preferences. Welcome to the club! At present time, there is no consensus on preferred autism terminology—whether you are autistic or not. This chapter offers food for thought regarding the preferred language when describing autism identity and using autism terminology. It seems to change every day. Ask someone with autism about the preferred nomenclature for your location and time if you have any doubts about best practices.

Person-first language has been the default language choice since the mid-1970s and was considered both a sign of respect and a social model for health professionals in research and clinical practice. Person-first language presents a condition as a neutral characteristic instead of a negative attribute. As a result of this way of looking at things, language that grouped people solely based on their unique conditions fell out of favor. Because of this, people with autism are no longer referred to as *autistics*, as they were in the old days. According to person-first language, saying *a person with autism* is the go-to description. Still, things have been changing, and *identity-first* language is becoming a preferred choice by many. Psychologists refer to this as a *minority model* where differences are considered a part of a person's traits. There is no reference to it being something that needs to be cured, and it is not considered a failing but embraces the condition as a natural variant of the human experience. With this, wording that implies someone is a victim or suffering from a condition is not used.

Identity-first language is also often seen as a reflection of pride in being described as autistic or having other conditions. An individual is referred to as an *autistic person* when using identity-first or condition-first language. Some autistic people will be happy to tell you that autism isn't something they *have*—instead, they may describe it as a foundational part of their core—not something they can put down or take off, like a purse. The degree to which people embrace using identity-first language varies along with their self-identity, which forms in different ways and at different times for everyone. A person who has grown up in a family full of relatives with autism has had a very different formative experience than a person who is the only one among their family or friends to have autism.

VOCABULARY MIX-UPS ARE OKAY

To make things even more confusing, mixed use of person-first and identity-first terminology has become increasingly commonplace. For example, magazine authors and editors writing for and about people with autism often report that mixing person-first and identity-first language in publications is an acceptable writing practice and that they defer to a writer's preferences. If someone is writing an article *about* people with autism, the current trend is to ask them how they would like to be identified. In their published recommendations for the American Psychological Association, Dunn and Andrews[4] recommended that psychologists use identity-first language alongside person-first constructions to respond to disability groups that advocate for all people to be treated with dignity while still upholding both scientific and professional standards. By embracing this practice, they held that stigmas associated with disabilities are reduced, stereotyping is minimized, and prejudice is lessened. In other words, they recommended people put the cookies on the table and not try to hide special conditions. The more frequently seen a condition is, the more everyone's thoughts and behaviors are shaped by their familiarity with it.[5]

The takeaway for cultural educators is to develop a nuanced understanding of when person-first language is appropriate and when an identity-first approach is preferred. A good rule of thumb is to play it safe and use person-first language in institutional communication. When working with program participants on a repeated basis, you may learn of a personal preference for identity-first language, which you can then use for that individual. The ADA National Network offers guidelines for writing about people with disabilities which reinforce this practice.[6] Keep in mind that social norms are ever-changing, and a generational shift can make one era's respectful terminology into the next era's outdated language. It is your responsibility to educate yourself and stay up to date.

PREFERRED VOCABULARY FOR DESCRIBING
AUTISM OR OTHER FORMS OF NEURODIVERSITY

After realizing there is no one answer to the question of the best choice regarding identity- or person-first language, things get even murkier. The word *autism* isn't the only preferred terminology to describe, well, autism.

Certain words are out, and others are in. For starters, some autism rights activists now rail against organizations that seek to promote cures for people with autism, such as the practice of locating biomarkers or genes that identify the condition of autism in utero. They argue that if or when it becomes possible to eliminate autism by terminating pregnancies, this practice would narrow the natural range of neurodiversity in humankind. They call for autistic people and their allies to join in celebrating the unique possibilities inherent in being neurodiverse.

In general, deficit-based models of many health conditions that fall outside normal ranges give way to strengths-based paradigms, such as the mental health movement Mad Pride and the neurodiversity movement Autistic Self Advocacy Network. These movements describe common differences, including how others should behave toward people with these conditions and interact with them rather than trying to repair something that movement members insist is not broken.[7] In the case of autism, instead of focusing on curbing the behaviors that have long been described as deficits—social, communication, and sensory differences—activists advocate for supporting the unique skill sets of autistic persons, such as having a deep focus, hypervigilance, and exceptional observational skills. According to autism advocates, it is all a matter of perspective.

VOCABULARY THAT IS OUT OF
FAVOR FOR DESCRIBING AUTISM

Along with learning the vast array of words that are encouraged when referring to autism, some words do not fit the current mind-set of autism activism and awareness. Here are a few pointers to help make some essential distinctions—and they are probably easier to identify and remove from your vocabulary than making complicated decisions on whether to go with person-first or identity-first language.

For starters, get rid of all notions that autism is a medical condition or that it is *special,* as in special education. *High-functioning* is another term on its way out the door. The idea of autism as a spectrum condition is more descriptive and doesn't create a hierarchy of levels of function. The condition of Asperger's syndrome or being an *Aspie* used to refer to individuals diagnosed with this condition, but nowadays, Asperger's syndrome is not considered a diagnosis— and it doesn't help matters that Dr. Asperger himself was reportedly a Nazi collaborator who contributed to the demise of countless "inferior" children.[8]

Terms describing things surrounding people with autism, such as *applied behavioral analysis* or *ABA,* have also become subject to scrutiny since they lean toward the cure versus acceptance paradigm. Interestingly, the month of April—long famous for being autism awareness month—has also taken a hit. Some autism activists feel that having acceptance instead of awareness is a better and clearer directive for people— it reflects the current mind-set of acceptance without trying to change.

So, what's left? Try your hand at words that reflect being different but not defective. Right now, the term *neurodiverse* is widespread, and this word choice is reflected throughout the book. *Neurodifferences* is a term that's also batted around. If a person has a variety of challenges, they might be considered as having a *neurodisorder*. Programming for neurodiverse people might be called *neuro-friendly*. Words have power, but no more power than people have. It's perfectly reasonable to voice your concerns about what to say and when. People with autism and their circle of family, friends, and coworkers can help you find your way, so don't be afraid to ask.[9]

Because we have stressed the importance of listening to and considering the viewpoints of all people, let's conclude this chapter by hearing what neurodivergent individuals have to say. Their comments in textbox 2.1 reflect a range of ways to describe the experience of autism.

TEXTBOX 2.1.
LEARNING FROM THE MASTERS: LANGUAGE
AUTISTIC PEOPLE USE WHEN DESCRIBING THEMSELVES

At Texas Woman's University, researchers asked autistic young adults the following question: *From your perspective, what kinds of social skills and behaviors do people with autism have that tend to impact their participation [in daily life]?*[1]

Their responses reflected various positions on this topic, from dwelling on the difficulties they experienced because of being autistic to feeling glad they were different from others. For some, embracing the differences inherent in being autistic was a developmental process that emerged over time.

According to one participant, "It's not easy for people with autism to come on and talk about themselves, but I'm slowly learning how to grow into manhood as a person with autism. It's not easy. I'll tell you that much. And it's pretty difficult . . . it's just a slow learning process."

Another respondent wrote about a different issue that frequently came up with young adults and said, "Some people choose not to ID [identify] because there's a stigma about it. But luckily, with my employees and with my community, I feel comfortable with that. And I think it's better [self-identifying autism] than not."

A third person expressed a different point of view, choosing to emphasize how autism isn't necessarily a bad thing, and said, "The special programs . . . at first, I thought since I was in the special program, I wasn't getting as good of stuff as the people in the normal program did, but then I found out people in the normal program did harder stuff. So, I was proud of being in a special one."

NOTE

1. Anonymous survey responses from unpublished research.

NOTES

1. Judy Singer, "What Is Neurodiversity?" *Reflections on Neurodiversity* (blog), accessed January 4, 2023, https://neurodiversity2.blogspot.com/p/what.html.
2. "Neurodiverse," *Oxford Learner's Dictionaries,* accessed January 4, 2023, https://www.oxfordlearnersdictionaries.com/us/definition/english/neurodi verse?q=neurodiverse.
3. Thomas Armstrong, *The Power of Neurodiversity: Unleashing the Advantages of Your Differently Wired Brain* (Boston: Da Capo, 2011).
4. Dana S. Dunn and Erin E. Andrews, "Person-First and Identity-First Language: Developing Psychologists' Cultural Competence Using Disability Language," *American Psychologist* 70, no. 3 (2015): 255–64, https://doi.org/10.1037/a0038636.
5. Jiedi Lei, Lauren Jones, and Mark Brosnan, "Exploring an e-Learning Community's Response to the Language and Terminology Use in Autism from Two Massive Open Online Courses on Autism Education and Technology Use," *Autism* 25, no. 5 (2021): 1349–67, https://doi.org/10.1177/1362361320987963.
6. ADA National Network, Guidelines for Writing about People with Disabilities, https://adata.org/factsheet/ADANN-writing.
7. Ginger A. Hoffman, "Public Mental Health without the Health? Challenges and Contributions from the Mad Pride and Neurodiversity Paradigms," *Developments in Neuroethics and Bioethics,* 2019: 289–326, https://doi.org/10.1016/bs.dnb.2019 .07.003.
8. Herwig Czech, "Hans Asperger, National Socialism, and "Race Hygiene" in Nazi-era Vienna," *Molecular Autism* 9, no. 1 (2018): 1-43, https://doi.org/10.1186 /s13229-018-0208-6.
9. Kristen Bottema-Beutel, Steven K. Kapp, Jessica Nina Lester, Noah J. Sasson, and Brittany N. Hand, "Avoiding Ableist Language: Suggestions for Autism Researchers," *Autism in Adulthood* 3, no. 1 (2021): 18–29, https://doi.org/10.1089 /aut.2020.0014; Silvana Galderisi, Andreas Heinz, Marianne Kastrup, Julian Beezhold, and Norman Sartorius, "Toward a New Definition of Mental Health," *World Psychiatry* 14, no. 2 (June 4, 2015): 231–33. https://doi.org/10.1002/wps.20231; May, Cynthia. "An Investigation of Attitude Change in Inclusive College Classes Including Young Adults with an Intellectual Disability." *Journal of Policy and Practice in Intellectual Disabilities* 9, no. 4 (2012): 240–46. https://doi.org/10.1111/jppi.12013.

Chapter Three

Nothing About Us Without Us

Co-creating with Neurodiverse Communities

In the United States, many of us were in an elementary school classroom when we first encountered the phrase "no taxation without representation." This political slogan, originating from the American Revolution, is taught to us as children to illustrate a pillar of American democracy—that no policy should be created without the representation and participation of those it affects.

While this principle is generally agreed upon as a point of fairness, the idea did not apply to disability communities until recent decades. Around the passage of the Americans with Disabilities Act (ADA) in 1990, the disabilities rights movements took up the rallying cry "nothing about us without us."[1] Activists with disabilities adopted this phrase to demand that their voices be included in the creation of legislation about them. Ultimately, more than four hundred individuals with disabilities have been credited as consultants and architects of the ADA.[2]

Thirty years later, this idea is now being championed and demanded in the cultural sector, particularly when designing programs and events for specialized audiences. From *serving* to *engaging*, arts and cultural institutions are moving away from the charitable model of interaction to a model of collaboration and equal partnership with community constituents. A foundational practice is *co-creation*, the process of partnering and designing with stakeholders who have lived experience.

While the idea of lived experience may seem simple, its importance cannot be overstated. Lived experience is the relationship between identity and personal knowledge of the world. Lived experience is like having a front-row seat, rather than a bird's eye view; it is with this perspective that one can see the nuances of experience beyond the dominant narrative. At the Dallas Museum of Art (DMA), the perspective of those with lived experience has been at the core of successful programming for neurodivergent visitors. After all, who better to answer the question, "What makes a good experience for neurodivergent visitors?" than neurodivergent visitors themselves?

This chapter discusses the importance of including neurodiverse voices in program planning in an authentic, meaningful way. Readers should expect to learn

- why co-creation with neurodiverse audiences is important;
- how educators can connect with co-creators through an example from the Dallas Museum of Art; and
- the six most important steps in the co-creation process.

SEEKING PARTNERSHIP, NOT VALIDATION

For co-creation to be authentic, it must happen at all levels of decision making. Ideally, co-creation is present from the beginning and develops somewhat organically. It happens when an authentic relationship is nurtured between your institution and your target community constituents. All specialized programming should begin with dialogue and relationship-building. When you are excited to engage with a new audience, holding off on program planning can be a challenge. However, it is of paramount importance that you listen to and learn from those with lived experience to create a foundation of knowledge before starting any program planning or ideation.

A common shortcoming in community collaboration is that institutions turn to those with lived experience for a rubber stamp of approval after an event or program has been designed—when it is too late to incorporate feedback or make any changes. Nothing damages trust between an institution and its co-creators like making one feel that their feedback isn't valuable, or that their identity is being used to merely give the appearance of community support.

FINDING CO-CREATORS

The idea for the DMA's autism programming first arose when a member of the museum's education team volunteered to support a sensory-friendly performance at the local children's theater, purely out of personal interest. At this performance, she saw the demand for sensory-friendly events and met many families who had children with autism or sensory-based needs. By continuing to volunteer at the children's theater, the DMA's staff member got to know some of the families who regularly attended the sensory-friendly performances. During informal conversations at the theater, the DMA educator shared where she worked and asked the families if they had ever gone to the museum. Many families shared the sentiment that they wanted to visit the museum but felt there were too many barriers for their children to be successful. After exchanging contact information with interested families, she continued the conversation over email and phone calls, learning what the families would want to do at the museum and what barriers stood in the way. It was through these interactions that museum staff found its first co-creators.

Just as museum staff found collaborators in the audience of the sensory-friendly theater, a great first step in finding co-creators is to identify local knowledge networks and interest groups. What other institutions are engaging with your intended audience? Are there local collectives or places commonly frequented by neurodiverse communities? Through a simple web search using the search term "sensory-friendly," you may find local movie theaters offering *low-sensory* film showings featuring house lights up and volume levels down, or special interest groups like Jazz Hands for Autism or the Musical Autist. Reach out to the groups that appear to share your values. Start attending or volunteering at their events to become a familiar face and part of their network.

As you begin offering programs and events for neurodiverse audiences, you will find valuable co-creators through your attendees. These individuals will be familiar with and invested in your institution. They are already coming to your institution and are motivated to improve programs and offerings for themselves and others. An added benefit is that co-creators tend to be tapped into local networks and can spread the word about your offerings. If you build trust and demonstrate that you value honest feedback, program attendees tend to be very giving of their time and perspective.

At the DMA, a valuable co-creator has been a young man who began attending our autism programming at the age of five. After turning sixteen, he began volunteering at the check-in table of our Sensory Days to fulfill service hour requirements for his school. While welcoming participants to the museum, he came up with several ideas to improve the experience. Now all attendees are greeted with a stress ball or plastic beaded necklace, which functions not only as a welcome gift but can be used as a fidget to help control stress during the event. When exiting the event, attendees can now vote on their favorite activity by placing a dot sticker on an image of what they liked best. Our co-creator's idea for audience feedback has brought in even more voices and made a co-creator out of every attendee, with minimal demand on their time.

Just as important, however, is the perspective of those who are not coming to your events or making use of your resources. This form of co-creation can be less demanding of the individual's time, taking the form of a casual conversation or response survey. Is the barrier simply a lack of familiarity with your institutional offerings or do other barriers stand in the way of participation? How could you not only remove barriers but entice participation? Make it known that you want to shape your institution into a place they would be comfortable and excited to visit.

While co-creation typically means partnering with individuals outside of your institution, it can also happen with others outside of your immediate team or department. An incredibly valuable co-creator has been someone from within our museum staff, an autistic Gallery Attendant Supervisor.[3] As his position is outside of the education team, this is someone we would not have worked with closely on our programs had he not self-identified as being autistic and offered his help. A certain level of trust between staff, as well as his knowledge and interest in our programming, led to this fruitful relationship. As a co-creator, he has helped develop staff training materials on the topic of creating positive experiences for neurodiverse audiences. Additionally, he has co-created communication cards that are used by gallery attendants to positively convey our rules to visitors during events for autistic audiences. His lived experience, as an autistic individual and someone with deep knowledge of the museum, has been vital. See figure 3.1 for an example of a rules-based communication card.

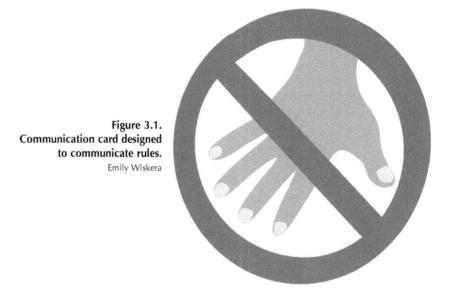

Figure 3.1.
Communication card designed
to communicate rules.
Emily Wiskera

Do not touch

THE SIX STEPS OF SUCCESSFUL CO-CREATION

When it comes to co-creation, the possibilities are limitless. Because this way of working can take so many forms, it can feel overwhelming and difficult to know where to start. The following six steps can help you co-create in your community on a scale that meets the particularities of your institution and community.

Step 1: Make Contact and Build Trust

The first step in co-creation is establishing a positive relationship with your potential collaborators. Just like any relationship, it is important to demonstrate shared values and a sincere interest in getting to know them. This can be done by nurturing a relationship with someone who already frequents your institution or identifying new co-creators by attending, supporting, and networking at local events that engage with your key constituents.

Step 2: Throw Preconceptions Out the Window

Co-creation is built on the knowledge that you can never understand someone's lived experience like the individual themselves. To really get to know your audience, it is important to ditch any preconceived notions and assumptions. Instead, frame these ideas as questions to your co-creator. If you assume that all people with autism have difficulty communicating, consider asking, "What are your preferred methods of communication? What things are helpful or make communication difficult?" Ask and really listen.

Step 3: Define the Scope

Co-creation can, and should, take many forms. At the DMA, the co-creation of autism programs has primarily occurred through community listening sessions, casual phone calls, email surveys, and project-based employment. Guest artists with autism have led demonstrations at Sensory Days. Neurodivergent musicians have performed low-sensory or modified sound and lighting sets at Family Festivals. Adults with autism have conducted sensory audits of the museum. Think critically about what forms of co-creation you have the resources to support and where it would be most beneficial for the visitor experience.

Step 4: Establish Roles and Expectations

Be direct with your co-creators about your goals and expectations. When working with a co-creator, you should be direct about individual roles, the scope of the project, expected time commitments, and what you can offer in return. This will vary based on the type of partnership, but even a phone call should start with, "This call will take about fifteen minutes of your time. I am asking for feedback to help positively shape our autism programs to better meet the interests of our participants." When fifteen minutes has elapsed, end the phone conversation. It is important to stick to your word, even if it means asking for a follow-up conversation where you restate goals and expectations for that secondary phone call.

For deeper collaborations, like internships, community advisory groups, and work opportunities, it is additionally important to define and manage expectations.[4] Just as you expect your co-creators to give honest feedback, open communication is equally important for institutional staff. Honesty about limitations of staff or resources can help you avoid disappointing co-creators with the result. Not all ideas may be feasible, or they may have a longer implementation timeline than your co-creator might anticipate.

Step 5: Center Neurodiverse Voices

A good collaborator amplifies community voices and speaks with, not for, them. An important aspect of co-creation is that it helps community members practice advocating for themselves and their community. Give your co-creators a platform to speak and give them due credit. After all, those with lived experience are the most important leaders in creating change.

Step 6: Continue the Conversation

Even though your program may have taken place, or your resource was produced, the work isn't over. Build in time for a debrief conversation with your co-creator. Your questions should not only be focused on the finished program or resource itself but should also be aimed at the experience of working with the institution. What went well? What was a challenge? What would improve the experience for co-creators in the future? How did your shared efforts impact your audience? Take a moment to document what you learned and share in your success. Then continue the process of co-creation. Listen, experiment, learn, and refine.

THE EXPONENTIAL BENEFITS OF CO-CREATION

Co-author of this book, Emily Wiskera, recalls a time when she became aware of the limits of her own perspective. Through the process of co-creation with neurodiverse visitors, Emily realized that she had been programming around her own sensory preferences. As someone who enjoys exploring textures and has a strong aversion to loud noises, the events Emily designed offered many tactile experiences in the art studio and prioritized keeping the event quiet. By designing programs with the input of co-creators, events now meet a wider range of sensory needs and preferences. Co-creators have designed engagement opportunities for sensory-seekers and sensory-avoiders of all types, resulting in flexible programs where attendees can choose to participate in ways that meet their own needs and desires.

Co-creation opens your creative process to a wide range of voices. Chief among these are your community constituents, the people who ultimately matter most. Each co-creator brings a unique perspective to the table, which will result in experiences that meet the needs and interests of a larger population.

Neurodiverse communities are practiced at speaking two languages—their experience and the system. They are aware of the gaps and solutions in the system and can speak directly to how changes would impact their experience. While the co-creation of our programs may be focused on better addressing the needs of people with disabilities, the real magic is that it allows us to think beyond disability.

No person is defined by a singular identity, and this is of course true of people with disabilities. We are all full people with unique skills, joys, challenges, and interests. Co-creation naturally helps our institutions take an intersectional approach. Our co-creators have helped us to learn about and better engage with various issues of identity, from what language is spoken at home, to common interests like comics and video games. By involving multiple perspectives, we can think beyond what is needed for basic access to what is wanted for an engaging and dynamic experience. The process of co-creation helps our institutions continually learn and improve, stay relevant to our communities, and celebrate the human experience in all its wonderful variations.

NOTES

1. Paul Harpur, "Nothing About Us Without Us: The UN Convention on The Rights of Persons with Disabilities," *Oxford Research Encyclopedia of Politics,* May 24, 2017, https://oxfordre.com/politics/view/10.1093/acrefore/9780190228637.001.0001/acre fore-9780190228637-e-245.

2. The full list appeared in the *Able* newspaper, July 2010 issue; portions were reprinted, with the names interspersed at the tops and bottoms of pages in the July 2015 issue, found at http://ablenews.com/wp-content/uploads/2015/06/ADA-pages-for-web site.pdf and http://ablenews.com/wp-content/uploads/2015/06/JULY-2015-LI-1.pdf.

3. The DMA typically defaults to people-first language. In this case, however, the individual prefers identity-first language.

4. One should be mindful that co-creators of access programs and resources should be paid on the same scale that has been established for collaborators, experts, or guest artists. The expertise that is being offered is just as valuable.

Part 2

LAYING THE GROUNDWORK FOR INCLUSIVE PROGRAMMING

Chapter Four

Opening the Doors

Planning from an Institutional Perspective

Since the Americans with Disabilities Act (ADA) was signed into law in 1990, following decades of advocacy by disability rights activists, many of the physical changes to our cityscapes—curb cuts, ramps, automatic doors—have become common features of our lives. But the preamble to the legislation may be read as a call to reach beyond these measures, identifying among the nation's goals the directive to provide equality of opportunity and full participation for individuals with disabilities.[1] President George H. W. Bush emphasized this broad call for change in his remarks upon signing the ADA into law, declaring, "Let the shameful walls of exclusion finally come tumbling down."[2] Cultural institutions serving the public have an opportunity—perhaps even a mandate—to seize upon this decree from the ADA in order to create a visitor experience that is welcoming, thoughtful, and adaptive for neurodivergent patrons.

This chapter offers a high-level view of the planning process from an institutional perspective and may be used as a tool for

- understanding the specific circumstances of your institution and developing a vision for programming;
- achieving buy-in from stakeholders; and
- developing a formative plan for programs and accommodations that will augment your mission to create meaningful experiences for neurodiverse visitors.

DETERMINING WHERE YOU ARE NOW

When developing something new, it helps to start with a realistic appraisal of the status quo. Take some time to reflect on your organization from the top down, beginning with your institutional mission. Does the mission affect which programs or projects take priority? How does your current work align with the mission, and how could an initiative serving neurodiverse audiences further this? Consider which individuals or groups hold power at your institution. What aspects of the mission are important to them, and how might they respond to what you have in mind? These factors should inform the objectives you develop for your program.

Beyond the ideals of the mission, what is the institutional culture? How staff members treat one another, interact with the public, and respond to change can be assets or obstacles in the process of advancing a new way of doing things. Think of other instances when new programs or policies were enacted as you envision how your efforts may be received. Speak with your colleagues to get a sense of their knowledge level regarding autism and neurodiversity. Compile a list of questions and topics that would enhance your understanding of these audiences, and what you would want others at your institution to learn.

Move away from your internal perspective to ascertain how someone with neuro differences might currently experience your space. An effective way to start is by gathering existing documentation or anecdotal accounts from staff who directly interact with neurodivergent visitors. Find out what has gone well, what challenges have arisen, and how visitors and staff have responded to their encounters. For the most accurate picture of the visitor experience, an audit of your space conducted by an expert or a focus group is an invaluable tool. As part of this process, pay attention to the noise and activity level on-site, the customer service tactics of frontline staff, the effectiveness and clarity of wayfinding tools, environmental factors such as temperature and light, and even the challenges that someone may encounter while traveling to your space. Spend time reviewing institutional policies that could impact visitors with autism. Certain event photography or video practices might interfere with the privacy of someone in a protected class, such as a minor or someone with a disability. Clearly articulated service animal policies and well-marked relief areas can greatly improve the quality of someone's visit, as can front-of-house staff who are trained on respectful interaction with service animals and their owners. Once you understand the factors that may affect an on-site experience for a visitor with autism, determine what you will be able to improve, what cannot be changed, and how you can help visitors navigate potential challenges.

For example, after working with the Dallas Sensory Consortium to evaluate its sensory-friendly offerings, a partner organization changed its event format by adding quiet hours to large festivals and developing programs outside of public hours with special activities designed for visitors with autism. Educators at the cultural institution also began working with a sensory certification service to train staff, reformulate on-site signage, and offer sensory kits featuring communication supports, headphones, and handheld manipulative objects for checkout.[3]

DEVELOPING A VISION

With a clear understanding of your institution's mission, stakeholders, culture, and conditions, you can begin to define your long-term vision and more immediate goals. Consider the following as you shape your vision: in five years, how do you hope people will engage with your institution? Think about what they might learn or take away from their experience and how you hope your institution will be perceived by these individuals, by the people who care about them, and by the general public. How do you want your institution to grow and change as a result of your initiative? How can you encourage staff at all levels to incorporate practices that promote access and equity into their work? Imagine how your efforts might contribute to a broader reach or deeper connection with your institutional mission.

Short- and medium-term goals should flow from this vision. In six months to a year, what specific measures will need to be in place? For example, having a certain percentage of staff participate in training, implementing basic changes based on a site audit, or hosting one special event could be attainable goals. Reflect on how these early accomplishments might evolve into more ambitious goals as you move forward. As part of this process, develop a set of metrics that will help you to track how effective your efforts have been and plan to revisit goals that may need to change over time. Build in time for evaluation and realignment on a regular basis, considering the needs of multiple parties: how can you better understand the experience of visitors with autism, of their companions, and of your staff?

ANTICIPATING CHALLENGES

Every challenge can become a learning opportunity when handled correctly. By creating a thorough map of the obstacles you may face and how you plan to address them, you will gain a helpful tool for achieving buy-in with institutional stakeholders. Some key issues include the investment of time, human and financial resources, risk of harm to visitors or to your space, and negative attitudes among staff or the public.

A well-executed program rides on the back of many hours of groundwork and preparation. When creating a timeline for reaching your goals, it may help to set a target date and work backward to determine if your plan is achievable. Do not underestimate the importance of staff training and the amount of time you will need to identify the right type of training for your needs. Consider also how long it may take for staff to process and adapt to new information. Building a shared understanding of the value of programs and accommodations for visitors with autism is the first step in working toward the implementation of best practices throughout the institution. In most cases, bringing in a knowledgeable outside source is the best strategy for initial training. Depending on your budget, you may choose to pay for a professional speaker, invite a specialist from a nearby university or school district (as described in the following example), or reach out to a colleague who has established sensory programming at their own organization.

Staff at the Nasher Sculpture Center, for instance, began the process of self-education by forming a partnership with the School of Occupational Therapy at Texas Woman's University, which allowed students to use the museum as a resource for research and service while museum staff could learn best practices for working with neurodiverse populations from the university. You may also want to research whether a sensory certification program is a fit for your institution.

Self-education will be key as you determine the best course of action, and you may find it helpful to build a portfolio of informative videos and readings to share with interested staff. Topics for training might include respectful and accurate language to use when speaking about autism, tactics for interacting with these visitors, and strategies for helping other members of the public to understand the perspective of people on the autism spectrum. As you develop a training schedule, include regular retraining sessions to refresh existing staff and bring new team members up to speed.

When planning for the implementation of your program, create a detailed list of any equipment and supplies you might need. Some items to consider are furnishings for a sensory space, fidgets, small handheld objects to help a person focus, other kit materials to help structure a visit, and supplies for gross- and fine-motor activities. As you list these items, take into account their physical weight and bulk. Where will you house them, and which staff will be responsible for managing them? As part of the Dallas Sensory Consortium, larger institutions like Texas Woman's University and the Dallas Museum of Art have been able to support smaller partners by storing or lending equipment for events.

The availability of human and financial resources can make or break a program, so try to create realistic estimates about what you will need. When developing a budget, include hours or stipends for the extra facilitators that will be required for synchronous, in-person programming. Refer to your list of equipment and estimate how much it will cost to purchase what you need. Allocate additional money and staff time to any items that may need to be professionally cleaned or replaced on a regular basis. Build in time and funding for staff training and include incidental travel or entertainment expenses that may be needed when hosting an outside speaker. Consider any loss of revenue from an event that limits paid visitation during open hours. Include any marketing costs that will be a part of your outreach plan and think about how much time you may need to spend on grassroots or word-of-mouth efforts. Anticipate printing costs to produce improved wayfinding materials and translation costs if you hope to offer access to audiences with limited English proficiency. And, finally, pay special attention to any additional spending that may be worthwhile to create an optimal experience for your visitors—complimentary transportation or parking, food and drink, or small items such as fidgets and headphones that could help them feel welcome in your space.

If you have performed a walkthrough of your space from the perspective of a neurodivergent visitor, you will already have a sense of the physical or environmental challenges people might encounter when they visit your space. Now, take the perspective of your institutional stakeholders. Are there areas that are at high risk for accidental damage? Are there other visitors who might create an uncomfortable situation for neurodivergent people, or give negative public feedback due to an encounter with a person whose behavior they found disruptive? Make a plan that helps to prevent these situations before they can occur. Some strategies may include enhanced signage, additional staff presence, success stories to help model expected behavior, special quiet hours, and well-marked sensory spaces where visitors may rest and recenter. A challenging situation occurred when educators at the Nasher Sculpture Center transitioned from a well-staffed sensory program held outside of normal museum hours to a self-guided program intended to reduce crowding during the COVID-19 pandemic. Because participants visited over multiple weeks instead of on a single afternoon, measures like enhanced signage and additional staffing were not in place. After a visitor had a physical interaction with an artwork, the museum's foundation of training and staff buy-in at all levels came into play. Front-of-house, curatorial, and education staff were able to work together to enact improved safety measures for the rest of the program period without the incident affecting the museum's commitment to serve neurodiverse audiences.

A final challenge that no one hopes to encounter is misconceptions or negative attitudes among internal staff. Every institution is different, so if you anticipate this being an issue, seek support from colleagues, program partners, or training entities. Educating yourself and having a carefully thought-out plan will be key factors in building the skills needed to effectively advocate for the work you hope to accomplish.

LAYING THE FOUNDATIONS

Once you have a vision in place for your program or initiative, begin to assemble the assets that will help you to achieve institutional buy-in and secure funding. Build a case for why an experience with your institution is valuable to neurodiverse visitors. What can you offer that others in the region cannot? What educational or social benefits might this experience create during a visit and after the visitor leaves?

Assemble a team of allies. Within your institution, identify colleagues from other departments who can offer essential support or helpful feedback. Work with these teammates to bring others in your institution up to your level of understanding about neuro differences, and to make staff at all levels aware of the new program you will be offering. Above all, find ways for everyone to feel invested and share in the success of your efforts. As you are laying these internal foundations, find ways to connect with like-minded organizations and consider how you might add to each other's strengths. Other cultural institutions, local colleges and universities, and autism specialists at area school districts are excellent places to start.

The planning and research you have undertaken will create a framework for a viable funding proposal. Funders who prioritize programming for neurodiverse audiences may not be the same as those who typically support cultural institutions, so it is important to be able to articulate the goals and benefits of your initiative. Create an outline or a short narrative describing the needs of your intended audience and how you plan to directly address them. Compile documentation and research to support both the demonstrated need for and the anticipated effectiveness of your proposed solution. Funders may be critical of proposals that merely include exposure to a cultural institution as an outcome, so consider the broader impact of your program and how you can prove that similar initiatives have succeeded. Include a detailed description of your evaluation plan and how your findings will inform the program going forward. Prepare an outline that defines how outside funding will enable specific program components. If you can only receive support for a portion of your expenses, what aspects of your program will be prioritized? Create a compelling story for a funder that anticipates their questions and eliminates doubt about the program's viability and sustainability.[4]

As you create a proposal, especially for a program in its infancy, avoid setting benchmarks for success that you may not be able to achieve. Rather than setting a specific attendance goal, begin with more qualitative metrics for success and be open to adjusting your practices based on participant feedback. You might start with a small-scale version of your program that requires only a modest budget. Once in place, this can be used as a scaffolding point for refining your practices, bringing additional support to the table, and reaching wider audiences.

Building awareness of your program in the community will require time and effort. Think first about your intended audience. Do you hope to reach children, adults, or both? Would your institution best serve family units or established groups of people who are participants in a class or structured program? Will you reach out to locals only or to those who may travel from a farther distance? Neurodiverse people and caregivers may follow special publications, social media, or online forums to learn about sensory-friendly programs and outings. Begin to spread the word by reaching out through program partners, entities that serve neurodivergent populations, and promotion in appropriate media. Build a contact list that will help you to communicate directly with people who show interest in your programming. Over time, especially if you demonstrate responsiveness to participants' needs and feedback, you should develop a substantial audience.

PLANNING FRAMEWORK

Using an outline like the one below may help you to organize your thoughts as you develop your program.

Vision
    How can experiences with your institution benefit visitors with autism?
    How does this initiative support your institutional mission?

Program Format
    Synchronous (time-based) event or asynchronous (ongoing) program?
    Special activities:
    Special resources or handouts:

Needs
    Training type:
    Training resources needed:
    Staff and volunteer needs:
    Supplies and equipment needs:
    Spaces used:
    Signage:
    Resources:
    Community partners:

Potential Challenges and Solutions
  Physical space
    Challenges:
    Solutions:
  Fragile or hazardous areas
    Challenges:
    Solutions:
  Internal attitudes
    Challenges:
    Solutions:
  Visitor attitudes
    Challenges:
    Solutions:

Audience Development
  Target audience type:
  Target audience size:
  Marketing outlets (email, institutional website, social media, print media):

Budget
  Training $_____
  Staff time $_____
  Contract staff $_____
  Equipment/supplies $_____
  Equipment maintenance $_____
  Marketing $_____
  Printing $_____
  Food and beverage $_____
  Other $_____
  Total funding needs $_____

Funding Plan
  Type of support sought:
  Demonstrated need:
  Intended outcomes:
  Documentation:
  Evaluation format:

Timeline
  Initial assessment: __/__/__
  Funding secured: __/__/__
  Staff training: __/__/__
  Program planning: __/__/__

Program marketing: __/__/__
Program resources complete: __/__/__
Program event date(s): __/__/__
Program evaluation: __/__/__

Evaluation
Initial audit plan:
Evaluation time frame:
Evaluation instruments:

INCLUSION BENEFITS EVERYONE

While you can never anticipate every eventuality, a thorough planning process will give you the tools you need to create a positive impact. As you learn more and begin to implement the practices you learn in this book, you are likely to find that neuro-friendly strategies benefit everyone. A quiet room designed as a sensory space may also provide a nursing retreat for parents of infants and a resting place for visitors with medical needs. Enhanced wayfinding materials can benefit visitors with learning differences or social anxiety. Training that helps staff develop empathy and clear communication skills will create a more positive experience for the general public and better serve visitors with disabilities, English language learners, and first-time visitors to a cultural institution. The plan you make today will pave the way for enhanced cultural engagement in the future. Let the walls come tumbling down!

NOTES

1. Americans with Disabilities Act of 1990, as amended with ADA Amendments Act of 2008, June 15, 2009, https://www.ada.gov/pubs/adastatute08.htm.
2. Remarks of President George H. W. Bush at the Signing of the Americans with Disabilities Act, July 26, 1990, https://www.ada.gov/ghw_bush_ada_remarks.html.
3. KultureCity is an example of an organization offering Sensory Inclusive™ certification, https://www.kulturecity.org/.
4. James Jillson (director of development, Nasher Sculpture Center) in discussion with Anna Smith, May 13, 2021.

Chapter Five

Something for Everyone

*Program Models and Examples
from Cultural Institutions*

If you work at a cultural institution, it is likely that you already offer educational programs to the public. Just as there are a variety of program formats for general audiences, such as summer camps, school tours, date nights, and academic lectures, there are many format options when creating experiences for neurodiverse communities. Programs and resources can be *synchronous*, meaning that they are offered during set dates and times, or *asynchronous*, meaning that they are available for anytime use on an ongoing basis. As with any educational experience, the format and frequency of your program will be determined by your specific goals.

This chapter offers examples of real-world program types that engage neurodiverse communities. It may be used as a tool for

- seeing the breadth of formats for educational programs and resources;
- understanding how factors such as format and frequency correlate with specific institutional goals; and
- discerning different categories of programs and resources so you can choose what is best for your resources and institutional goals.

Please note that programs are described using the same terminology as the presenting institution.

SYNCHRONOUS EVENTS

Synchronous events allow the most control over a visitor's experience and how they interact with the activities and resources your institution has to offer. This type of event can be the most rewarding for staff, who get the chance to directly interface with neurodiverse visitors, but can also require the greatest output of staff time and financial resources. Below is a sampling of programs following a synchronous model.

Open House or Family Day Event

Attendance: Attendance limited based on footprint of participating institution. Dallas Museum of Art and the Nasher Sculpture Center cap attendance at five hundred, while partner institution the Dallas Zoo caps attendance at a thousand.

Age: All ages

Frequency: Four times per year

Goals and Format: Drop-in style events for families are often formatted with a variety of activities for participants of different age and skill levels. These are a popular way of connecting with a broad range of families who wish to socialize and learn together at a cultural institution. This event format may attract first-time visitors to the institution.

Case Examples: When developing the idea for its first tailored program for neurodiverse communities, staff from the DMA spoke with potential participants and parents about what they would want from this event. Statements from parents indicated desires "to introduce [their] child to a new place and have it be a positive experience," "to enjoy time with [their] child in a judgment-free zone," "to connect with like-minded parents," and "to learn strategies and find resources for [their] child." When neurodivergent children were asked what they would want to do at the museum, they responded: "make friends," "play," "see cool stuff," and simply "have fun!"

The following common considerations from parents also emerged:

- having a child who is easily overstimulated and needs space and trained staff to help them calm down;
- the need to be able to bring a whole family, not just the neurodivergent child;
- having a child who has difficulty going to new places because of fear of the unknown;
- difficulties adhering to a schedule that requires exact timing and preferring a format that allows families to come and go as needed;
- cost as a barrier to participation; and
- neurodivergent children already have enough school and therapy in their lives and need activities that are fun and enjoyable.

> Based on these conversations and stated participant goals, the DMA developed a family day event, which after several name changes is now simply called Sensory Day. During this event, the museum opens two hours early

for families to explore the galleries and enjoy additional activities before public hours. Event-specific success stories are sent to families in advance of the program to help parents prepare their child and reduce anxiety about the unknown. The event, including parking, is free, but to reduce sensory overload, registration is limited to the first five hundred participants. Occupational therapy students from Texas Woman's University (TWU) staff the event, and while they are not administering therapy, their specialized knowledge can help them anticipate and respond to participants' needs. Visitors can explore at their own pace, choosing from a range of drop-in activities and recharging in a low-sensory space as needed. Activities are designed around a variety of sensory preferences, can be enjoyed by all ages and all members of the family, promote social interaction, and most important, encourage fun.

The DMA's neighbor, Nasher Sculpture Center, started offering synchronous sensory-friendly events in 2018 after shadowing events at the DMA and consulting with Texas Woman's University about best practices for its spaces. From the start, the Nasher invited Dallas institutions that had advised them in the planning process to be a part of their sensory program launch, a decision which has benefited all involved. The public enjoyed a variety of activities presented by partners, participating institutions made new community connections, and the Nasher was able to offer more activities than they would have been able to alone. This consortium model took off and was eventually formalized into the Dallas Sensory Consortium.

Since then, the number of consortium partners has grown, and participating institutions take turns hosting Sensory Day events and contributing an activity when they are not hosting. While this event has evolved over time, its goal has remained the same—to remove barriers to participation, encourage engagement within our community, and promote fun. Its success has caused nearby Fort Worth institutions to inquire about the consortium's structure and create something similar in their city.

Recurring Programs for Specific Ages

Attendance: Small group of about ten participants, sometimes with accompanying adult

Age: 13 to 18

Frequency: Monthly

Goals and Format: This type of program may be structured as a workshop, tour, meet-up, or performance with focused content geared toward children, teens, or adults. The series format creates opportunities for relationship-building between participants and cultural institution staff, and among peer groups. With repeat visitation, participants may be able to reach more specific goals related to learning or developing social skills.

Case Examples: Based on feedback from parents and participants of Sensory Day, the DMA learned there was a strong need in the community for programming specifically tailored to neurodivergent teenagers. While museums and other cultural institutions were increasingly offering programs for neurodivergent children, there were very few programs designed for teens as they begin navigating the challenges of adulthood. The Sensory Day feedback demonstrated the need for an informal learning environment where adolescents could strengthen their social skills. Neurodivergent teen participants at the DMA expressed that they often had difficulty understanding what other people were thinking, making social interactions a challenge. These social skills, however, can be learned through practice, especially during adolescent years when neurodivergent individuals have the tendency to become more aware of their own social isolation.

In January 2017, the DMA established Sensory Scouts, a monthly thematic workshop designed specifically around the interests and goals of neurodivergent teenagers. This program allows participants to explore works of art through gallery discussion, sensory explorations, art making in the studio, and social skills activities designed in collaboration with a specialist. Participants can attend the program independently, but if participants are not comfortable attending unaccompanied, parents and caregivers are always welcome. At the beginning of each program, museum staff explain the day's activities with an illustrated schedule. The pictures in the schedule depict the day's events in easily identifiable graphics, which can help alleviate participants' anxiety. The theme of the program changes each month, but always focuses on a specific social skill. For example, participants have learned about expressing their own feelings and understanding the moods of others in the Emotions in Art program. In the Stories in Art program, participants practice improvised speech through storytelling. Following each program, parents and caregivers are provided with a summary of the conversations and skills explored during the program, including related art making and discussion prompts for extended learning.

In Sensory Scouts, the museum functions differently from a typical classroom. Museum staff act as facilitators rather than teachers and consider themselves to be among a community of learners along with the program participants. The staff enables and encourages the learning process through dialogue and engagement in which participants bring value to the program through their unique identities and experiences. Group identity is encouraged through collaborative gallery activities and discussion. While works of art act as the catalyst for conversation, staff members do not place great importance on participants acquiring a discrete body of facts, such as the artwork title or date of creation. Rather, the value lies in the participants contributing to a learning community and forging individually meaningful pathways to make connections between the art and the world around them. Following time in the galleries, participants return to the studio for a hands-on art activity. Art projects are designed to relate to the program's theme and emphasize experimentation and discovery over a final product. For the Stories in Art lesson, participants created *story dice*, wooden blocks on which they drew images to represent the different elements of a story, such as character and setting. Then participants took turns rolling their dice and telling stories to one another in a way that combined their story dice elements. Through art projects such as this, participants of Sensory Scouts explore their self-identity and have the opportunity to express themselves creatively to others.

One of the ongoing challenges with Sensory Scouts has been unpredictable attendance from program to program. While participants are asked to register in advance, program attendance rarely mirrors the registration list. It is understandable that teenagers have many competing obligations or, on the day of the program, may simply not feel like participating. However, this has led to staff ordering too many art supplies in anticipation of a larger group, and a few awkward programs with only a couple of participants. Since the program relies on mutual exchange among a community of learners, the group benefits from a more robust attendance number.

This challenge has been successfully mitigated in similar programs at many museums by partnering with another organization that has a preexisting group of participants. A special education teacher of a local high school reached out to the DMA to create a monthly program for her classroom of twelve neurodivergent students. Each month, education staff from the museum create a lesson plan in conjunction with the teacher. Within the lesson plan, students interact with art to practice and reinforce their understanding of topics that are concurrently being covered in the classroom. Topics can be somewhat unusual, such as "going to get a haircut" or "storm preparedness," but museum staff always find creative connections between the learning objective and the art collection. For example, students practiced the topic of "getting dressed for the day" by looking at landscape paintings that depict different types of weather and selecting an outfit from a costume trunk of various options. Since the visit is treated as a fun field trip where students do not receive grades, participants can translate their classroom knowledge to another environment and can practice applying it without the pressure of tests and grading.

The Montreal Museum of Fine Arts (MMFA) likewise found great success in partnering with another organization with a preexisting group of participants. Since 2017, the MMFA has collaborated with *Autisme sans limites* to create an ongoing art therapy group for young autistic adults. In the program, participants are led through gallery discussions and art making by the MMFA's full-time art therapist. Outside of the MMFA's program, the participants of this group regularly engage in other group activities such as cooking classes, gardening, going to the movies, and dining at local restaurants. The participants of the museum's program benefit from an established knowledge and level of trust between themselves fostered through previous interactions offered by *Autisme sans limites*.

Summer Camp

Attendance: Typically less than fifteen, or a size that maintains a manageable child-to-staff ratio.

Age: Varies, but typically a limited age range corresponding with the learning level of themes and skills developed in the camp.

Frequency: Varies, but typically offered as a weeklong, full- or half-day camp that is offered once during summer months.

Goals and Format: Many cultural institutions offer weeklong summer camps for school-aged children who are on summer break. Camps are popular among working parents who need to keep their child supervised by an adult and engaged with activities during the weekdays. Summer camps at most cultural institutions are offered for specified age ranges and designed around a specialized theme or focus. Typically, camps for neurodiverse children are no different, but may employ specially trained staff who can plan and implement accommodations or modifications that will improve the experience of participants.

Case Examples: The Dallas Museum of Art offers Hands-On Art Camp, a weeklong camp for neurodiverse children ages 8–12. This camp is co-taught with a contract autism specialist who incorporates resources and supports into the camp. These include a designated sensory space in the classroom and the use of visual communication cards to give students a preview of the day's activities. In a previous year, the camp was themed around animals. Campers learned about animal patterns and habitats through the artwork in the galleries and had a visit from a zookeeper who spoke about their career caring for animals. Throughout the week, campers make artwork inspired by the daily topic, which they showcase to their families during the Friday summer camp exhibition in the classroom.

The Virginia Museum of Fine Arts offers a bite-sized summer camp experience for children with autism, accompanied by their caregiver. During a one-hour workshop session, budding artists ages 5–12 explore the museum's collections, experiment with art materials, learn through specialized teaching methods, and interact with peers. At the Glazer Children's Museum of Tampa, Florida, campers can choose from multiple autism-affirming weeklong camps each summer. These camps, designed for ages 5–10, have featured themes such as Make a Masterpiece, Time Travel, and Maker Mania. In addition to usual camp programming, the Glazer's autism-affirming camps also include behavior and speech specialists on-site, sensory-friendly tools and resources, consistent schedule and routine, an optional precamp orientation tour for parents and campers, adjacent quiet room, and smaller class sizes.

Increasingly, cultural institutions are recognizing the need for additional resources and support in all camps, not just those designed for neurodivergent campers. At the Perot Museum of Nature and Science, summer camps are popular with neurodivergent children who have a focused interest in one of the many scientific topics featured in the museum's exhibition hall, such as paleontology, robotics, ornithology, and astronomy. Although parents were not disclosing if their child was neurodivergent, it was apparent that many children needed additional resources to have an enjoyable summer camp experience. Staff reached out to co-author Tina Fletcher for help. Tina recalls working creatively with the Perot's existing resources to create a better camp experience for children who were becoming overwhelmed with sensory stimuli and social interactions over the course of the week:

> Staff at the Perot shared multiple instances involving children who struggled with transitioning from one activity to another, eating only specific snack and lunch foods, and having difficulties successfully interacting with other campers. Usually by the second or third day of camp, they were emotionally depleted, on sensory overload, and oftentimes engaged in some acting out. To offset this, staffers devised a plan to offer each camper, not just the ones who were struggling, an option for a daily supervised on-demand fifteen-minute break. The museum had half a dozen 6 × 8 foot fiberglass turtle shells that were left over from an exhibit, so we created little relaxation havens in the shells that campers could visit by exchanging a pass for a break. We called it Turtle Time and offered campers different shell environments and configurations to select from. This included using weighted blankets and computer monitors featuring trippy screensavers and naturescapes. Because museum staff believed some of the volunteer counselors lived with the same challenges certain campers experienced, Turtle Time was offered as a counselor break, too.

The Perot Museum's implementation of a sensory space greatly benefited both neurodiverse and neurotypical summer campers, as well as camp staff. As is the case with all accessible resources, Turtle Time perfectly illustrates the ripple effect of even the simplest solution. What is necessary for some typically benefits all.

Sensory-Friendly Performances and Story Times

Attendance: Varies, depending on venue footprint and staff to attendee ratio.
Age: All ages.

Frequency: Varies widely based on institutional event calendar and capacity.

Goals and Format: Many movie theaters, libraries, and performance venues, including ballet theaters and symphony halls, now offer sensory-friendly performances and story times for attendees who have specific sensory needs. Sensory-friendly performances and story times typically include environmental modifications, specially trained staff, and relaxed rules—all designed to create a safe, nonjudgmental experience.

Case Examples: For each of their productions, Dallas Children's Theater offers multiple sensory-friendly performances. During the sensory-friendly plays, guests will encounter several environmental modifications: the intensity of lighting and sound effects is reduced, house lights are dimmed rather than completely off, and a quiet area is provided in the lobby. Additional trained volunteers are on hand to assist with patron needs. The theater has a more relaxed atmosphere, where visitors are allowed to freely enter and exit their seats during the performance and use digital devices, with the understanding that nonverbal audience members may need them to communicate. Additionally, adjustments are made to the script and story to maximize audience comprehension. With advance purchase of a ticket to a sensory-friendly performance at DCT, attendees are automatically emailed a success story showing what can be expected when visiting the theater, a parent tip sheet, and a short synopsis about what happens in the play.

Sensory-friendly performances are another great example of how something developed for a specific disability has benefited the wider population. Sensory-friendly movies and performances are frequently attended by neurotypical young children and their parents who appreciate the nonjudgmental atmosphere. They are also commonly attended by those who have adverse reactions to unexpected sensory stimuli. Someone who has encountered a traumatic event, such as a combat veteran or a child who experienced family violence, may prefer to attend a performance without sudden loud noises or flashing lights. Sensory-friendly performances are also popular with first-time attendees who may have trepidation about what to expect from their first play or symphony. The popularity and effectiveness of sensory-friendly performances is demonstrated by their abundant availability in every big city across the United States.

Advisory Groups

Attendance: Small working group, typically comprised of less than ten neurodiverse advisors and allies.

Age: Teen to adult.

Frequency: Varies, but typically meet one to two times per quarter or more frequently if needed while developing a specific project.

Goals and Format: As discussed in chapter 3, the practice of co-creating with community constituents is incredibly beneficial to the quality of your institution's programs and resources. Co-creation opens your creative process to a wider range of perspectives. In particular, offerings that are co-created with neurodiverse communities tend to be of exceptionally high quality because they were developed with the expertise and considerations of your target audience.

Case Examples: The Montreal Museum of Fine Arts's advisory group, the Committee for Neurodiversity, consists of roughly a dozen community stakeholders who each bring a unique perspective to the table. The group is composed of neurodivergent individuals as well as allies, including parents and caregivers, special education teachers, researchers, and representatives from partnering foundations. The Committee for Neurodiversity has not only helped to develop and pilot sensory-friendly programs and resources, but their perspective has shaped some of the museum's daily practices. The committee continues to inform many of the museum's approaches, such as which terms are used to describe neurodiversity and how to create sensory-friendly spaces throughout the museum. Likewise, the GFA (Guggenheim for All) Advisory Committee is comprised of teachers, parents, and professionals both with and without autism who work together to evaluate the museum's current practices, develop new offerings, and inform daily approaches related to autism.

The frequency of advisory group meetings varies greatly from institution to institution. A specific advisory group may have a set frequency of recurring meetings, with additional working sessions as needed while projects are in development. At the DMA, an internal advisory group of staff with disabilities and allies meet on a monthly basis to identify opportunities to increase access to the museum. Additionally, the DMA assembles project-based advisory groups to bring in the perspectives of community constituents when developing offerings for specific audiences or when reimagining its galleries. Since project-based advisory groups meet for a limited duration of time in pursuit of a well-defined goal, the DMA is able to pay its advisory members an honorarium for their time and perspective.

ASYNCHRONOUS EVENTS AND RESOURCES

For times when staff may not be available to facilitate a synchronous event for neurodiverse visitors, asynchronous programming allows for a positive, self-directed experience. This may take the form of a handout, a kit, or a digital resource to help someone make the most of their visit. In many cases, asynchronous resources are designed for a wider age range than synchronous events and can be enjoyed at the user's own pace. The following are a variety of asynchronous offerings from cultural institutions.

Resource Tote Bags and Backpacks

Goals and Format: Sensory bags, totes, or kits may be offered to neurodiverse individuals or families taking part in a self-directed visit to a cultural institution. These may include tools for communication or sensory and behavioral self-regulation provided with the goal of making a neurodivergent visitor's experience more manageable and enjoyable.

Case Examples: Nasher Sculpture Center makes sensory kits for neurodiverse visitors available at the entrance desk. These kits take the form of lightweight backpacks filled with materials provided by KultureCity, a nonprofit organization that offers training and certification related to sensory inclusivity. Kits include helpful tools like communication cards indicating basic needs or questions, headphone-style ear defenders, and fidgets or other handheld objects used to keep the hands busy and reduce sensory overload. Having this bag readily available allows individuals to self-select the resource as part of their experience in the space. When the Nasher began its partnership with KultureCity, they were the second institution in Dallas to become certified. Now there are many locations that have that designation. The public's awareness and experience with the sensory bag at other venues has promoted a comfort level wherever they are seen and consistently used.

Another museum that offers sensory backpacks is the Houston Museum of Natural Science. They can be rented, free-of-charge, at the Museum Services Desk for use during operating hours. The backpacks were created and gifted to the museum by local Boy Scout Alex Hightower, and include fidgets, stuffed animals, ear defenders, and sunglasses, among other things, to ensure that visitors of all ages have a comfortable, sensory-friendly visit.

Sensory backpacks created unforeseen challenges during the COVID-19 pandemic, when health advisories encouraged sanitized surfaces on all commonly used surfaces in institutions. One-time usage materials became the standard because it was difficult to ensure that resources would be germ-free between users. To address this situation, members of the Dallas Sensory Consortium created a one-time usage sensory tote that was distributed to guests during the two-year period that the CDC recommended enhanced sanitation measures. All the institutions in the consortium pooled resources to make these kits. Hundreds were made and each participating institution offered them at their entrances for neurodiverse guests. In addition to the materials included in the sensory backpacks described above, these single-use totes included information about all the institutions in the consortium, self-guided activity sheets, a timer, and disposable earplugs (instead of the acoustic headphones typically offered by many institutions). Although each institution focused on different subjects and began with different core audiences, the totes were designed to promote cross-visitation and a feeling of safety and consistency for visitors at a time when nothing seemed certain.

Sensory Maps, Visual Communication, and Digital Resources

Goals and Format: Digital resources such as sensory maps and success stories can provide essential information to support the success of a visitor before they even step foot through your doors. These may be provided in a digital format via an institution's website or through an on-site quick response (QR) code that visitors scan, or they may be distributed as hard copies near an entrance, performance hall, or special exhibit. Sensory maps with recognizable icons showing spaces that have high or low levels of sensory stimuli throughout an institution's building and grounds may help visitors maximize their time and positive experience.

Case Examples: The Nasher Sculpture Center's website features easy navigation to its success story, parking directions, and building map. The map indicates need-to-know locations like the restrooms, elevators, and quiet spaces marked with universal icons. Upon arrival, families can find the same directional icons as well as specific signage for recommended headphone zones to help those affected by loud sounds created by fountains, bustling cafés, echoes, and ambient garden noises. Having a page that is dedicated to accessibility concerns makes it easy for families to land on the information they need with the fewest number of clicks. The Nasher also links content in this area to information about sensory-friendly events and online projects and videos designed for neurodiverse learners.

The Pushkin State Fine Arts Museum in Moscow, Russia, offers a resource that they refer to as a sensory security map. The sensory security map helps visitors plan their visit around their own sensory preferences by indicating the various sensory stimuli present in each exhibit hall. Factors that are indicated on the map include lighting and noise levels, areas where smells from the café can linger, and spaces where visitors can touch interactives or engage with activities.

New York City's Intrepid Sea, Air, & Space Museum offers a variety of resources for visitors to plan and manage their visit, many of which are available digitally on their website as well as on-site resources. These are listed simply as accessibility resources, available for any visitor who finds them useful. The Intrepid's interactive digital guide allows visitors to preview exhibits from home or use at the museum to avoid crowding around labels. The digital guide includes full label text, additional photos, and captioned videos for each stop. The museum also offers visual communication cards for visitors to get a sense of what to expect, plan their visit, and introduce new vocabulary paired with photographs for terms such as "galley" and "flight deck."

There are many more varieties of programs for neurodiverse learners, as well as many ways to customize and riff on the models described in this chapter. We offer the examples in this chapter as a reference point for the more detailed strategies that are presented in subsequent chapters of this book. As you read on, you might consider how a sensory space, schedule, or visual support would integrate with a drop-in event, workshop, or self-directed experience in your space.

Chapter Six

Know Where You're Going

Developing Participant and Institutional Goals

Cultural institutions are dynamic places full of ideas that lead to various programs. Along the way, many decisions need to be made about allocating finances and staff resources. Part of that process is developing well-formulated goals that provide a solid basis for planning and measuring work as it moves forward. Creating measurable goals can help your institution pursue grants and program funding more successfully, as measurable goals are often required in grant applications.

This chapter details a method for creating goals that are *specific, measurable, attainable, relevant,* and *time-sensitive,* also known as SMART goals. The practice of using SMART goals gives planners a way to break long-term plans into manageable actions and ensures that everyone is on the same page when designing and measuring program effectiveness. Research about SMART goals also shows that while many people can articulate actions and time frames when constructing their goals, they often miss the mark when it comes to creating measurable outcomes.[1] It has also shown that when people have SMART goals to guide them, their actions are more focused, aligned, and diligent, so despite the difficulties some may have when first developing them, SMART goals pay off.[2]

In the following pages, we explore the process of creating SMART goals for a special event created for neurodiverse audiences, with content focused on

- goal planning for a variety of stakeholders;
- creating measurable and attainable objectives; and
- sample SMART goals for a drop-in style sensory-friendly event.

51

START PLANNING BY THINKING THINGS THROUGH

One of the first steps toward creating any event is to think it through. This may seem self-evident, but taking time to be intentional about a new program will make it a meaningful and productive experience for everyone involved. As you develop your goals, consider that they need to be specific enough to make them understandable to people within and outside your organization, and clear enough to make sense to stakeholders with deep knowledge about autism and sensory programming and also to those who are new to the idea. Next, the hard part: the goals must be measurable, and this means you must see them to be able to measure them. And to add to that, not only do the goals have to be observable and measurable, but they also must be achievable, not just a set of idealistic platitudes or big ideas. While you are trying to create these observable, measurable, and achievable goals, they also need to be relevant, or people won't be interested in participating. All your hard work will be for nothing.

First, you should ask yourself if all stakeholders have the same goals for the program or event. It may be possible that your administrative team, educators, and visitors all have different goals for the same event. You will need to account for that in your planning. And finally, what is your allotted time to make these goals happen? Measuring time frames can get tricky, so ensure you are not creating an impossible or difficult situation for yourself or your team.

EVERYONE HAS NEEDS: SETTING GOALS
FOR A VARIETY OF STAKEHOLDERS

If you have done your due diligence in program planning, you should know who the stakeholders are for your initiative. For a sensory-friendly event, these might be the institution, the participants, and, in the case of youth events, the participants' caregivers. Suppose you are hosting an event that will be open to the public. In that case, it will be impossible to know what's on the minds of every person who signs up—what their needs, wants, abilities, and challenges may be, and what they specifically hope to gain or experience by attending. It may be safe to assume some broad strokes that can help define more specific program objectives.

For neurodivergent visitors and their companions, some of the biggest goals may be promoting social participation, using context-appropriate social behavior, developing functional communication skills, practicing behavioral self-regulation, and increasing understanding of ways to ensure personal safety. The only way to know for sure is to ask. When voiced by your attendees, they may state their goals are simply "to make friends," "to have fun," or "to learn something new." This won't give you a lot to work with in terms of creating goals. Consider arranging a preprogram survey or focus group to better understand your visitors' goals as part of your goal-setting process, but be mindful of the ethics of privacy if you do so, ensuring that your inquiries don't breach their privacy or cause unintentional harm such as personal embarrassment or ridicule by others.

Institutional goals may be divided between those that serve the institution itself and those that serve event participants. In addition to metrics-related institutional goals—attendance, reach, participation levels, interactions with event-related marketing, and other items that may interest funders—there may be mission-based goals that will be important to internal stakeholders. Some great news from the cultural field is that in recent years, calls to action driven by advocates for social justice have caused many institutions and professional organizations to create or revisit existing Diversity, Equity, Access, and Inclusion statements.[3] These statements, while often broad in scope, can be useful in understanding how high-level stakeholders at the executive or board level envision their institution's role in connecting with underinvited communities, which can include neurodiverse audiences. The American Zoological Association (AZA), for instance, noted in their 2020 Diversity, Equity, Access & Inclusion Position Statement, "There is an expectation that all individual members, member institutions and AZA staff will proactively work toward greater diversity, equity, access and inclusion in all that they do."[4] Program staff may have specific goals related to the visitor experience, such as creating an environment that promotes equal access to cultural resources or offers multimodal learning opportunities. One model of this can be found within the Dallas Sensory Consortium's Partner Agreement, which includes a set of Institutional Inclusion Goals that promise to make institutions an inclusive place, a welcoming place, and a safe place.

Whomever you are hoping to satisfy, goals should be addressed transparently and be well-documented. Suppose an initial goal that drives decisions toward sensory-friendly planning is met. In that case, other goals may become more compelling as the institution's understanding of the event or experience with program planning grows. Goals are not set in stone and will change with time and experience.

Back to our original goals set for sensory-friendly planning—let's use them to create a set of SMART goals. Based on key visitor and institutional goals, we can see that the following components may be at the heart of such events: to provide opportunities and support to increase social participation, practice social behavior, engage in functional communication, develop and practice behavioral self-regulation skills, and to be safe. Our event planners may want to use some of the following tools to meet these goals. Keep in mind we are moving from abstract ideas and platitudes toward measurable and attainable actions, so we can measure how well we met the mark.

To help visitors increase social participation and promote social behavior, we might offer success stories to demystify the event, communicate expectations, and suggest strategies and actions for a successful visit. We might also consider planning for activities that promote social participation and social interaction, such as by offering a handful of imaginative play or cooperative play activities to encourage social engagement. To provide opportunities for visitors to practice social behavior, we might offer parent tip sheets for information about on-site etiquette and potential challenges.

To help visitors engage in functional communication, we can create a variety of visual and verbal supports, including web-based planning documents for kids. To promote behavioral self-regulation, we can build spaces to offer sensory-based ways to calm and soothe jangled nervous systems, and finally, to promote safety, we might include information on potential hazards and user-friendly solutions within tip sheets and success stories.

KEEPING IT REAL: MAKING THINGS VISIBLE AND MEASURABLE

Now that we have worked our way through some of the strategies that support visitors on sensory-friendly event days, we can go back to original assumptions about the event, what the goals are, and some of the ways we can help visitors meet these goals. We now have things to observe and measure. What kinds of goals can we create? We can measure observable actions, such as increasing or decreasing, creating or saving, or improving something. Still, we cannot measure factors we can't see, such as thinking, believing, hoping, understanding, knowing, or feeling something.

Here are some examples of ways to measure components of goals: we can measure the degree of success with which a participant completes an activity, the amount of staff preparation and training time invested in the event, the number of environmental supports implemented, the number of interactions strategies such as communication cards used, the number of materials and resources developed, and the degree of supervision needed for participation in activities we designed. Remember the success stories we offered to visitors? Staff may consider the most important goals for these resources, such as promoting safe behavior to protect the space and the visitor, and enhancing social participation by making expectations clear, and prioritize these items from the outset. You might then measure the time spent developing the success story, how frequently visitors were seen referring to it, and the degree of success with which safety instructions were followed.

CREATING UNITS OF RELEVANT
AND ATTAINABLE MEASUREMENT

This chapter has worked through some ways to describe the objective or target of the goal, but how do you know if you have met it? Like getting a score on a report card, you've still got to have a measurable criterion for success. From a practical standpoint, you've got to keep things relevant and attainable, too. It's easy to get ambitious during planning when goals are on paper, but keep in mind they will be measured by people who are busy doing many things simultaneously. As a result, goals should be user-friendly. So see what you can create to make a condition and a measurement. Consider the following snippets or phrases that can be added to a goal to make it measurable: during three observations, for ten minutes, on arrival and departure, when entering activity stations, when asked, and when prompted are all excellent starting points.

As you develop your goals, set your sights on things your institution can control versus what individuals may experience separately in relation to their own needs. Cultural educators are not equipped to develop individualized goals for neurodivergent visitors, nor, in most cases, would they have the means and capacity to do so. To make things more relevant and attainable, goal-setters must keep the focus narrow enough to make it realistic. As an example, for social participation goals, measure social participation at the event only or in one room of the location, measure social participation with one group only, such as other visitors, institution staff, or family members, measure functional participation for the event in visible ways, such as asking for help, directions, information, or communicating basic needs for bathrooms and water. If goal-setters have a goal for self-regulation, it should be specific to the environment, social interactions, or activities. Ideas in a museum setting might include using an inside voice during a gallery tour, handling personal art supplies only, or walking instead of running in the art room.

SAMPLE SMART GOALS FOR
A SENSORY-FRIENDLY EVENT

See if you can find the specific, measurable, attainable, realistic, and timely elements in these sample sensory-friendly event goals that promote communication, safety, and social participation.

- Communication: Event staff will be able to describe three ways to communicate with neurodivergent visitors, including word cards, nonverbal cards, and speaking in plain language. Evaluator will observe staff using two of these three methods during the event.
- Safety: Before the event, staff will discuss two ways for visitors to stay safe by pointing out two danger zones and stating two desired safe behaviors at those zones, such as hands to sides and walking. After the event, staff will self-report instances when unsafe behavior was observed and how visitors were redirected.
- Social Participation: The event will include at least three channels for making expectations clear, such as online preparatory information, pre-event communication, on-site signage, and success stories.

THE GOOD NEWS ABOUT WRITING SMART GOALS

Practice improves goal writing. Beginner goals are difficult to understand and measure and often have impractical time frames. As you try your hand at writing SMART goals, keep thinking realistically and ask yourself if someone else who walked in on the situation could understand the desired behaviors and the criteria for meeting the goal. With practice, scenarios and choices become more reasonable and show growth in professional reasoning. In the meantime, finding a practice partner who can read and appraise goals and talk through them with the goal-writing team is helpful. The only way to learn if SMART goals are working is to put them into practice and measure away. Start with a low-stakes event that doesn't rely too heavily on goal setting and work your way into higher-stakes events. With practice, your efforts will pay off, and your documentation practices will become more efficient and realistic.

NOTES

1. Osahon Ogbeiwi, "Why Written Objectives Need to Be Really SMART," *British Journal of Healthcare Management* 23, no. 7 (2017): 324–36, https://doi .org/10.12968/bjhc.2017.23.7.324.

2. Amish Aghera, Matt Emery, Richard Bounds, Colleen Bush, R. Brent Stansfield, Brian Gillett, and Sally A. Santen, "A Randomized Trial of SMART Goal Enhanced Debriefing after Simulation to Promote Educational Actions," *Western Journal of Emergency Medicine* 19, no. 1 (2018): 112, https://doi.org/10.5811%2Fw estjem.2017.11.36524.

3. Excellence in DEAI Report, American Alliance of Museums, 2022, https://www .aam-us.org/wp-content/uploads/2022/07/AAM-Excellence-in-DEAI-Report.pdf.

4. Diversity, Equity, Access & Inclusion Position Statement, Association of Zoos and Aquariums, November 2, 2020, https://assets.speakcdn.com/assets/2332/aza _bod_statement_deai.pdf.

Part 3

PREPARING RESOURCES FOR NEURODIVERSE AUDIENCES

Chapter Seven

Speaking Their Language

Communicating with Neurodivergent Visitors

While knowledge of neurodiversity is changing as new research unfolds, one thing that remains the same is that neurodivergent people tend to communicate differently from most. What can be challenging for administrators and educators at cultural institutions who want to create inclusive environments is that it's not easy to predict a visitor's communication skills. For example, some neurodivergent visitors might not talk or appear to have any form of communication, and yet they may have rich and nuanced understandings they simply can't convey to others. Others may struggle with interaction difficulties such as the "cocktail party problem" many of us may have witnessed—for many neurodivergent people, it's often difficult to comprehend what one person is saying while others are talking, or background noise is present. Some may also have expressive communication differences such as irregular voice pitch or volume, making limited eye contact, staying on conversational topics, or using unusual speech rhythms.[1]

While it isn't within the scope of practice of cultural workers to identify these difficulties, it is reasonable for them to plan for some of the most common challenges experienced by neurodivergent visitors and, when the situation calls for it, to have an educated support team who can help when resources are stretched to their limits. It can be especially important—and comforting—to have advisors such as neurodivergent individuals, special educators, or therapists available to provide practical advice.[2]

In this chapter, we reflect upon how cultural institutions can and should communicate with their audiences, with content that includes

- understanding the purposes of communication between cultural institutions and visitors;

- crafting messages that can be widely understood using plain language and clear graphics;
- adapting communication for special audiences; and
- ensuring that rules and expectations are clear to all visitors.

FOUNDATIONS OF COMMUNICATION
BETWEEN INSTITUTIONS AND VISITORS

To begin with, we will work from three general assumptions about communication practices for cultural institutions: they need to communicate information that benefits all visitors, they need to communicate information relevant to certain subsets of visitors, and they need to communicate information such as rules and procedures that protect the institution and its holdings. We will align these with some of the overarching goals of cultural institutions as visitor-oriented institutions, using museums as the primary example. According to the American Alliance of Museums,[3] all museums should strive to work with and serve the physical, intellectual, and social needs of key stakeholders locally, statewide, nationally, and internationally. To achieve this goal, museums and other cultural entities should do all they can to minimize frustration, discomfort, and fatigue. They should also remove any barriers to effective communication as a standard practice.

Our first assumption is that *cultural institutions must communicate basic information that meets all visitors' needs* using clear and precise visual and written language, with levels of interpretation that are understandable to the majority of visitors. This includes signage written in the dominant language of the culture and images that augment the text. Content in this category is offered to ensure that everyone has what they need to navigate their experience and can include information about exhibitions, programming, and infrastructure, including considerations of visitor comfort (restrooms, cafés, and shops) and safety (exits and sheltering).

Our second assumption is that *cultural institutions often communicate information about special services and events not used by all visitors.* This includes event planning for specific populations such as neurodivergent visitors. In this case, information about relaxed openings, special performances that music venues sometimes offer, specific hours for special events, unique features such as pop-up spaces or activities, and instructions for registration, attendance, and feedback mechanisms. Not all visitors will need to access this information, and those who do may need additional support to understand it. As an example of an Internet-based preplanning resource designed for neurodiverse visitors, the

Metropolitan Museum of Art in New York City offers a visual checklist that is customizable by offering cut-and-paste images that can be attached to a preplanning schedule and picture cards to help communicate basic needs such as taking a break, using the restroom, or checking off an "All done" schedule.[4]

Our third assumption is that while cultural institutions endeavor to be as visitor-centered as possible, *interactions between visitors and institutions will have rules.* Cultural institutions are interested in meeting the needs and goals of all visitors. Still, they are also concerned about their collections, including how to preserve, display, and interpret them and offer them for study or use by others. In this case, while understanding what visitors expect from their experience, they must also make their institution's expectations of visitors clearly understood. According to the American Alliance of Museums guideline 15.1, "All museums should adopt and publish or post a formal list of Rules of Decorum, which outline to the public the rules of the museum."[5] In the spirit of the show must go on, other institutions, such as those that feature live performances, must factor in the real-time visitor experience and logistics related to segmenting portions of the audience who need accommodations that won't detract from the event itself. Places that feature transitions between indoor and outdoor experiences must manage safety considerations and climate control, and in places with living animals or plants, their safety and comfort, as well.

In addition to operating under the assumption that institutions must communicate well with visitors about general and special considerations, as well as fulfilling other responsibilities regarding their mission, they should also base their planning on research-based strategies for communicating with neurodivergent visitors.

First, public-facing institutions should *communicate in a variety of ways.* Multimodal communication will support comprehension in visitors with a wide variety of speech and language needs that aren't easily predicted. One way to ensure effective multimodal communication is to use *universal design for learning,* or UDL. UDL can be thought of as the educational counterpart of *universal design,* or UD, which is a series of guidelines developed for ensuring spaces are physically accessible, such as curb cuts for wheelchairs.[6]

Second, cultural institutions can use *plain English* or *plain language* as a pathway for enhanced communication.[7] Plain English or language is a practice of creating direct communication that doesn't diminish the information being presented but instead standardizes best practices for communication. The principles are common sense and easily implemented in various contexts, including museums. With these considerations of UDL and plain English or language in mind, let's revisit our basic assumptions.

CULTURAL INSTITUTIONS MUST COMMUNICATE BASIC INFORMATION THAT MEETS ALL VISITORS' NEEDS

Of the many ways cultural institutions communicate with the public—an email, a friendly face, a brochure—signage is perhaps the most visible and pervasive. If you have ever wandered into a public space cluttered with an overwhelming number of signs, or into one completely devoid of helpful directions, you have some idea of the value of well-crafted signage. This section will focus on the importance of clarity when posting information for the benefit of all visitors to a cultural institution.

The Science of Signage

In 2017, Australian researchers Meis and Kashima[8] detailed some of the most significant differences between signs, prompts, and symbols to change or influence people's behavior. They made a distinction between signage and mass media, and pointed out that while signs can be expensive and high-tech, they don't have to be to do their job, which typically entails giving directions, warning about potential danger, identifying things, and advising people to perform certain actions. They found that signs are most effective when they are displayed close to where actions are needed and are relatively convenient. They also found that there is not a clear answer as to whether polite, nondemanding versus bossy, or demanding language improves people's tendencies to do what the sign tells them to. In other words, they determined that people tend to obey "Do not litter" signs when they are displayed where littering might occur, especially when a trash can is conveniently located close to the sign. Still, they could not conclude whether it is more effective to say "Do not litter" or "*Please* do not litter" to get the job done. This simple adjustment to signage may become important when we explore principles guiding the use of plain English or language, which places an emphasis on keeping things simple and brief to ensure understandability.

One of the most important aspects of the research we are exploring relates to how cultural organizations use the Internet versus signage in their physical space to communicate with visitors. Beyond the littering scenario, another example might be the common challenge of managing sound in interior spaces. Telling people on the institution's website that they will be asked to monitor their noise levels while visiting may be useful for promoting on-site etiquette because it provides time for those neurodivergent individuals who plan their visit online to practice using strategies such as speaking with a soft volume or an "indoor voice." For others, posting this information in areas with sound-level problems will be more effective. Still, others might argue that Internet posts plus physical signage on-site are best-practice multimodal strategies for enhancing communication. There is no one-size-fits-most solution to the effectiveness of communicating basic information to all audiences.[9]

Saying It with Symbols

A second consideration for communicating information to a broad audience is whether using text or symbols and icons is preferred. According to UDL principles of providing multiple means of engagement and multiple means of representation, the best practice is to use both strategies. When visitors have different ways to ascertain information, a greater number are more likely to produce the desired physical actions or understand the information.

One caveat with symbols is that they may not be as universal as they seem. As an American who just returned from an extended visit to several countries where English is not the primary language, co-author Tina Fletcher found in her visits to over a dozen museums that signage such as universal symbols for toilets was found in all locations. Still, their location-specific customization can make them difficult to understand for literal or concrete thinkers. A case in point is the women's toilet icon.[10] In Portugal, the icon sports a little windswept hairstyle and curvy figure—and no arms. When displayed next to the male icon for toilets, to Tina's American eyes, she looked like she was on a date. Interestingly, when the Portuguese woman symbol is portrayed taking an elevator ride (displayed as a box with up and down arrows), in addition to losing her arms, she also loses her head. When she is displayed in a family restroom sign, the foreshortening of an icon for the baby in her lap looks like she is wearing a breastplate instead of holding a baby. The same set of circumstances in Austria yields a tall and hairless icon wearing a short dress, also standing by a man, but the business-like appearance of the side-by-side couple does not look like a date. The Austrian elevator image only shows men—with heads. One observed family restroom sign bore a striking resemblance to a male doctor examining a small patient on a table rather than a father changing his child's diaper. While these images undoubtedly make sense to most locals, a person traveling from one culture to another might have a harder time interpreting the nuances.

The moral of the story is to think through the symbols you choose. If an image is difficult for the average visitor to decode, it may be a frustrating source of confusion for someone who is neurodivergent. Consider what will make the most sense to the most people and how a symbol might be misinterpreted. A good rule of practice is to run any graphics past a formal or informal focus group including both neurotypical and neurodivergent people of different ages and cultural backgrounds in order to check for understanding.

Humor Is Tricky

An additional consideration is efforts by sign designers not to sound too bossy or strict by adding humorous visual elements. Some signs depict hats flying off the heads of people who are falling, tripping—or dancing. Lightning bolts fly out of fingers presumably pinched in doorways—or showing superpowers. Bathrooms depict humorous text communications cautioning toilet users not to flush their hopes and dreams—or goldfish—down toilets and are accompanied by images of toy cars flying into—or out of—toilets. This can also be exacerbated by adding elements of local color, such as cowboy boots, Hawaiian muumuus, or Tyrolean hats, and walking sticks to the standard icons. In other words, adding additional elements might lighten an overly directive message, but they can also add to confusion or limit comprehension for visitors in unfamiliar territory who are attempting to manage various communication challenges. Figure 7.1 shows some confusing images from a variety of settings.

Figure 7.1.   Confusing images from a variety of settings.
Tina Fletcher

The Value of Plain Language

Lastly, when posting information for all visitors, institutions should consider posting information in both the dominant vernacular and in plain language. Consider that by offering a simpler version of the same information, more visitors can use both sets of information to understand the content. It is also helpful for non-English readers to anticipate whether their language will be used, and in which order it will appear. As a museum visitor in Barcelona, co-author Tina Fletcher found English was often displayed as one of four posted languages, but not consistently. On occasion, it was replaced with Catalonian. As an American living close to Mexico and familiar with Spanish signage, she attempted to read Spanish words when no English was available. Under these circumstances, she would have gladly welcomed *plain Spanish* to support her surprisingly limited understanding of the signage. Table 7.1 shows a checklist for using plain English or language. In situations where a cultural institution's brand is playful, and staff want signage to have a friendlier tone, visual imagery or icons can help to convey an idea that is not strictly expressed in plain language. Figure 7.2 shows an example of signage with playful headings accompanied by recognizable icons, followed by explanatory information in plain language. These instructions are displayed on the elevator to the main entrance of the museum.

Reviewing all information for literal meanings does not mean information needs dumbing down. Consider including the following practices when you review information for clarity and conciseness, and apply these strategies to both print sources and digital media scripts for podcasts and videos[11]:

1. Avoid idioms such as "We are going to *tackle* Pop art and technology" or "You are *fishing* for compliments." Expressions may confuse neurodiverse audiences that take phrases literally.
2. Avoid jargon such as *Pop art* without defining it. In the case of Pop art, a literal thinker might think of a popping sound and not connect the word to *pop*ular culture.
3. Avoid using slang, which creates confusing descriptors and compliments, such as *hunky dory* or *groovy*.
4. Replace nicknames such as *Art Star* or *Warhol* with complete and literal names.
5. Reduce word salad. Paring down the number of words used in certain situations can go a long way to giving the neurodivergent person an opportunity to comprehend information. The following example compares a wordy sentence with a concise counterpart.

Table 7.1. Plain English or Language Checklist

Did/Did Not	Think of the person reading the information. (Make it clear. Avoid using "I," "we," and "you" when possible.)
Did/Did Not	Be direct and use the active voice most of the time. ("We will decide on your application soon," instead of "A decision on your application will be made soon.")
Did/Did Not	Avoid unnecessary jargon and technical terms. If not possible, use definitions for terms. ("No food and drink in this area," instead of "No food and drink on the portico.")
Did/Did Not	Define unfamiliar abbreviations and acronyms. ("Enjoy Free First Friday," instead of "Enjoy FFF.")
Did/Did Not	Avoid Latin, French, or Spanish expressions. (Readers can confuse *e.g.*, *i.e.*, and *etc.* Use full terms such as "for example.")
Did/Did Not	Each sentence should have 15 to 20 words or fewer. (Keep sentences to a minimum and use shorter, snappier sentences for variety.)
Did/Did Not	Remove unnecessary words and phrases. (Use words such as "before" instead of "in advance of.")
Did/Did Not	Avoid using nouns made from verbs (nominalizations). ("Please remove shoes when you enter," instead of "Please remove shoes upon entry.")
Did/Did Not	Break up dense text. (Use bulleted format for subheadings.)
Did/Did Not	Use any color images appropriately. Use clear and readable fonts. (Use a clear font, do not have more than three distinct fonts, and align text correctly on the left side of the document.)
Did/Did Not	Emphasize text carefully. (Use only **bold** to emphasize text, keep capital letters to a minimum.)
Comments:	

DMA
museum guidelines

PLAY BY THE RULES

 Keep Your Distance

Feel free to look, **but please do not touch the art or furniture on display**. Works of art are fragile, so keep a safe distance *(two feet is great)*.

 Lighten Up!

Please **check backpacks and umbrellas** at the **Coat Check**. *Front baby carriers and shoulder diaper bags are allowed in the galleries.*

 Strike a Pose

Photography without a flash is allowed in the galleries unless otherwise indicated. To protect the artwork, **monopods and tripods are not allowed**.

 Got Kids?

All children 12 and under must be supervised by an adult caregiver at all times. We recommend holding hands in the galleries with the youngest and fastest children.

Figure 7.2. Multimodal museum standards for etiquette posted near a museum entrance.
Image courtesy of Nasher Sculpture Center

a. Wordy sentence: I want to conclude by making a final point that we can agree on—hard work brings success.
b. Concise sentence: Finally, hard work brings success.

6. Stay focused on the reader, not the writer. Eliminate unnecessary self-references to keep the focus on the reader.

   a. Self-reference example: The Education Team at the Museum of Magical Thinking thanks you for visiting.
   b. Concise sentence: Thank you for visiting.

7. Let technology work for you. A variety of programs to check reading levels and sentence complexity exist. When many people contribute to written visual supports, different writing styles appear.

To determine how similar their reading level and complexity are, upload text to an online program such as a Flesch Kincaid Calculator for reading levels or a Lexile analyzer. While reading level analysis will provide a grade level, a Lexile analyzer includes information on word complexity and stylistic differences. One example regarding the different types of information provided by each is an analysis of Ernest Hemingway's work, which has a low reading level due to simple word use but has high complexity due to writing style. The only way to know which type of analysis works for your institution is to try several systems to see which results align with your needs. With practice, your team will learn how to adjust their styles to provide consistent results.

CULTURAL INSTITUTIONS COMMUNICATE SPECIAL SERVICES AND EVENTS NOT USED BY ALL VISITORS

In revisiting our chapter's second assumption of communicating with certain subsets of the public (such as neurodivergent visitors), two factors come into play. Cultural institutions may offer time-specific events, including temporary web information and signage, and ongoing events or resources. Each may have special considerations such as registration locations or times, programs, equipment, or supplies that are either taken home after the event or that should remain in place, and other unique factors such as how the challenge of hosting multiple service animals in one location should be handled. Sensory spaces and other special equipment may be available and require instruction on how to use them. There may also be questions about the goals of the event, which can include providing opportunities for neurodivergent individuals and their families to meet others, learn about local resources, practice being with visitors who tolerate behavioral differences, or learn how to interact with cultural personnel. Institutions that communicate this information in various ways will help visitors experience less confusion and provide more enjoyable experiences.

Cultural educators can communicate directly with local autism centers, school special education departments, and area therapists to learn information about how signage is posted in their centers. A great example of this is information regarding headphone use. Creating *headphone zone* signage to indicate noisy areas where people might choose to wear headphones is helpful, and creating signs using the same graphic style as schools and autism centers is even more helpful. Neurodivergent students and educators use a variety of software programs, and depending on the center or school, they will also have preferred icons or images from these programs that they use heavily. In the interest of making visits good experiences for neurodivergent visitors and their companions or helpers, some places may provide copies of their favorite images. Still, others may offer more basic information and recommend that the cultural institution purchase its software package. One primary concern for institutions that post this information on their own websites is to ensure they follow copyright and fair use guidelines. Textbox 7.1 shows a variety of programs used for visual communication support.

An additional consideration when providing information on special events or services is not to hide or gatekeep this information. Although a sensory space, for example, may be reserved for certain visitors, it can be helpful for everyone to know about it. Openly communicating what is offered to neurodivergent visitors normalizes their presence at your institution and signals that all are welcome.

TEXTBOX 7.1.
PROGRAMS USED FOR VISUAL COMMUNICATION SUPPORTS

BOARDMAKER

This program allows and focuses on augmentative communication products in which it completes a special education platform that allows consumers to access support in education, access, and social-emotional needs. There is a wide variety of information that extends to educators, parents, therapists, and administrators for their visual support needs. Boardmaker provides training and support to run this program with ease as it offers helpful tips and ideas on how to use the product effectively and efficiently. There is a variety of solutions with low- and high-tech augmentative and alternative communication (ACC) tools and software for purchase.

https://goboardmaker.com/collections/all

(continued)

TEXTBOX 7.1. *Continued*

PICTO4ME

Picto4me is a powerful web app that allows users to create, play, share, and chat with ACC pictograph boards. This software has over 80,000 images and is still continuing to grow; within the app, it contains cells that allow users to pick an image and select their desired visual representation coupled with a QR code that is given for quick access. This program can be downloaded onto a personal mobile device or can be managed on a web browser. It is available to any individual with a free account, but it also allows for better features by upgrading to pro or premium accounts.

https://www.picto4.me/site

SYMBOXSTIX

SymbolStix brands itself as a new and dynamic symbol set using "stick figures with an attitude." One unique feature is that the 11,000 figures can be depicted without reference to gender, age, or culturally specific attributes to avoid distraction by detail. SymbolStix also provides options to portray a range of famous individuals including William Shakespeare.

https://www.cricksoft.com/us/symbol-sets/symbolstix

VISUAL ESSENTIALS SOFTWARE

The Photo Essential Software contains over 3,500 pictures that include layouts and templates that can be easily created as visual supports. These visual supports can be aligned with demonstrating appropriate and inappropriate behaviors. This essential software includes ASL, community signs, and photos with a wide variety of category illustrations for the desired targeted behavior. The software is $69.99.

https://nationalautismresources.com/visual-essentials-software-with-3-500
-photos/

VISUALS TO GO

Visuals2Go is an all-in-one app created to support communication and learning difficulties, as it can be used for verbal and nonverbal users. The app was developed with the collaboration of speech pathologists and parents. It allows access to a variety of visuals to support communication needs. The application is always being updated with new images, free resources, therapy support, training, and tutorials for use. The app is free but has in-app purchases or with a subscription of $9.99 for a month or $79.99 annually.

https://www.visuals2go.com

INTERACTIONS BETWEEN VISITORS AND CULTURAL INSTITUTIONS WILL HAVE RULES

Now that we have explored communications about what visitors want to know, it's essential to spend a moment with what cultural institutions will need them to know. A study published in *Tourism Management* by Taiwanese researchers Sheng and Chen[12] analyzed 425 survey returns detailing what visitors wanted from museums. They found responses clustered around five categories; visitors wanted fun and easy visits, cultural entertainment, a sense of personal identification with the exhibits and museum, the experience of historical reminiscing, and escapism. They recalled the 1992 work of Dierking and Falk[13] exploring the appeal of interactive environments that make visitors feel a part of their museum experience. While visitors are busy enjoying their cultural outing, they may be less focused on how they are affecting their environment. By effectively communicating rules and expectations to everyone, cultural institutions can help to maintain safe conditions with limited disruptions to the visitor experience.

Reflecting on the need for clear language when communicating expectations, co-author Tina Fletcher conducted a little research focused on museum expectations for good behavior. She used English-language search phrases "museum etiquette," "museum manners," and "how to act in a museum" in her computer search browser and was rewarded with pages of responses. She found new etiquette guidelines in the first twenty-one responses and continued until she examined twenty-five and found no new guidelines. She then categorized the guidelines and found five overarching themes, then she reexamined each theme finding what would be considered clear signage, such as "Leave backpacks at the front desk," and those that are less easily understood or defined, such as "Keep noise at a country club level"). Table 7.2 shows how some aspects of etiquette, such as noise and physical behavior, are objective, while others, such as touching and respecting viewing distances, need to be communicated with definitions of what is meant.

While this list is an informal compilation, it is easy to see that some of these items are subject to personal interpretation—unless a definition is provided to the viewer. A literal thinker might wonder if horses are involved with "horseplay" or houses are involved in "roughhousing." Referring to our first study on signage, the authors found that everyday actions need only a prompt or reminder from a sign. These might include "Don't touch" or "Don't chew gum." The challenges arise when new knowledge is being transmitted by signage. The signs either need to carry more information, be specific, and keep the language free of nuances. Examples of this might include, "Do not cross rope barriers or stanchions (e.g., an upright post forming a barrier),"

Table 7.2.   Etiquette Guideline by Category, Definition, and Measurability

Category	Language Used on Website	How the Language Can Be Measured
Copyright and Intellectual Property	Don't do a mini photoshoot. Don't post artworks without crediting the artist. Check guidelines for sketching. Put phones away.	Measure with a yes or no or how many times the actions are witnessed: photographing, posting, sketching, or using a phone.
Physical Actions	Don't touch. Avoid touching unless it's interactive. Don't go over barriers. Don't sit on ledges. Beware of movement. Respect space. Avoid horseplay.	Measure with a yes or no or how many times the actions are witnessed: touching, going over barriers, and sitting on ledges. Be more specific and describe terms with visible actions: beware of movement, respect space, and avoid horseplay.
Social Behaviors and Impacting Others	Manage time. Follow current health and safety guidelines. No littering. Observe safety. Practice hygiene. Have appropriate behavior. Don't flirt with your significant other. Dress appropriately. Don't take too long taking photos of installations.	Measure with a yes or no or how many times the actions are witnessed: manage time, follow guidelines, don't litter. Be more specific and describe terms with visible actions: observe safety, practice hygiene, have appropriate behavior, don't flirt with your significant other, dress appropriately, and don't take too long taking photos of installations.

followed by a photograph or clear illustration of which side of the barrier or stanchion the person is expected to stand on. Co-author Tina Fletcher once had an autistic museum visitor explain that they thought they could lean across a barrier if the artwork was covered in glass. A photograph of the de-sired action would help correct such faulty interpretations of directives.

WHEN IN DOUBT, ASK

Community members can explore their resources to develop the signage they need to minimize frustration, discomfort, and fatigue and remove any barri-ers to effective communication. When they collaborate with local experts and neurodivergent people, they can create signs and information postings that are targeted and effective and avoid spending time on signage that either misses the mark because there is a mismatch between the reading level of the sign and the communication skills of the visitor, or they lack the visual appeal to grab and focus attention. Asking neurodivergent people and their families for their opinions and insights can go a long way to designing effective signage, but so is taking the time to watch and learn from how they spend their time in your cultural institution.

NOTES

1. Mari Wiklund, "Interactional Challenges in Conversations with Autistic Preadolescents: The Role of Prosody and Non-Verbal Communication in Other-Initiated Repairs," *Journal of Pragmatics* 94 (2016): 76–97, https://doi.org/10.1016/j.pragma.2016.01.008; Daniel Oberfeld, and Felicitas Klöckner-Nowotny, "Individual Differences in Selective Attention Predict Speech Identification at a Cocktail Party," *eLife* 5 (2016), https://doi.org/10.7554/elife.16747; Adelbert W. Bronkhorst, "The Cocktail-Party Problem Revisited: Early Processing and Selection of Multi-Talker Speech," *Attention, Perception, & Psychophysics* 77, no. 5 (2015): 1465–87. https://doi.org/10.3758/s13414-015-0882-9.

2. "Visual Supports at Home and in the Community for Individuals with Autism Spectrum Disorders: A Scoping Review," *Autism* 24, no. 2 (2019): 447–69, https://doi.org/10.1177/1362361319871756.

3. "Diversity, Equity, Accessibility and Inclusion," American Alliance of Museums, November 30, 2017, https://www.aam-us.org/programs/diversity-equity-accessibility-and-inclusion/.

4. Metropolitan Museum of Art, "My Met Tour: A Visual Checklist for Visitors on the Autism Spectrum," https://www.metmuseum.org/-/media/files/events/programs/progs-for-visitors-with-disabilities/my-met-tour.pdf.

5. The Museum, Library and Cultural Properties Council of ASIS International, and the Museum Association Security Committee of the American Association of Museums, "Suggested Practices for Museum Security," June 2008, https://www.aam-us.org/wp-content/uploads/2018/01/suggested-practices-for-museum-security.pdf.

6. "The UDL Guidelines," UDL, October 15, 2021, https://udlguidelines.cast.org/.

7. "Plain Language Principles," U.S. Food and Drug Administration, accessed June 18, 2022, https://www.fda.gov/about-fda/plain-writing-its-law/plain-language-principles.

8. Julia Meis and Yoshihisa Kashima, "Signage as a Tool for Behavioral Change: Direct and Indirect Routes to Understanding the Meaning of a Sign," *PLOS ONE* 12, no. 8 (2017), https://doi.org/10.1371/journal.pone.0182975.

9. "Signage as Non-Verbal Communications," Hanafizulkipli blogspot, October 19, 2015, http://hanafizulkipli92.blogspot.com/2015/10/signage-as-non-verbal-communications.html.

10. Alissa Walker, "The Story behind the Universal Icons That Came Long before Emoji," *Gizmodo*, November 7, 2015, https://gizmodo.com/the-story-behind-the-univer sal-icons-that-came-long-bef-1592800916.

11. For insights on the lived experience of communication with autism, see Temple Grandin and Oliver Sacks, *Thinking in Pictures: And Other Reports from My Life with Autism,* (New York: Vintage Books, 2020). To learn more about communication styles, see "Autism: 10 Ways to Make Communication Easier," https://www.youtube .com/watch?v=94aW1AfDug8.

12. Chieh-Wen Sheng and Ming-Chia Chen, "A Study of Experience Expectations of Museum Visitors," *Tourism Management* 33, no. 1 (February 2012): 53–60, https:// doi.org/10.1016/j.tourman.2011.01.023.

13. L. D. Dierking and J. H. Falk, "Redefining the Museum Experience: The Inter-active Experience Model," *Visitor Studies* 4, no. 1 (1992): 173–76.

Chapter Eight

Show and Tell

Creating and Using Visual Supports

When visiting a cultural institution, many neurodivergent visitors will appreciate some *visual supports*, usually in the form of images displayed on walls, in handouts, or posted online. While the term might be new to some readers, the practice of providing visual supports is common for those who have worked as educators. Supports can include pictures, emojis, written words, physical objects, photographs, schedules, maps, and labels.

In this chapter, you will learn

- what visual supports are and how they are used;
- effective placement of visual supports;
- differences between literal and abstract visual supports; and
- how to develop tip sheets for projects and experiences.

MANY TYPES OF PEOPLE BENEFIT FROM VISUAL SUPPORTS

Some visual supports can be highly personalized for specific individuals, and others can be more general. Personalized supports make heavy use of familiar photographs, words, and images, and are likely to be implemented in cases where the interests and experiences of a neurodivergent person are well known. General visual supports are widely understood by many people and can be found throughout our everyday lives. Familiar examples of everyday general supports include stop signs, traffic lights, car dashboard icons, and information postings. Familiar examples from cultural institutions may include graphic signage, printed handouts, and digital guides.

Well-designed visual supports can benefit everyone as they learn about expectations and activities. For example, while some visual supports have neurodivergent visitors in mind, those featuring pictures, graphic images, or icons can also benefit non-English readers. Simple graphics paired with words can be helpful for beginning readers. Presenting concepts and ideas in multiple ways is a valuable way to communicate with neurodivergent visitors who may either have language or intellectual barriers to understanding.[1] Think about a harried mother pointing out a posted picture to help her small child understand expectations created by a place, and that it's not just the mom being bossy.

Figure 8.1.   Simple word and image pair.
Tina Fletcher

Figure 8.2.   The concept of headphones moves from literal (top image) to abstract (bottom image).
Tina Fletcher

LOCATION, LOCATION, LOCATION!

Remember that old saying about leading a horse to water but not making it drink? Like many adages created in the spirit of providing something that isn't used, we could express a similar idea regarding visual supports. You can post a sign to share information, but you can't make visitors read it.

You can improve your chances of your visual support being seen with predictable placement. If visitors have an expectation of where information will be posted, they are more likely to look for it. Many community venues have a lot of things on walls, from maps and signs to exhibits and related infographics. Decor, while seen by most as a positive addition to a venue, might prove distracting or confusing to a neurodivergent visitor. To minimize the need for visitors to go on a visual scavenger hunt to find helpful information, venues can develop the habit of consistently placing signage at eye level, creating signage that is consistent in size, format, and layout, and decluttering the space around posted signs.

Hopefully, ascertaining information from the sign is self-explanatory, but if it is not, a helpful human presence may go a long way to smoothing that process. This is particularly true in cases where symbols or colors are used to represent something, such as noise levels or whether an exhibit may be touched. A friendly staff member can point out or reinforce the message posted on the visual support. Informing frontline staff such as gallery attendants or ushers of temporary signage placement may also go a long way toward having their help in directing people to the information, as well as preventing trips or falls resulting from visitor encounters with the signs.

Visual supports are also helpful in places or events when noise makes it hard to hear what other people are saying. Classic examples of noisy environments are conference halls, food courts, packed transportation systems, and large tour groups. Wind, weather, or background music can make it difficult to hear and comprehend information in places where noise levels are not exceptionally high. For these reasons, visual supports are significant in conveying information to all visitors, not just those who are neurodivergent.

LITERAL AND ABSTRACT: TWO SIDES OF THE SAME COIN

Over time, an understanding of the effectiveness of visual supports has developed. Two main ideas can represent a hierarchy of visual representation. The first idea is that visual supports are most easily understood when they are literal. Examples include using videos, photographs, tangible objects, and objects that are smaller but similar to what they represent. The second idea is that visual supports can move from literal things to abstract concepts such as text or printed words as individuals expand their ability to conceptualize ideas.

Be as Literal as Possible

Some concepts are not based on actual objects, and they are more challenging to conceptualize. One example is the word *understand*. A sentence reading, "Skylar *understands* the impact of technology on Pop art," could be illustrated in many ways. An illustrated concept of *understands* might be a photograph of Skylar holding her hand under her chin in the style of Rodin's *The Thinker*. Still, a more literal illustration of the main idea would be an image of Skylar reading a labeled or illustrated text on technology and Pop art. In this case, a more literal sentence would say, "Skylar *reads* about the impact of technology on Pop art." We can describe the concept of reading much more quickly than the idea of understanding.

In a cultural setting, this example might translate into the use of visual supports that remind visitors not to touch something. Figure 8.1 shows an example of some commonly used pictures that could be potentially confusing.

Figure 8.3.   Graphic images of "Do Not Touch" can have other meanings. Could these images also mean point, pick up, and stop?
Anna Smith

Each of these is identified as a *Do Not Touch* image. Yet close examination shows how they could also refer to pointing, picking something up, indicating stop, and other unintended concepts. What is intended to be a simple, straightforward message could be an unexpected source of frustration. While there may not be a perfect image to convey the idea of not performing a specific action to any number of different objects of spaces, consistency and compassion can go a long way. Use the same image to express the same idea throughout your space, share expectations with visitors when they arrive, and remember the power of a helpful human presence for moments when a picture isn't enough.

Striking a Balance

Many neurodivergent people prefer and are most successful communicating with literal concepts, including accurate word choices. For these individuals, sarcasm, jokes, puns, and wordplay are often very difficult to comprehend. Examples of confusing requests include *hop to it* (start working), *hold your horses* (wait), *keep your eye on me* (watch me), and *don't break your arm patting yourself on the back* (don't overpraise yourself). Those who interpret words literally can find product names like *ear defenders* (headphones), *fidgets* (handheld manipulative objects), and *sneakers* (athletic shoes) confusing. As people mature and their ability to process more abstract information develops, their needs for literal visual images may diminish. As an example, a young adult with a cartoon-based picture story or schedule may be using this because they have always used images in this style, not because it is the most developmentally appropriate for them. With maturation, they may no longer need illustrations to understand a concept and can process text quite well without them.

In a cultural setting serving a wide variety of visitors, it may be difficult or impossible to gauge individual processing ability. In this case offering a range of visual supports may be helpful, such as one version of a tip sheet with activity instructions for readers and one for nonreaders. For reference, the following list is one way to look at the ranking of visual supports, and as an example, how viewers interpret them relative to a person preparing to visit a sensory-friendly art-making event. The top of the list shows literal items that could be used to convey an idea, and the bottom shows abstract items that express the same information:

1. real items (stretched canvas, painting, snack)
2. portions of actual items (piece of canvas, painting, snack food item wrapper)
3. miniature versions of actual items (dollhouse version of a canvas, painting, snack)

4. photograph of actual items (photos of a canvas, painting, and snack)
5. computer-generated image or icon of items (canvas, painting, and snack)
6. single words attached to illustrations (canvas, painting, and snack)
7. written words only (canvas, painting, and snack)

From a practical perspective, educators can use what makes the most sense to their institution. Sometimes it isn't easy to use real items owing to issues like size or perishability. Instead, many people begin by using a photograph, followed by an icon with a word. The only way you will know is to experiment and get advice from someone who works with people you anticipate hosting.

TIP SHEETS: BREAKING THINGS DOWN

A *tip sheet* is a short guide offering information in an easily digestible format, such as bullet points, numbered lists, or graphics. This form of visual support can be a useful tool when giving instructions for multistep activities to program participants. An activity-focused tip sheet is an invaluable addition to verbal instructions and demonstrations, allowing participants and their companions an opportunity to review instructions and process them at their own pace. For this type of resource, it is helpful to break down the individual steps that make up the project, describe them in plain language, and pair them with images showing how that step is completed. Keep in mind the distinction between literal and abstract when creating these instructions, and what format will promote comprehension for the greatest number of participants. These sheets can then be displayed as a sign near the corresponding activity station or as a handout, which frees up staff to communicate more directly with visitors. A helpful bonus to creating a process-oriented tip sheet is that writing out the steps can help you discover if a project is too complex and needs to be adapted.

PULLING IT ALL TOGETHER

The goal of this chapter is to encourage you to try your hand at providing multiple means of communication for all visitors, including neurodiverse audiences, nonreaders and beginning readers, harried and hurried visitors, and non-English speakers and readers. Implementing the same communication practices that other similar or nearby institutions use can promote consistency and ease the code shifting that can distract from a visit. The only way to know if your efforts have paid off is to devise simple methods of collecting data that are not burdensome for either employees or visitors. Starting simple and systematically introducing visual supports is the easiest way to explore the impact of each addition. Ultimately, the adage less is more should be the goal for institutions as they introduce ways to help their visitors engage with and not be overwhelmed by communication and comprehension options.

NOTE

1. Universal design for learning, or UDL, is a concept that aims to provide easily understood teaching and learning methods for all learners, despite any limitations in comprehension or expression. To learn more about UDL guidelines and methods, see CAST at www.cast.org for downloadable teaching and program design aids.

Chapter Nine

Happily Ever After

Writing Effective Success Stories

Success stories can go a long way in helping people understand unfamiliar and potentially challenging events. As opposed to the traditional concept of a success story being a rag-to-riches tale, the type of success stories you'll want to use are physical or digital documents that provide guidance to help anyone have a successful experience when visiting your venue. Sometimes, if a person is in a new environment with unfamiliar rules, both stated and implied, it is helpful to have someone spell out what is happening. Some autistic or neurodivergent people in particular have difficulty reading the facial expressions of others and won't respond to social cues such as a meaningful look or withering glance from others. To counteract this, they can review a success story to learn what typically happens at an event or in a place, find out what people tend to be thinking about, and prepare strategies regarding potentially tricky situations that might arise.

This chapter presents the basics for staff members at cultural institutions who wish to create their own success stories, including

- why success stories are a helpful tool for neurodivergent visitors;
- what makes an effective success story;
- examples of written and visual success stories; and
- common topics included in success stories and how to approach them.

PURPOSES OF SUCCESS STORIES

Cultural institutions might create success stories to teach visitors about social niceties such as using an indoor voice despite the temptingly bouncy ambient sound, figuring out how far to stay back from an exhibit, learning how to gauge

83

what the standards for crowding are, and figuring out what can or cannot be touched. In nature and outdoor venues, success stories offer help for understanding how to respond when animals hurt each other, nurse their young, defecate, mate, or make thunderous sounds. One zookeeper, for instance, shared his continual problem with the public's response to a harpy eagle hanging entrails on their enclosure fence during the eagle's dinner time. Considering these scenarios, it is easy to see that a person doesn't need to be autistic to appreciate a friendly explanation of site-specific norms and rules before any trouble begins.

While they may appear deceptively simple, a good story carefully interweaves ample neutral descriptions of the event and place. It refrains from giving orders or directives to the neurodivergent reader or listener. Instead, it provides typical situations and strategies that can meet them. Stories can be crafted predictably and use consistent approaches to providing information and processes. In addition to providing information about a place or situation, a well-crafted story can also supply information about what is expected from the visitor, considering a variety of conditions and potential outcomes that may happen. Some neurodivergent visitors may be able to read a story, while others will listen to someone else read it. In some cases, the story can even become a script for a video. In stories and videos, the protagonist can be an anonymous individual or the person themself.

WE'RE NEVER TOO OLD FOR A STORY: ANATOMY OF A STORY

This section details creating stories. While the focus of story writing in this chapter is on creating general success stories, some readers may also be familiar with the term *Social Story*. While a success story follows similar parameters, a Social Story is a trademarked product created by special education teacher Carole Gray, who directs users that the term should be written as a proper noun. One way to differentiate them is that *success story* is a broad category, but a *Social Story* follows a specific recipe, including a title and introduction that identifies the topic, a body that adds detail to the scenario, and a conclusion that reinforces and summarizes the information. A Social Story comprises sentences that are descriptive, perspective, directive, affirmative, and cooperative.[1] These stories also utilize ratios of different types of sentences to achieve their goal. For an example of sentences that follow this format, see table 9.1. Social Stories are widely used and effective, but developing them requires training, certification, and practice. For this reason, many community members appreciate them but recognize that creating general success stories may align more closely with their realities of available time and resources.

As a rule, the recipe for a success story begins by describing a place or event. Following a general description, the story can move into telling what other visitors are doing and may include what their feelings or thoughts might be.

Table 9.1. Descriptive, Directive, Perspective, and Affirmative Sentences in a Social Story

Title: Riding the Bus to the Museum			
Sentence Type	*Sentence Description*	*Usual Place in Social Story*	*Sample Sentences*
Descriptive	Neutral description	Used throughout the story—at least two descriptive sentences are used for each directive sentence	• My class will go to the museum on Monday. • We will ride the bus with our teacher. • The bus and museum have rules for good manners. • Using an inside voice is a way to show good manners.
Directive	Gives actions that can be followed or coaches the reader	Follows descriptive sentences	• I can use my inside voice to show good manners on the bus and in the museum.
Perspective	Describes what others are thinking	Follows descriptive and directive sentences	• The bus driver and my teacher appreciate it when I have good manners.
Affirmative	Describes important rules or laws and can provide a cause-and-effect pattern	Follows descriptive and directive sentences	• Using good manners on the bus keeps me safe. • Using good manners in the museum is a way to be a good citizen.
My class will go to the museum on Monday. We will ride the bus with our teacher. The bus and museum have rules for good manners. Using an inside voice is a way to show good manners. I can use my inside voice to show good manners on the bus and in the museum. The bus driver and my teacher appreciate it when I have good manners. Using good manners on the bus keeps me safe. Using good manners in the museum is a way to be a good citizen.			

Sometimes emphasizing things that are not visible can be very helpful to a neurodivergent person because being able to anticipate another person's feelings or identify reasons for their actions is not always easy for some. One common scenario in museums is whether an artwork can be touched. While a sign may use words or images to direct people not to touch, the desired behavior may still not be evident. Including a picture of a person not touching the artwork can include the distance they should stand back from the art, along with actions indicating they will avoid touching it, such as holding their hands behind their back or crossing their arms across their chest. An accompanying caption can further explain these actions. Let's look at two images that show this common scenario illustrated in two different ways. Figure 9.1 uses a literal image in the

Figure 9.1.   Modeling desired behavior with literal images. The sign on the floor says "Do Not Touch," and this visitor is not touching. This visitor is two steps away from the art and has his arms behind his back to remind himself not to touch it.
Anna Smith

form of a photograph. The sign on the floor says *Do Not Touch*, and the person in the image is not touching. The person is two steps away from the art and has his hands behind his back to remind himself not to touch it. Figure 9.2 is from a success story that uses illustrations to give visual cues about desired behavior. Which image and instruction pair would be best for your visitors?

I will look at art from 2 feet away.

Figure 9.2.   Modeling desired behavior with graphic images.
Anna Smith

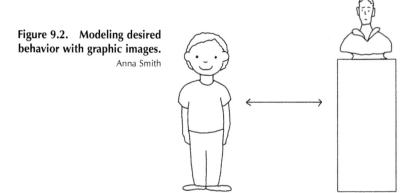

HELP WITH IMAGES

While there is no formula for delivering ideas through images, it is common to see computer software–generated graphics and icons commonly associated with educational instruction in schools. Boardmaker and Symbolstix are two programs that have widely used software programs in schools and other educational settings attended by neurodivergent visitors. These programs are both based on subscription services, but other image options can be found by downloading symbols, images, and icons from copyright-free servers.[2] Hand-drawn illustrations may also be effective and need not be complicated, so long as they are clear and straightforward. Figure 9.3 provides an example of an illustrated success story from an art museum with images drawn by a staff member. Cultural institutions can also provide scripts online that families and friends of neurodivergent people can personalize with images found on the Internet, photographs they take, drawings they create, or use without any images at all. The more personalized the story is, the more likely it is for people with different intellectual capabilities to understand and remember it.

PLAN AND PRACTICE

As a learning tool, here are the basics of writing good stories for people who are neurodivergent—and anyone else who could use a little guidance and encouragement for their visit.

Create a Goal for the Story: Usually, it is to help the reader/listener understand an unfamiliar or challenging event and detail strategies they might need to have in place.

Consider the Perspective and Voice: Tell the story from the reader/listener's perspective, as if they were reading it to someone else. The tone of the story should be encouraging and helpful.

Write the Steps:

1. Break the story into parts.
2. Decide how long or involved the story should be. The level of detail can be tailored to individual needs.
3. Choose the most appropriate level of visual supports and whether visual supports are needed at all. Consider whether it is necessary to personalize them, such as using the neurodivergent person as the model.
4. Describe what's happening and suggest strategies for behavior, action, and thinking throughout the story. Place the most significant emphasis on describing.
5. Keep the tone positive and encouraging.
6. Reinforce or praise the reader/listener's understanding or efforts.
7. Practice!

Success Story

I am going to the Nasher Sculpture Center.	Signs and maps help me find my way around.	If I stay close to my group, I won't get lost.
I shouldn't touch the art or the walls.	I will look at art from 2 feet away.	I can talk about the art in a quiet voice.
I can walk on the grass, but I shouldn't climb the walls.	I will see water outside, but I shouldn't touch it.	If there is noise, I can wear headphones.
I can use a pencil to do the activities in my kit.	Sometimes, I need to use the restroom.	There is a quiet room to take a break.

 **Today was a good day!**

Nasher Sculpture Center

Figure 9.3.   Success story with hand-drawn illustrations.
Anna Smith

BREAKING DOWN THE SCENARIO
INTO MANAGEABLE CHUNKS

The only way to learn about success stories is to build them repeatedly. Stories are easy to read, and many writers assume they will be easy to write. It takes a lot of practice to make a well-structured and crafted story that accurately hits the targeted behaviors and suggested actions and leaves off the bossy tone. Writers are often surprised at how hard a simple story is to craft. In this example, the scenario is about attending a sensory-friendly art-making workshop at a museum. Here is what the event might look like from a staff perspective:

8:30–9:30   Everyone arrives and makes small talk.
9:30–10:00 People move into art-making stations.
10:00–11:00 Everyone makes art in their stations.
11:00–12:00 People can talk about their art with the group.
12:00–12:30 Everyone says goodbye and leaves.

What might not be apparent to unprepared staff in this scenario is that two of the most challenging aspects of this experience for neurodivergent participants are making small talk and sharing art because social interactions and communication are often tricky and can be the least self-evident of all event components. For this reason, a story can explain the nuances of making small talk since there are no clear rules or standards to explain or help with that aspect. From this, the story writer can break events into smaller parts if this kind of microanalysis is needed. Here is an example of the many things that may occur in the first thirty minutes of this sensory-friendly art-making experience alone, the part for 8:30–9:30 when everyone arrives and makes small talk. The list can go on and on:

1. Arrive at the museum.
2. Smile and greet people.
3. Put away coats, umbrellas, and other personal items.
4. Find a place to sit.
5. Select something from the snack area or vending machine.
6. Join others in small talk (ask a few questions, answer a few questions, make a few statements, listen to what other people say, and respond to them).
7. Clean the area.
8. Move to the art-making stations . . .
   . . . and then the story moves on to what is happening in the next increment.

Making Sure the Story Is Right

Writers can verify their lists with regular visitors or facilitators of this event and decide which steps to analyze and emphasize to the reader/listener, paying particular attention to events or things that may not be explicit, such as the many subtle components of greeting one another. Greetings may entail many factors, such as identifying oneself, looking at a person, offering to shake hands or bump fists, and exchanging greetings with others.

At this point, it may be obvious that a story can have as much or as little information and suggestions or strategies as the reader or listener needs to experience the event successfully. The writer determines how complex and lengthy the story should be and if and how illustrations will be used. The following example shows how a story can be used to explain the same experience of sensory-friendly art-making time at a museum. Figure 9.4 shows one example of how one portion of this story can be illustrated using photographs.

Sensory-Friendly Art-Making Time at the Museum

Many museums have sensory-friendly art-making times. People might greet each other in many ways when they get to the museum. They can shake hands, bump fists, or wave or smile instead. If my arm or shoulder gets patted, I remember the pat will usually last a second. I can rub my arm or shoulder later, but if I rub it, then people might have their feelings hurt.

After greeting others, people can enjoy snacks if they want to. I can figure out how much to eat and drink so that I won't take too much. Enjoying refreshment time is a big part of being with other visitors at the art-making time and can be fun.

It's 9:30, and the time for eating and drinking is over until next month's meeting. It's time to go to the art stations. Before I go, I can put my cup in the sink, my napkin in the trash, and push my chair up to the table. This is being respectful.

We all go to our art stations and make art for an hour. When the time to make art is over, everyone helps clean up the art supplies and makes sure our art is in a safe place or ready to go home with us. After this, we can return to the refreshment room and discuss the art. This is when people talk with others in friendly ways but can also talk about things they are worried about or excited about. Some people might decide to listen to other people but not talk. This is okay.

Most people aren't sorry the art-making time is over because they might be with each other next time. If I am sad to leave sensory-friendly art-making time, I can remember that it happens every month, and I am welcome to come back again.

The End

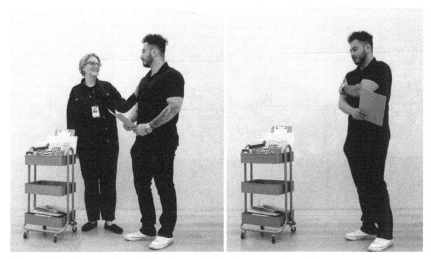

Figure 9.4. Success story illustrations with text passage. From the success story: many museums have sensory-friendly art-making times. When people get to the museum, they might greet each other in many ways. They can shake hands, bump fists, or they might wave or smile instead. If my arm or shoulder gets patted, I can remember the pat will usually just last a second. I can rub my arm or shoulder later. If I rub it then, people might have their feelings hurt.

Anna Smith

Notice the tone of the story is personal, descriptive, and positive—it is not a list of rules or regulations. The images that accompany the story also stick closely to the point. If the story is about selecting a beverage from a vending machine, the provided image should focus on a photo, icon, or drawing of a person selecting something from a vending machine, deemphasize the surroundings, and reduce the amount of excess information about the environment or presence of other people in favor of focusing on the vending machine and the visitor. Figure 9.5 shows an example of a zoomed-in shot of this scenario.

COMMON TOPICS FOR SUCCESS STORIES

There are a variety of situations that a visitor may encounter when attending a cultural institution. A science museum workshop will differ significantly from an art museum tour, a symphony performance, or a trip to the zoo. However, common sensory and social needs of neurodivergent visitors can help cultural educators to plan some content that will be relevant to most readers of a success story.

Figure 9.5. Comparing a zoomed-in versus zoomed-out photograph. If a story is about selecting a beverage from a vending machine, the accompanying image should focus on the image of a person selecting something from a vending machine and deemphasize the surroundings.

Anna Smith

Start to Finish

A broad overview of an experience at a cultural institution can help someone to prepare for their entire visit. Consider every step of the visit sequence from when the visitor arrives at your space until they leave. What might their first impression be? Where should they enter, and what should they do next? What may be brought into your space and what rules should be followed? Include pictures of the building, admission staff, and security team they may meet, as well as examples of things they are likely to see, smell, touch, hear or move through. Indicate where people may rest, eat, and meet if they are connecting with a group. Information is key to anyone planning an experience, and a comprehensive success story can be a useful tool for alleviating anxiety.

How Loud Is Loud?

Some common scenarios in cultural institutions involve subjective considerations, such as gauging how loud one can be or whether they are blocking other visitors' lines of sight to installations or displays. In these situations, providing visitors with objective measures can help them adhere to the rules. An example some neurodivergent visitors might appreciate is a link to a decibel reader app and a target range for loudness.

Decibel readers are readily available as free or low-cost apps for digital devices. Simple teacher apps used to manage classroom volume or student noise levels while on field trips are easy to use and provide graphic images of sound levels that are understandable to students with a wide range of abilities. Some classroom noise monitor apps even have an alarm feature. The app sends a visual or audible alert or warning when noise meets a predetermined threshold. Other apps are user-driven, such as behavior counters, in which target behaviors are monitored and tallied by the app user, much like a gallery tally counter.

One example of measurable behavior is shouting or screaming. It is helpful to reference a familiar noise to indicate the volume of different decibel ranges. For example, 60 decibels is the volume level of conversations. Seventy decibels is as loud as the sound of a vacuum cleaner or hair dryer. An image table or picture of the sound level they can use in a museum can help visitors gauge their volume. Allowing neurodivergent visitors to practice with the noise level app before a visit can also help them self-manage their noise level.

Another strategy to help visitors who can't gauge their loudness can be to remind them that their voice should not be heard in the next room or gallery. Allowing neurodivergent visitors to practice using appropriate volume levels before opening times or in another location can be helpful. Explicit instruction in the story and practice gauging their volume, practicing safe viewing distances, and even wayfinding can be beneficial and align expectations between cultural institution personnel and visitors.

Crowd Control: The Good, the Bad, and the Ugly

Another potentially confusing situation for some neurodivergent visitors that can be tackled in a story is understanding how crowd control can be managed from one location to another. Stanchions (short posts with ropes or cords), retractable belts, traffic cones, barricades, barriers, crowd blockers, and safety barriers have a wide range of appearances, and the many ways they are used can also contribute to confusion on the part of neurodivergent visitors. While it may seem logical to use a practice of putting stanchions in front of all canvas works and not putting them in front of glass-covered works because they are already protected, a neurodivergent visitor may interpret the absence of the stanchion in front of some works as meaning it is permissible to get close to or touch the stanchion-free artwork. Simple solutions for this dilemma are to put stanchions or other consistent crowd control measures in place for all art or to explain their purposes, such as a sign with a photo and description. This information is also helpful to new visitors who may need to learn the unwritten etiquette of particular settings.

Emotional States: Don't Make People Guess

Spelling out reasons for emotional states and resultant behaviors in other visitors in stories can also go a long way in helping a neurodivergent person understand their underlying emotions and the behaviors that often accompany them. Helping them understand these behaviors and providing examples of how people tend to respond to the circumstance or events can help them and the people they might share stories with. In the case of the reader/listener lapsing into behaviors considered inappropriate to the situation, the story can help by redirecting people to the central ideas or topic of the story. The story may be tailored to the reader/listener's needs and provide them with specific sentences or prompts that they have used in similar situations. Because they are meant to be helpful and not punitive, stories are written in a cheerful voice and avoid using bossy or controlling statements, reprimands, or familiar phrases. A common phrase that might run through stories can read something like, "In the museum (or café, stairwell, parking garage, restrooms, or elevator), I will remember to use my inside voice" instead of a more controlling sentence that reads, "In the museum, I will keep my lips zipped, and not bother other people."

PREPARE IN ADVANCE

Providing the reader/listener with the story well in advance of the circumstance or event helps them prepare by referring to it whenever related questions arise. For a success story meant to prepare someone for a standard visit to a cultural institution, online access is likely to be the most effective. Finding a prominent place on the institutional website to post the success story and linking back to it from other relevant sections of the website will help to ensure that the people who wish to use it can find it. You may also find it helpful to include the link in any confirmation messaging generated by online ticketing. For special events, sharing the success story in any "know before you go" communication will help visitors to read and prepare in advance. In addition to these measures, having hard copies of the success story available at your front desk or box office will offer reinforcement of the digital content or at least an opportunity for anyone who missed the digital versions to use the story on-site.

One cultural institution visitor recounted her practice of laminating a legal-size one-page version of a story for each family member and then using them as placemats for family mealtimes. Even when the neurodivergent person cannot communicate with words, they can often benefit from hearing family or friends go over the story.

A SUCCESS STORY OF YOUR OWN

In closing, well-crafted success stories help neurodivergent visitors better understand the place or situation and what usually happens. The most important considerations of the context and format include determining the level of specificity the story should have and how personalized it needs to be effective. Understanding the wants and needs of your visitors, your goals for their experience, and the specific circumstances you want your story to cover will be key as you develop this type of support. No matter the story, the neurodivergent visitor will most likely have a more successful visit than if one was not used.

NOTES

1. Carole Gray, *New Social Story Book, revised and expanded 15th Anniversary Edition* (Arlington, TX: Future Horizons, 2015).
2. For more information see Boardmaker, https://goboardmaker.com/; SymbolStix 9, https://www.n2y.com/symbolstix-prime/, and copyright-free images at https://publicdomainvectors.org and https://openclipart.org/search/?query=no+touch.

Chapter Ten

First Things First

Schedules for Neurodiverse Visitors

Some readers may feel like creating a story is more than they want or need to do for a specific event or component of a visit. This is when creating and using schedules comes into play. A schedule can be a straightforward way of sharing information to help someone structure a visit or experience in a format that is familiar to most visitors.

In this chapter, we will share

- why schedules are a helpful tool;
- how to effectively structure a schedule for neurodivergent visitors; and
- different types of schedules and their uses.

SCHEDULES AND STORIES ARE FIRST COUSINS

Commonly referred to in schools as picture schedules or visual schedules, schedules are excellent ways to organize the day, provide structure to events, and help with downtimes such as waiting in admission or bathroom lines. Like stories, they can have a variety of configurations, ranging from being very detailed to being broad and overarching, depending on the needs, skills, and interests of the person using them. They can use the same visuals as a story or take on a different look. For example, some visitors to natural history museums will only want a general schedule of locations, such as each floor in the building. Still, other visitors with deep interests in dinosaurs may wish to allocate time to each dinosaur and prefer that these times are in their schedule.

SCHEDULES FOR SPECIFIC OR ONGOING EVENTS

Instead of telling a story, a schedule emphasizes two things; specific events that occur in a given period and ongoing events or those without firm time frames, especially in outdoor venues like zoos and arboretums that follow seasonal changes in weather and daylight. Specific events might include a talk or performance as part of a more significant event. Ongoing events are usually structured to match the predicted sequence in which the activity will occur, possibly on a route or map, no matter how small the activity is. In this case, the organizing feature is the passage of time. The beauty of schedules is that they provide a familiar sense of structure for neurodivergent visitors even when they are in an unfamiliar place, and they foster a sense of control or mastery during visits as they check off items on their schedule or, in the case of object schedules, peel off completed items affixed by sticky tabs to their schedule. Figure 10.1 shows an event-based schedule from a program at the Dallas Museum of Art.

art studio: sensory game stations

9:00 - 11:00 a.m.

Create pixel art, play games, and explore multisensory stations in the art studio!

fleischner courtyard

9:00 - 11:00 a.m.

Explore our outside space with activities from TWU Occupational Therapy students!

Chiptunes 4 Autism: fleischner courtyard

9:00 - 11:00 a.m.

Join *Chiptunes 4 Autism* as they play electronic music inspired by video games. Try out a variety of electronic instruments in hands-on stations.

c3 theater: interactive musical performance

10:00 - 10:30 a.m.

Join us for an interactive performance with our music therapist, Diane Powell!

Figure 10.1.   Event-based schedule used at a museum sensory program.
Emily Wiskera

SCHEDULES MAKE TRANSITIONS EASIER

People accompanying a visitor using the schedule are also provided with a way to encourage transitioning from one activity to another by showing or reminding them what is next. When ambient noise and crowding may jangle visitors' nerves or make verbal communication difficult, a visual schedule can provide a multisensory way of negotiating spaces. Schedules can also be used in conjunction with timers to help visitors keep on track. Watches, timer apps, phones, and tiny hourglass timers can provide reminders or cues for event times to provide an even greater sense of scheduling. Museums can offer inexpensive minute timers to larger five-minute hourglass timers to check out in conjunction with schedules for neurodivergent visitors as part of their visitor services.

ANATOMY OF A SCHEDULE

Educators can follow a series of predictable steps to make a consistent and reproducible schedule. They can use a numerical schedule or show options spatially on a map. If both options are offered, visitor preferences will be quickly determined, and future events can rely on that method.

1. Break the event into small sections.
2. Describe the events one after another.
3. Work with the person to follow the schedule and adjust it if necessary. They may not use the schedule without some help.
4. Determine how things will be marked as completed. Using a marker or wipe-off pen to check a box or cross out completed items are common strategies. If the items are attached to a page with sticky tape, they can be pulled off.
5. Practice and revise if needed. It's hard to get it right the first time.
6. Finish with a nice wrap-up.

After deciding to go with a schedule, there are several considerations for which type of schedule is the best. The following section details the types of schedules and factors to consider when choosing one. Table 10.1 gives an overview of these schedule types along with their uses, benefits, and problems.

Table 10.1. Types of Schedules

Type of Schedule	Characteristics	Benefits	Problems	Uses
Object and binder schedule	Concrete, uses actual objects or miniature versions of objects.	Reaches a wide range of users.	Difficult to transport, bulky.	Wide range of users, good for nonreaders, non-English speakers, and concrete thinkers.
Touch-oriented binder schedule	Uses actual objects with a variety of textures; provides a stand-in for objects that can't be touched.	Allows visitors to explore textures without handling actual objects.	Difficult to transport, bulky.	Wide range of users.
First-then schedule	Simple communication, *first* represents something less appealing, *then* represents the reward.	Simple concept, motivates users.	Relies on motivation and being able to delay gratification.	Useful when some unpopular things occur, such as cleaning up or waiting a turn.
Photo, picture, icon, word schedule	Progresses through an array of concrete to abstract options.	Easily customized for differing intellectual abilities.	Requires multiple versions to reach a wide audience.	Benefits nonreaders. Allows for customization.
Tiny and flip book schedule	Pocket-sized, multiple pages.	Portable, customizable, engaging.	May be fragile and easily damaged.	Scavenger hunt, souvenir, can be taken home to share experience with others. Can be used as a fidget.

OBJECT AND BINDER SCHEDULES

Object schedules are the most concrete of all schedules and use actual objects for cueing the user about events and activities. Both verbal and nonverbal visitors tend to understand object schedules. For example, in an event like sensory-friendly art-making day, refreshments might be signaled by a plastic fork or a coin used in a vending machine, cleanup might be indicated by a small piece of sponge, and the art-making station might be represented by an actual crayon, all attached to pages of the schedule. There are multiple examples of binder schedules on the Internet. Google the term *binder schedule* and click on Images to see many concept variations. Whatever your plans are, it is a practical idea to create only one binder, pilot it with visitors, and see what the wear and tear plus transport factors are.

For less-literal representations, small objects can be used to represent larger objects, such as a tiny paintbrush or short pencil representing art supplies. People creating the schedule must determine how literal the image must be to be an effective communication tool. For example, it would be easier to slice a little soccer ball in half and attach the half-ball to a schedule than to use a round ball. However, the question is whether the half-ball will carry the message of soccer to the schedule user. Furthermore, will seeing a ball sliced in half upset someone who cares deeply about soccer?

SCHEDULES COME IN ALL SIZES AND SHAPES

Practically speaking, object schedules can be challenging to create, transport, and store. Depending on the objects they use, they can also be expensive to make—as in the case of dinosaur schedules. Many opt to create object schedules using pages inserted into plastic sleeves, then place them in binders, which can also help in windy or wet environments. Binder schedules can get heavy. The heavier the weight on each page, the more likely they are to rip out. It may be easier to use cardboard "pages" that are less likely to tear. On the plus side, object schedules can immediately impact the user and reach a broad audience, especially nonreaders.

DO-IT-YOURSELF SCHEDULES HAVE THEIR PLACE

If cultural institutions wish to create their own object and binder schedules, this can provide a nice way to offer visitors opportunities to touch or scrutinize facsimiles, objects, or texture and material samples that may be off-limits for

handling in exhibits. Having touch-oriented binder schedules ready also eliminates the visitor hassle of transporting their schedules during an already busy
and often complicated process. The advantage of having these materials available is that they undoubtedly provide more significant insights and variety in
their binders than many visitors may have considered or been able to do with
their versions. In outdoor venues, as a fun introductory activity, during the art-
making time, visitors can create sand, oil, or gel timers from plastic beverage
bottles to use in conjunction with schedules.

Check with your cultural institution to determine the rules for transporting
these items throughout the space. Popular crafting sites on the Internet feature
several do-it-yourself timers, and consideration should be related to the materials used to create them. Look for items that rely on small containers rather
than two-liter drink bottles, which are more likely to break apart if dropped.
Water beads may be a simple timer item, unlike those with oils, gels, water,
and dyes. It's a good idea to find a toddler to road-test the things before they
are used in your space. This also provides cultural educators an excellent opportunity to talk about the day's activities and show visitors how to use their
schedules. Figure 10.2 shows a binder schedule for textures that will be seen
during wayfinding in a sculpture museum. When fully opened, the facing page
of the binder includes a key to the different materials and where they are found.

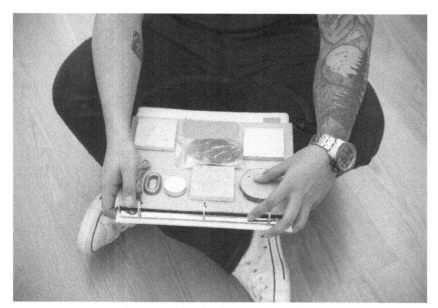

**Figure 10.2. A texture binder schedule used during wayfinding. Samples of textures can
be placed in a binder, and arranged in order of when they will be found in the museum.**
Anna Smith

FIRST-THEN SCHEDULES

First-then schedules are like object and binder schedules in that they are considered among the simplest and most basic of schedules. These schedules state what someone should do *first*, followed by what they may do *then* once the first action is completed. They are usually image-based but can also have accompanying text. In many cases, they focus on one concept at a time. Examples from a sensory-friendly art-making workshop example could include paired first-then concepts.

First, say hello—then eat snacks.
First, listen to instructions—then make art.
First, clean up—then see friends.

Notice in these first-then pairs that the second item of each pair seems more fun or is rewarding. First-then schedules are especially helpful in pairing the more difficult or less pleasant *first* items, such as greeting strangers or cleaning up, with the more interesting, fun, or exciting *then* items, such as having snacks or making art. For this reason, first-then schedules work best with visitors who are motivated and able to respond to the provided information. These schedules are also helpful in supporting transitions from one activity to another, which is a complicated or unpleasant process for some neurodivergent people. The first-then schedules take some tweaking to identify the components seen as undesirable, followed by those seen as preferred or rewarding. One of the biggest challenges of first-then schedules is identifying positives and negatives. For further information, investigate writing a behavior intervention plan (BIP), which focuses on systematically developing rewards and sanctions. The focus is preventing problematic behavior, teaching appropriate behaviors, recognizing appropriate behaviors, and not reinforcing problem behaviors. Multiple Internet sites feature templates for these plans.

Like a well-crafted story, first-then schedules stem from the idea that visitors will be successful once they understand their choices and options. First-then schedules can also go a long way toward staving off anxiety, heading off behavioral outbursts, and increasing a neurodivergent visitor's staying power. For a neurodivergent visitor who responds well to the concepts of working through something less pleasant toward something they prefer, a final option might be to provide them with a choice board at the end of their experience in which they can select a reward for doing a great job.

From a practical standpoint, first-then schedules are like object-binder schedules in that they can be bulky, often with only one pair of prompts per page, and may need several prompt pairs to span an event. Ideally, they should be evident to the neurodivergent visitor to remind them of what they are working through and toward. This can have ramifications of the schedules being in the way, being awkward to carry and display simultaneously, and having only one visual concept at a time. On the other hand, they are highly effective communication tools. They can move the visitor toward independence as they meet first-then goals and need less reinforcement to make their visits successful.

From a cultural institution's perspective, if group members have similar motivations, educators can implement some general first-then prompts in classes or small groups. As educators learn more about their groups, they are more likely to develop practical first-then communication resources that can be reused over time.

PHOTO, PICTURE, ICON, AND WORD SCHEDULES

Graphics can contribute to a wide array of schedules. A few organizing thoughts may make it easier to avoid immediately defaulting to the myriad of free items on the Internet used for illustrating schedules. Many free images are like what students use in school, but they may miss the mark regarding the neurodivergent person's developmental readiness and needs. While following the *literal to abstract* guidelines mentioned previously, it is also always wise to attach text to any items presented because the development of word comprehension may not be easy to gauge in some people and opportunities for learning words may be passed by if they are not put in place. From a practical standpoint, text-based schedules are portable and not likely to be incorrectly interpreted by the neurodivergent person or others if they are literate and can read the language.

Educators can build and print schedules; users can then cross off items with a pen, pencil, or marker. Folding dog ears into page corners or covering images with removable sticky strips are mark-off alternatives when visitors are not permitted to use writing tools. If users desire more durability, they can laminate the schedule and use a dry-erase marker to cross out items. Many people prefer to use loop-and-pile sticky strips on a page and create a vertical schedule with removable events attached to them. Schedules can also be made with the help of an app and then used on a pad or phone. Other people prefer cutting out laminated images, punching a hole in each, and then threading them onto a ring or clip. As the event occurs, the idea moves to the back of the stack. The ring of images itself can be attached to a belt loop, lanyard, or backpack for easy access.

SCHEDULES CAN GROW UP WITH YOU

It is easy to think that people who are neurodivergent may grow out of their need to use schedules, but many neurotypical people use schedules all of their lives. In the cases where the need for a visual schedule remains present, the formatting of the schedule can change in complexity and the presentation of images or text. In fact, rather than becoming more complex, the schedule may become more straightforward as a person matures and needs fewer visual supports.

TINY SCHEDULES CAN DO BIG THINGS

A scavenger hunt–style schedule flip-book is an entertaining and engaging version of a schedule that keeps people moving from one station to another. Instead of cutting the tiny book pages out, educators can create an origami-style flip-book using one of many Internet patterns. Once the schedule designer adjusts images and text to fit the layout, the scavenger hunt–style schedule can be printed, folded, and distributed. These little books often become little security objects neurodivergent visitors enjoy thumbing through and holding as they make their way through the space. As an extra touch, creating scavenger hunt–style books can be made more difficult by adding riddles and puzzles or made more straightforward by deemphasizing text and focusing on photographs of actual objects in the setting. Scavenger-style books make following a schedule both comforting and fun. From a practical standpoint, they can also help visitors avoid bottlenecks and crowds in parts of the building by encouraging movement around them. Scavenger-style books also become souvenirs of the event and a conversation starter if the same place hosts another event. Some venues may create simple flip-books from stacks of thumbed-through office notes. Alternatively, a simple eight-page origami mini-book requires one snip; the rest is history.

From a cultural institution's perspective, having both special events and everyday schedules physically available and posted on the institution's website can be helpful. People who need much preparation and time for events will appreciate having early access to schedules. Many event visitors will enjoy having something in their hands as they move through the space. Figure 10.3 shows the unassembled and assembled eight-page origami mini flip-book.

Figure 10.3.   Origami mini flip-book.
Tina Fletcher

Chapter Eleven

Best Foot Forward

Training and Educating Staff and Volunteers

The plans are in place, the event date is selected, and the activities are in place. The staff and volunteers have their tasks. You think things are ready, but you aren't quite sure your team is. You may be right.

When working with the public, chaos theory is at play. Even seasoned staff members at cultural institutions may tell you that they have experienced every unexpected situation that could happen . . . so far. A sudden bout of severe weather, a visitor meltdown, a last-minute change of location, or even a printer malfunction can derail an event if the people running it don't know how to respond and guide the visitor experience. What can set a smooth event apart from a disaster is thorough and thoughtful staff training and education.

This chapter focuses on strategies for preparing staff at a cultural institution for interactions with neurodivergent visitors. In it, we share

- a discussion of the distinction between training and education;
- goals, strategies, and suggested content for guided staff training and education sessions; and
- resources for self-directed learning about autism and neurodiversity.

TRAINING VERSUS EDUCATION

Required workshops and continuing education experiences can be a grind. Most of us have been students or teachers in these experiences, which can seem to drag on forever. The good news is that some schools of thought will make the process more relevant and exciting and result in deeper and more engaged learning. One of the first distinctions we should make is *training* versus *educating* staff and volunteers.

For our purposes, training is teaching people the skills they need to do specific jobs, such as training front-of-house staff in particular strategies for communicating with nonverbal visitors. Education is a process of developing knowledge and skills from a program of study. People who receive an education can strategize, plan, and critically appraise situations. It is a process that takes time and imparts a nuanced understanding of the topic. In the case of frontline employees like educators and admissions staff interacting with nonverbal visitors, an educated staffer would be able to make proactive decisions about factors that might facilitate or impede communication, adjust their strategies accordingly, and plan for future communication experiences. Employees in positions that are part-time or have higher turnover, such as ushers or gallery attendants, will benefit from training on how to best interact with neurodivergent visitors and who on staff to turn to for support. Training can take place within a single workshop but may be repeated regularly to reinforce skills. Only some people need to be *educated* to meet the needs of neurodivergent visitors, but they should be actively involved in ensuring that everyone is *trained*. We will explore how some individuals might become trained while others follow the education route.

GUIDED STAFF TRAINING AND EDUCATION

Regardless of whether you hope your colleagues will come away from a guided professional development session trained with basic skills or educated about working with neurodivergent visitors, you will want to be sure that the session's content is thoughtfully designed. Think carefully about what you hope staff will learn, what impact that knowledge will have on visitor experience, and how you will encourage staff to retain knowledge and continue learning. Table 11.1 gives an example of content that might be included in a staff training versus a more in-depth educational presentation. A key difference is who leads the session: training may be easily led by a fellow staff member, while an educational presentation may be better suited to an outside speaker who has expertise in working with neurodiverse populations.

Finding an Outside Speaker and External Resources

If you hope to present an in-depth education session for staff, bringing in someone with expertise in working with neurodivergent people can be useful. When searching for the right presenter, a solid strategy is to start local, then broaden your search as needed. School districts and universities in your area may have faculty with credentials related to autism and neurodiversity who could visit your site to conduct staff training. Looking more broadly, your

Table 11.1. Training versus Education in the Context of a Guided Program for Staff

Guided Staff Training	Guided Staff Education
Led by: Staff member who works with the institution's programming for neurodivergent visitors.	Led by: Speaker with expertise in working with neurodiverse populations, such as school psychologist, occupational therapist, or university professor.
Scope: Narrow	Scope: Broad
Format: Inservice or workshop for practical skill development. One or more sessions.	Format: Classroom learning for developing theoretical concepts. Extends over time.
Goals: Performance oriented— train frontline staff in key skills for respectfully interacting with neurodivergent visitors.	Goals: To develop reasoning and expand decision-making capacity—empower staff to engage and communicate with neurodivergent visitors based on an understanding of their wants and needs.
Possible topics: • What is autism / what is neurodiversity • What behaviors might you expect to see • What resources does the institution offer for neurodivergent visitors • How to respond to common situations involving neurodivergent visitors • Who on staff can offer support when needed • Appropriate terminology to use	Possible topics: • What is autism / what is neurodiversity • What drives common behaviors in neurodivergent individuals • How to develop and facilitate use of resources such as sensory spaces, communication cards, or sensory kits • Troubleshooting complex situations with neurodivergent visitors • Current trends in terminology • Resources for further study

region's ADA Disability and Business Technical Assistance Center[1] may offer resources and support, or national organizations such as the Kennedy Center Leadership Exchange in Arts and Disability[2] may help to connect you with the right presenter for your needs.

Costs associated with an outside speaker should be built into your budget in advance. These may include a speaker's fee and expenses associated with travel and lodging. If staff within your institution are comfortable with technology, offering training in a virtual format can reduce costs and cut down on staff time expended on arranging travel and setting up a training space. An additional bonus to virtual training is that, with the speaker's permission, the session can be recorded and used as a resource for future staff onboarding.

However you choose to set up a presentation, you will want to ensure that your speaker's priorities and style align with your institution's needs. If you hope for participatory learning, make sure your speaker is comfortable facilitating discussion. Be clear about your goals when approaching a speaker. If you want a session focused on preparing resources that connect deeply with neurodivergent learners, for example, don't hire an expert on ADA law. A suggested goal for training might be learning to accommodate and welcome neurodiverse visitors, in which case someone who specializes in applied behavior analysis or emphasizes treating or curing sensory processing disorders will be a bad fit.

Best Practices for Adult Learners

Educator Malcolm Knowles developed *andragogy*—the art and science of educating adult learners—over a half-century ago.[3] It is a credit to his work that very little has changed regarding the theoretical underpinnings of teaching adults. According to the tenets of andragogy, adult learners have specific traits. They are self-motivated and, as a result, can be self-directed. Adult learners have a variety of experiences they bring to the table, and because of this they have different needs and wants regarding what they are learning. Adult learners tend to be practical and learn well through problem-based material or active learning. They need to understand why they are learning something and will be most interested if it is relevant to their work. Adult learners must also be engaged in critical thinking and reflection and find meaning in working collaboratively.

To paraphrase these tenets in ways most relevant to cultural educators, adult learners want to understand why or how the content relates to their work. If they find meaning in the content, they will learn things in their way and with their team. Adult learners will think deeply about the content if they believe it is meaningful and then will contribute their understanding to others. They will also not take well to being considered passive vessels who receive knowledge without question, won't appreciate dull learning environments that lack innovation (better figure out ways to educate others beyond the digital slideshow format), and won't like being told what to do. While negotiations between adult students and educators aren't always comfortable, they are a common feature of andragogy. It will also take some of the more orderly and compliant adult learners a little time to adjust to the fact that their opinions matter and are factored into decisions made about course content and delivery. When the messiness of the adult education process is acknowledged and celebrated, the business of learning can get exciting and meaningful.

As an example of andragogy, Joe attended a workshop on preparing for autistic zoo summer campers. Judging by his body language of tightly folded arms, sitting slumped in his chair, and wearing a hat low over his eyes, he seemed to be indicating to his peers he didn't want to be there—until the program leader specifically asked him to provide the group with a dilemma he faced as the big cat keeper. He casually mentioned that it was a perpetual problem for visitors who became upset when he fed dead animals to the tigers. Seizing this opportunity, the leader asked the group if they would like to create a visitor story about animals eating other animals and instantly had their full attention. In this case, the relevance of Joe's situation energized everyone regarding a practical skill the program could teach them. Soon, all twelve workshop attendees were working in teams, describing their challenges and collectively choosing the words they needed to write about them positively. They were engaged enough to let the group leader sneak a few facts and figures into their workshop, which, while not in the "need to know" category, were definitely "nice to know." See table 11.2 for a recap of andragogy as related to the cultural staff and volunteer education.

Table 11.2. Andragogy as Related to Cultural Staff and Volunteer Education

Andragogy Principle	Education Practice
Favors self-motivated, self-directed learning	Provide students with a menu of course offerings and let them select topics of interest.
Offers a variety of experiences	Provide students with an opportunity to design or participate in training sessions where they have expertise.
Addresses different wants and needs	Create a knowledge rating scale and let students create an action plan based on what the group learns about their needs.
Conveys practical information and skills	Ensure that all activities have a visible and measurable connection to students' work.
Teaches through problem-based material or active learning	Create real-life scenarios with neurodivergent people to develop skills and understandings that directly relate to participants' work.
Allows participants to understand why they are doing something	Be transparent in designing activities by including a rationale for training topic and method of content delivery.
Promotes critical thinking	Provide opportunities for discussion and debate so students may share power and use their insights in planning.
Encourages collaborative work	Use the power of the group. Either purposefully select the group or give them parameters for group formation.

Cafeteria-style Learning

Cafeteria-style education or *cafeteria learning* is a practice that puts the control in the learner's hands. Remember the principle of andragogy that says adult learners want to be self-directed? Cafeteria education is a way that self-directed learning can happen. In teaching staff about neurodivergent visitors, cultural educators can offer short educational programs related to the "need to know" modules presented to cover essential background information. These topics can be paired with a series of "nice to know" issues that may spark varying degrees of interest and relevance for the learner's setting, background, or tasks, which we presume they know more about than we do.

Recall the case of Joe and the flesh-eating tiger. It would have been tough to anticipate that being a challenge the group should have covered. When designing workshops, you can offer a few nice-to-know mini-workshops and, like someone going through the cafeteria line and picking out their favorite flavor of the jiggly dessert, ask your learners to select one of those options. Some employees will undoubtedly say they don't know which to choose. In this case, it's a good practice to let them take a private quiz for their eyes only or to complete a modified KWL (What I Know, Want to Know, and Learn) about neurodiversity so they can design the second half of their learning experience. If a topic is new to learners, completing a KWL will help people who don't know enough about the topic to form some opinions and goals related to their learning. Operating under the assumption that adult learners can learn well together while selecting options they feel meet their own needs, they are likely to have a more successful learning experience. Table 11.3 shows how a training workshop can combine principles of andragogy with cafeteria planning.

Making It Stick

Almost anyone who has ever been a student has had the experience of feeling confident about their grasp on the material right up until it's time to take the test or put the knowledge into action. Ensuring that training is effective from the start will go a long way toward motivating staff to participate and help them retain what they learn. Consider that you may be teaching a group of people with different roles, different levels of experience, and different learning styles. Think through who will be attending and what factors will make the content feel relevant to them. Look for ways to connect the presentation to their prior knowledge and areas of expertise. Remember to create opportunities for small-group or full-group discussion and participation in the learning process, and don't forget to check for understanding with the group as a way

Table 11.3.   How a Morning Training Workshop Can Be Designed Combining Andragogy with Cafeteria Planning

8:00	Introductions and Self-Quiz or Knowledge Rating Scale	Goal: To assess present understandings of neurodiversity and plan attendance for optional sessions. Learners select goals for their workshop participation.
9:00	Must Know Session 1: Basic Facts about Neurodiversity	Goal: To learn the basic facts about neurodiversity and how they impact practice. Brainstorm and analyze visitor challenges during institutional walk-through with a neurodivergent advisor.
10:00	Must Know Session 2: Communicating with Neurodivergent Visitors	Goal: Establish the relationship between neurodiversity and communication via talking, writing, or signage. Small groups cover each of these three subtopics. Determine who attends which one of the next workshop choices.
11:00	Nice to Know Option 1: Sensory Processing OR Nice to Know Option 2: Behavior and Self-Regulation	Goal: Small groups can divide and conquer information that will impact their practice. Depending on their interest or need, some will manage factors of sensory-friendly programming, while others will provide information on preventing and managing behavioral differences and outbursts.
12:00	Self-assessment via ungraded quiz plus action plans for the future—discussion of online versus face-to-face follow-up for continuing education. Set goals for future learning.	Goal: Learners will have input into the contents of the next workshop including whether it is face-to-face or hybrid. Topics will be presented, and learners can request certain selections.

of prompting recall. You can make this entertaining with a game-like quiz, small rewards for correct answers, or even a little friendly competition.

It also doesn't hurt to assess the group's prior knowledge and their expectations for a training right at the beginning. Co-author Tina Fletcher recalls a time when one of her training modules fell flat due to a simple misconception:

I was excited to create and implement a neurodiversity training session for volunteer docents at the Dallas Museum of Art. Since I have a doctorate in educational design and curriculum instruction, I felt I had the necessary skills to deliver content to this group in a meaningful and interesting way. Armed with handouts and interactive materials, I began my session with a dozen docents of all ages. About two hours into our session, one of the docents timidly raised her hand and asked why communication cards were necessary to help artistic children at the museum. To my chagrin, I realized that she had participated in the training session thinking she was going to develop skills for helping *artistic,* as opposed to *autistic* visitors. When I realized our miscommunication, I asked the group how many of them thought the workshop was for artistic visitors, and three more sheepishly raised their hands. From that point forward I was tasked with the challenge of reteaching materials while introducing the rest of the content educators at the museum I deemed important. If I had asked for more audience input during the session, I believe I would have uncovered this miscommunication early on.

When working with an outside speaker, find out how they plan to present information. If the speaker is more comfortable delivering a straightforward lecture, provide time for staff-led reflection activities and discussion afterward. Be sure to find out in advance what a speaker's tech support needs may be, such as Internet access or audio amplification. There is nothing more awkward than watching a potential speaker attempt to energize their audience with an online version of Jeopardy! or Kahoot!, only to find your facility doesn't have the bandwidth to support the choice.

Whether training is staff-led or presented by an outside speaker, chances are that a certain number of attendees will not give their full attention, while others may listen closely but still not retain as much information as you would hope for. A familiar example of the need for retraining and reinforcing information is cardiopulmonary resuscitation (CPR), a specific skill set that someone learns as part of their job but may not use every day. Because the application of this technique can have life-or-death consequences, the American Red Cross Scientific Advisory Council recommends retraining on an annual basis after finding significant decay of CPR skills after three to twelve months.[4] Most of us are likely to forget skills that we do not use on a daily basis, and while the stakes when interacting with neurodiverse populations might not be quite as high as in a situation that necessitates CPR, the need for consistent and repeated training holds true.

To maintain a core of important knowledge institution-wide, you might fold neuro-friendliness skills into orientation materials, ensuring that knowledge isn't lost due to staff turnover. Presenting annual refreshers is also a good idea. These can take the format of formal training or can be approached more playfully through an engaging video, self-directed quiz, group discussion, or with a combination of these strategies. Making training materials such as an outline or slide deck accessible to staff after a training can help support those who are not avid notetakers, and creating an easy-to-digest tip sheet or quick reference guide will help anyone who needs to refresh their knowledge at a moment's notice. Textbox 11.1 is an example of a tip sheet on welcoming neurodivergent visitors that could be printed and kept on file at a front desk or security station.

TEXTBOX 11.1.
TIP SHEET: GUIDE TO WELCOMING
NEURODIVERSE VISITORS FOR FRONTLINE STAFF

UNDERSTANDING NEURODIVERSITY AND AUTISM

Neurodivergent people are those whose brain functioning and development differ from *neurotypical* people. Autism falls into the category of neurodiversity. People who are neurodivergent may have these needs:

• Communication difficulties or differences
• Challenges with social engagement
• Sensory needs or issues, such as sound sensitivity

INTERACTING WITH NEURODIVERGENT VISITORS

Being prepared to welcome neurodivergent visitors and helping them to know what to expect during their visit will improve the experience of both staff and guests.

Start Off on the Right Foot

A visitor on the autism spectrum may not make eye contact with you, but that does not mean that you should only address their companions or care partners. Greet the group warmly and include everyone as you speak. When speaking directly with neurodivergent visitors, break up directions into individual steps, using short sentences or making use of visual communication cards. When sharing the rules for your space, use positive instructions like "the rule is to stay two feet away from artworks," or "please keep your hands to yourself," instead of "don't touch," or "stop that."[1]

Help Visitors Plan Ahead

Offer a map, success story, or other resources that will help someone structure their visit. Explain in clear, friendly language where facilities like restrooms or sensory spaces are, as well as any areas where visitors should be especially careful. Let the visitors know who they can ask for assistance and how staff might respond if an issue arises.

Help Staff to Be Sensitive

Discreetly let other front-of-house staff know to expect a visitor or group that may need extra support or sensitivity. Try to avoid making visitors feel that they are being shadowed or profiled during their visit.

(continued)

TEXTBOX 11.1.   *Continued*

When Someone Needs Space

If a visitor seems to be upset, overwhelmed, or having a meltdown, stay calm and ask if they would like to take a break. Keep your voice slow and steady, and be concise with your words since excessive talking can be overwhelming. If they would like to do so, direct or escort them to the nearest sensory space. Refrain from touching the visitor unless absolutely necessary.

Terms to Know:

meltdown–An emotional reaction to anxiety that comes from an unexpected change in routine. A meltdown can include strong emotional responses such as anger, fear, and crying.

sensory space–A designated quiet room, sensory haven, or secluded area where someone may remove themselves from a stressful situation in order to become calm.

success story–A document with words and pictures that walks someone through an experience so that they know what they might encounter and what behaviors are expected.

NOTE

1. Another useful tip sheet for communicating with neurodivergent people can be found at https://www.autism.org.uk/advice-and-guidance/topics/communication/tips.

Co-author Tina Fletcher shares some of the recommendations she makes to the PhD students who attend her classes in teaching and learning:

Being a practical person, I like having a book that I can keep in my purse and read while I have a little downtime, especially when I am creating a new course, or refining one that already exists. Hands down, *McKeachie's Teaching Tips*[5] is my favorite. There are many editions of this book, but I always recommend people buy the most current edition because it reflects current technology and teaching practices, such as online learning or student-directed learning theories. My other favorites are the *Teaching Naked*[6] book and workbook, which commingle educational theories with teaching practice ideas that emphasize adult learners. If you feel disinclined to carry around a large lime green workbook with the words *Teaching Naked* emblazoned on the cover, you might be interested in learning more about the concepts of *Small Teaching*[7] and *Small Teaching Online*,[8] which emphasize making small changes to courses you already have in place. What's most important is that the books you select should focus on meeting the needs and interests of the adult learners that reflect your museum staff or other learner demographics.

SELF-DIRECTED EDUCATION

While guided staff training and education are critical tools for promoting collective understanding and coherence in public-facing practices, self-directed learning can be a driver for progress and institutional change. Especially in small institutions or those with few staff members devoted to accessibility initiatives, someone with the time to dig deeper and build expertise can become a champion for neurodivergent visitors. This section details how and where a motivated learner can build essential knowledge.

Accessing Content from Colleges and Universities

Higher education environments are competitive these days. Colleges and universities find themselves in positions that require them to maintain an edge over their peers, and this often includes marketing themselves to potential students. One of the outcomes of this process is that many colleges have wisely paid attention to research-driven trends for creating above-average or value-added educational experiences. Some of them can benefit cultural institutions that want to educate and train their employees.

One such method of content delivery is to provide *microcredentialing* such as minidegrees, certificate programs, or digital badge certifications.[9] Essentially, a microcredential is created by an expert in the content area, which can then be awarded to those who participate in all facets of the training. A 2023 review of literature related to microcredentials showed that learners perceived them as motivating factors for completing digital learning courses, and as a positive means for flexible and equitable access to knowledge. Employers saw microcredential courses as a valuable way to close skill gaps, so long as they were verifiable and offered by a reputable source. Additionally, *Inside Higher Education* reported that in 2023, Collegis Education and the Association for College and University Leaders in Online and Professional Continuing Education (UPCEA), conducted a survey to determine whether employers found digital badging and microcredentialing useful and found that 95 percent support the process and see benefits to their employees.

In some cases, universities offer microcredentials to people who want to earn credits that can be used in a degree plan. Microcredentials often involve taking competency exams, completing certain hours of training, attending specific courses, or having particular experiences. To make matters even more interesting, microcredentials can be *stacked*, meaning they belong to a specific category or type and are usually part of a path toward a more significant type of credentialing. Some institutions also require learners to

Table 11.4.   Microcredentials for Education and Autism

Credential	Institution	Content	Information
Understanding Federal Policies to Support Exceptional Students	National Education Association	Federal legislation, IDEA, student learning, behavior plans, universal design for learning	Stack of six 15-minute-long microcredentials, blended learning format
Autism: Contemporary Diagnostic Frameworks	University of Western Australia	Key indicators of autism with each respective diagnostic criterion and diagnostic criteria for autism	Certificate of Achievement plus transcript listing all successfully completed microcredentials
Understanding Autism	University of Kent	Autism, social communication, sensory issues, categorization, and case studies	Certificate of Completion available
Good Practice in Autism Education	University of Bath	Understanding of autism, developing effective and inclusive teaching practices	Certificate of Completion available

create portfolios to earn a microcredential. Currently, museum science micro-credentials are available through several educational institutions, and autism microcredentials are available through both universities and professional organizations.[10] Table 11.4 shows some microcredential programs that are relevant to the goals of this book.

Accessing Preexisting Educational Materials

Our last consideration for this chapter is whether a cultural institution has to design the educational experiences they intend to provide from scratch. It may be that while giving some introductory workshops, the institution has discovered a few employees who are interested in taking a deeper dive into the subjects of autism and neurodiversity and would like to learn more. When this is achieved, the institution can enjoy having an in-house expert. The world of massive online open courses (MOOCs) might provide the options the deep-diving employees want.

While andragogy as a learning theory has been around for a half-century, MOOCs are the new kids on the block and are considered by many to be a part of open educational resources (OER).[11] Developed around 2010, MOOCs have taken advantage of advances in the science of learning technology and have exploded on the Internet. As a result of their increasing sophistication,

MOOCs have challenged educators to think about how they teach and also challenged the notion of what constitutes a good education.

Additionally, MOOCs can provide tremendous, globe-spanning opportunities for people to learn with others but will not feature a personal connection with an instructor. Women in countries that restrict their education have celebrated MOOCs, residents of remote locations can partner with digital peers both near and far, and all have the opportunity to learn about a stunning array of topics. MOOC users also report that the credentialing process of some MOOCs has even challenged their beliefs about whether college degrees are essential paths to their professional life.

On the *Educause Review* website, researchers Hollands and Kazi[12] reported the results of an online survey they developed to find whether over three thousand MOOC learners who participated in a microcredentialing process felt they benefited from their studies and learned several interesting things. The researchers discovered that MOOCs have been used equally by men and women and that various racial groups have used MOOCs similarly. They found the average age of learners who responded to their survey was 35 and that the 30- to 44-year-old group was the largest, which shows MOOCs aren't just for young technology wizards. They also learned that many of the respondents participated in MOOCs as a workplace initiative, and their employer paid for their participation and education.

Some MOOCs allow students to audit them at no cost, while others charge for competency testing at the end of the course, and others charge for the entire educational experience. MOOCs are also offered by a variety of institutions, including edX, Coursera, and the Khan Academy, so different formatting choices are available to meet diverse learner needs. Table 11.5 shows some of the MOOCs related to autism.

TAKEAWAY CONSIDERATIONS FOR TRAINING AND EDUCATING STAFF AND VOLUNTEERS

Without a doubt, educational practices have improved as the needs and interests of adult learners are considered in educational planning and implementation. New academic research methods have provided the world with better ways to implement instruction and design educational content. Increased global connections have also provided new ways to connect, ensure consistency, and plan for the future. Considering all these changes, cultural institutions might want to reconfigure staff training methods to align with what research shows works—and celebrate the future. It will undoubtedly continue to improve and challenge our ways of learning and thinking.

Table 11.5.   Massive Online Open Courses for Learning about Autism

Name	Platform	Institution	Prerequisite	Cost
Autism Spectrum Disorders	Coursera	University of California, Davis	None	Coursera subscription options
Understanding Autism	Future Learn	University of Kent	None	Free plus upgrade available
SMART-ASD, Matching Autistic People with Technology Resources (Spanish or English)	Future Learn	University of Bath	None	Free plus upgrade available
Understanding Autism, Asperger's & ADHD	Canvas	University of Derby	None	Free
Autism and Related Disorders	iTunes	Yale University	Students	Free
Treatment-Guided Research: Helping People Now with Humility, Respect, and Boldness	MIT Open Courseware	Massachusetts Institute of Technology	Parents, Practitioners	Free
Autism Internet Modules (AIM)	Ashland Course Platform	Ashland University	None	Free

More information can be found at https://www.early-childhood-education-degrees.com/moocs-learning-autism/.

NOTES

1. For contact information about regional ADA Centers, see https://disabilityinfo.org/fact-sheet-library/legal/ada-disability-and-business-technical-assistance-center/.

2. For information about the Kennedy Center's Leadership Exchange in Arts and Disability (LEAD), see https://www.kennedy-center.org/education/networks-conferences-and-research/conferences-and-events/lead-conference/.

3. Katherine Cumings Mansfield and Jaime Stacy, "Preparing Practitioners to Conduct Educational Research and Evaluation: What the Research Says and What Our Experiences Taught Us," *Journal of Research on Leadership Education* 12, no. 3 (2016): 302–34, https://doi.org/10.1177/1942775116668524.

4. Education Subcouncil, American Red Cross Scientific Advisory Council, "CPR Skill Retention," American Red Cross, updated June 2022, https://arc-phss

.my.salesforce.com/sfc/p/#d0000000bxKz/a/0V0000019lr6/WNVfckgXDBbuBT1X KL.OsD1BBHPiAzBceqvhJFS4d0s.

5. M. D. Svinicki, W. J. McKeachie, et al., *McKeachie's Teaching Tips: Strategies, Research, and Theory for College and University Teachers* (Boston: Wadsworth, Cengage Learning, 2014).

6. Jose A. Bowen, *Teaching Naked* (New York: John Wiley & Sons, 2012).

7. James M. Lang, *Small Teaching: Everyday Lessons from the Science of Learning*, 2nd. ed. (San Francisco: Jossey-Bass, Wiley & Sons, 2021).

8. Flower Darby, with James M. Lang, *Small Teaching Online: Applying Learning Science in Online Classes* (San Francisco: Jossey-Bass, Wiley & Sons, 2019).

9. Patti Dyjur and Gabrielle Lindstrom, "Perceptions and Uses of Digital Badges for Professional Learning Development in Higher Education," *TechTrends* 61, no. 4 (2017): 386–92, https://doi.org/10.1007/s11528-017-0168-2.

10. One familiar example is KultureCity, a service that works with a variety of consumer groups and organizations to implement sensory-friendly programming. See www.kulturecity.org for more information.

11. Christian M. Stracke, Stephen Downes, Grainne Conole, Daniel Burgos, and Fabio Nascimbeni, "Are MOOCs Open Educational Resources? A Literature Review on History, Definitions and Typologies of OER and MOOCs," *Open Praxis* 11, no. 4 (2019): 331–41.

12. Fiona Hollands and Aasiya Kazi, "MOOC-Based Alternative Credentials: What's the Value for the Learner?" *Educause Review*, June 3, 2019, https:// er.educause.edu/articles/2019/6/mooc-based-alternative-credentials-whats-the-value -for-the-learner.

Part 4

MAKING ADJUSTMENTS
FOR DIFFERENCES IN
SENSORY PROCESSING

Chapter Twelve

Making Sense of It All

Sensory Processing and Sensory Processing Disorders

Have you ever entered a building where a ceiling fan hums or squeaks away? Most of us notice the noise, then turn our attention to other things, and even if the sound continues to grate on our nerves, we can still function. How about when you step into a homey little restaurant that smells like cooked cabbage and you don't like that smell? Again, most customers register the scent and react to it but can enjoy their dining experience without it drastically affecting their ability to function.

Now, think about the first time you saw your favorite work of art, stepped up to the glass at an aquarium, or heard the opening notes of a live symphonic performance. When experiencing the best that cultural institutions have to offer, the senses are the gateway to excitement and enrichment. This chapter explores what's behind negative or distracting sensory reactions and how we can work to minimize their impact on visitors, clearing the way for the best and most meaningful use of their senses.

Content within this chapter focuses on

- what defines a *sensory processing disorder*;
- how the senses function in people with sensory processing disorders; and
- which senses are the most powerful in these instances.

SENSORY PROCESSING DISORDERS

For some neurodivergent people, registering sensory input such as sounds and smells is a complex process. Individuals who are sensitive to sensory input may even need to leave the immediate area to escape it. If they can't, they may become agitated or anxious and not be able to get anything else done. They may have what is known as a *sensory processing disorder*, or SPD. Some researchers speculate that SPDs or simpler sensory aversions may affect nearly one in twenty people.[1] People with SPD generally have difficulty managing their responses to sensory input. Luckily, when it comes to sensory regulation, many people do outgrow their childhood sensitivities, or at least figure out their strategies for coexisting with sounds, smells, and other sensory input that might have set off a screaming fit when they were younger.[2]

TACKLING SPD HEAD-ON

The good news is that there are ways to help people with sensory processing disorders and aversions work around their challenges. For example, occupational therapists often work with neurodivergent individuals to develop coping strategies for sensory processing challenges.[3] Not everyone needs or wants therapy to work through their sensory sensitivities. Still, since we can't tell the world to be quiet or stop spinning, it's essential to help neurodivergent people navigate situations where managing responses and reactions to sensory input are crucial. Let's first look at the eight sensory systems, the many ways people process and react to them, and how we can help people with sensory processing disorders and aversions manage them when they are almost too much to handle.

THE FIVE SPECIAL SENSES

When asked how many senses there are, most people can report on the five basic senses of vision, hearing, taste, smell, and touch. While the first four systems have organs designed to act as receptors for senses—our eyes, ears, tongues, and noses—the touch or tactile system, as it is often known, is much more complicated. Skin is the unique receptor for touch, making the tactile system the largest in our body. It provides a vast number of touch receptors that give us more information about the kind of touch being received. In a nutshell, our different touch receptors let us know whether the touch is light (like the brush of a feather—or a crawling bug) or deep (like a bear hug), whether something is vibrating, if something is hot or cold, or if one or two points are touching us. Light touch has benefits—it alerts us to danger and often calls us to act. Deep touch is considered the most calming of touch receptors—think of the cozy comfort of crawling under a bed piled high with quilts or holding a baby close to your chest.

THE BIG THREE SENSES

In addition to the five basic senses just detailed, there are three more senses that are less well known but equally important. The first is a *vestibular system*, a grouping of tiny little spirals in our inner ears that provides our bodies with information about the movement of our head and its relationship to gravity. You activate that system when you spin on a dance floor, and you stress it when you are in the backseat of a car that's bouncing down a country road and you can't see out the front window.[4]

Staff at cultural institutions can help visitors with vestibular issues to navigate spaces by being aware of areas within the venue that may be problematic. A dramatic architectural staircase, for example, may pose a challenge. In this instance, having clearly marked elevators and helpful staff to direct people to them is a simple solution.

Scattered throughout the entire body is the second system, the *proprioceptive system*. Like the tactile system, it's big. It consists of sensory receptors in joints, tendons, and muscles that tell us the position of body parts without us having to look at them. More specifically, proprioception contributes to our body posture, and movement, and responds to changes in equilibrium by receptors that tell us the position, weight, and push and pull of objects in relation to our bodies. It is often referred to as the position in space. Gymnasts make heavy use of proprioception and the sense of joint position when they perform. They never look at their body as they go through their routines because they get plenty of input from both their proprioceptive systems. Figure 12.1 shows

Figure 12.1. The interplay between the vestibular and proprioceptive sensory systems. Note that both visitors use their vestibular systems to hold their heads upright and their proprioceptive systems to automatically move their arms, legs, trunks, spines, and hands as needed to maintain their positions on these mobile surfaces.
Tina Fletcher, Anna Smith

the interplay between vestibular and proprioceptive input as visitors try out an interactive kinetic sculpture. Notice the visitors holding their heads upright while they gauge how much movement is needed from their arms, legs, spines, and hands to remain on the sculpture. They don't have to consciously think about doing these things; their vestibular and proprioceptive sensory systems have done the job for them.

Francesca Bacci and Francesco Pavani in *The Multisensory Museum* discuss how proprioception may come into play within a museum space:

> Once again, embodying what is on display can provide a new self-awareness, which in turn has the power to deeply affect our experience of art. We are not made to be only viewers but rather fully sentient entities with a personal understanding of the art—not only at a high cognitive level but also at a more basic, yet rich, sensory level.[5]

Cultural educators may capitalize on this by being aware of what a visitor's body is doing when experiencing a space. Encouraging bodily movements in response to an artwork, exhibit, or performance can be one way of connecting with visitors via their bodies.

The third of the big three is the *interoception system*, which tells us how our body feels inside, whether thirsty, in pain, tired, or hungry. Interoception is often ignored but can significantly impact our activity levels and feelings of well-being. Children are often most prone to misinterpreting the feeling their bodies send them. In particular, neurodivergent children reportedly tend to ignore pain, thirst, and tiredness not only in themselves but also in their perceptions of others.[6] Think of the many times you have heard an exhausted child whine that they are not tired, then are sound asleep a few minutes later. Likewise, think of the times you may have been pestered to death by a child who simply cannot gauge how tired or fatigued you might be. You simply must spell it out for them.[7]

Staff at cultural institutions can help visitors in these instances in several ways. First, for those attending as part of the general public, providing a map with clearly marked locations for restrooms, cafés, seating areas, and sensory spaces will allow visitors to find the amenities they need to take care of self-regulation. For those taking part in a special event, building in frequent breaks specifically designed for attending to biological needs is helpful. Staff may choose to be proactive and provide snacks, visit restrooms as a group, or schedule designated quiet times to ensure all participants' needs are met.

To recap, vestibular senses help us maintain our balance on uneven surfaces or moving structures, and proprioception enables us to be coordinated and use the right amount of force needed to interact with the world around us. Interoception tells us what we need to do to tend to our bodily needs.

MEET THE POWER SENSES!

Knowing what we do about the eight senses, this is when things get interesting. Three of these form what some refer to as the *power senses*. Tactile, vestibular, and proprioceptive senses work together and become integrated to provide a foundation for our behaviors and actions. When they don't work together, they lead to several complications, such as

- being sensory defensive (experiencing distressed responses to input most people don't find offensive);
- having poor sensory modulation (not being able to form an appropriate mental or physical response to sensory input);
- having poor sensory registration (over- or under-registering sensory input); or
- having impaired sensory integration (physically responding to sensory input in a dysfunctional way).

All of these can lead to different behaviors or internal states that cause us to either check out what is around us or to go into fight or flight mode, in which our actions are so focused on managing our emotions that it is nearly impossible to attend to anything else, much less enjoy it. The upshot of this information is that if community venues want to promote a calm and organized environment, they should evoke the power senses by providing visitors ways to stimulate their tactile, specifically deep pressure touch, vestibular, and proprioceptive systems. Think of creating opportunities for gentle back-and-forth head movement, or offering gliders, washable weighted lap pads, and places that safely offer a tight squeeze or the feeling of being held close. These resources should be self-administered by visitors so they can gauge their own needs and avoid overstimulation.

When in doubt about what is appropriate, consult with an expert on autism and neurodiversity, such as an occupational therapist, who can share strategies specific to your needs. No one expects cultural institutions to become therapy centers, but having a general understanding of what can contribute to a person's sensory well-being can help planners make informed decisions about designing environments that promote relaxed and alert engagement, and to troubleshoot problematic environmental irritants that need to be adjusted or removed.

NOTES

1. For more information about sensory processing challenges in the general population see Maria Panagiotidi, Paul G. Overton, and Tom Stafford, "The Relationship

between ADHD Traits and Sensory Sensitivity in the General Population," *Comprehensive Psychiatry* 80 (2018): 179–85, https://doi.org/10.1016/j.comppsych.2017.10.008.

2. See the STAR Institute's checklist for more information about sensory processing disorder, https://sensoryhealth.org/basic/symptoms-checklist.

3. Visit the American Occupational Therapy Association at https://www.aota .org/community/special-interest-sections/sensory-integration-and-processing for more information about how occupational therapists help people with sensory processing disorders.

4. For more about motion sickness and the vestibular system read Giovanni Bertolini and Dominik Straumann,"Moving in a Moving World: A Review on Vestibular Motion Sickness," *Frontiers in Neurology* 7 (2016): 14, https://doi.org/10.3389 /fneur.2016.00014.

5. Francesca Bacci and Francesco Pavani, "'First Hand,' Not 'First Eye' Knowledge: Bodily Experience in Museums," chap. 2 in *The Multisensory Museum: Cross-Disciplinary Perspectives on Touch, Sound, Smell, Memory, and Space*, edited by Nina Levent and Alvaro Pascual-Leone (Lanham, MD: Rowman & Littlefield, 2014).

6. To learn more about interoception in autistic children and adults, see Toby Nicholson, David Williams, Katie Carpenter, and Aimilia Kallitsounaki, "Interoception Is Impaired in Children, but Not Adults, with Autism Spectrum Disorder," *Journal of Autism and Developmental Disorders* 49, no. 9 (2019): 3625–37, https://doi .org/10.1007/s10803-019-04079-w.

7. The Autism Research Institute reports on interoception in children with autism. See https://www.autism.org/interoception-impaired-asd/.

Chapter Thirteen

Know Your Space

Learning from Sensory Audits

Being a part of a community means getting out there and participating in what it offers, whether that means going to a cultural institution, the grocery store, or a football game. Sometimes it's just impossible to adjust sensory input to a tolerable level. Instead, an alternative is knowing what to expect and planning for it. Knowledge can be power.

This chapter will help cultural educators plan a *sensory audit*, which is a tool to help understand how a venue is experienced by neurodiverse visitors. Readers can expect to learn

- how to build an audit team;
- how to develop effective tools to capture auditor feedback;
- what factors auditors should be asked to respond to; and
- what a sensory audit report and action plan should look like.

MAKING OBJECTIVE AND MEASURABLE ASSESSMENTS OF ENVIRONMENTAL FRIENDLINESS

A sensory audit, sometimes known as an autism audit, can provide planners a structured way to observe and make note of sensory, communication, and social factors in a community environment. An audit ensures that the space or environment, including toilets, parking lots, elevators, drinking fountains, and break areas, is as accommodating as possible for neurodivergent visitors. While anyone can assess the sensory-friendliness of their venue, it is helpful to have auditors who have practiced and learned something about the components of neurodiverse friendliness assist with this process. These auditors could be special educators, occupational therapists, or speech and language pathologists. Equally important are the real experts in the field—people who are neurodivergent. Through all the processes discussed in previous chapters, having a neurodivergent advisor or community partner to provide input and advice will give authenticity to any programming, documents, activities, and environment where you intend to work.

Assembling the Auditing Team

In the case of environmental accessibility audits, whenever possible, it is helpful to have a team of neurodivergent and neurotypical auditors collaborate. One example might be a special education teacher with a few of their students. Another team can be members of a family who accompany a neurodivergent visitor. The school team will draw on their knowledge gained by exposure to many types of neurodiversity, but the teacher will not have the experience of living it day in and out. The family team may have the limitations of their personal experiences informing their decisions but have the benefit of deep learning brought on by having the daily lived experience. If the neurodivergent auditor needs assistance to participate in the audit, they can team up with a helper to accompany them; it's worth the effort! Another valuable member of an auditing team is someone from another museum because they have insights into the interaction of the environment and functionality of the space.

Using the Tools

Auditors can rate factors embedded in a digital survey tool such as Google Forms with neutral statements (meaning things are okay) about sensory, communication, and social factors and dropdown menu options on a five-point agree/disagree Likert scale. For example, a neutral comment can read:

At [. . .], the smells of the environment inside were okay.
1. Highly agree
2. Agree
3. Disagree
4. Highly disagree
5. Not applicable, or doesn't apply

Comments:

Factors for this process are derived from research evidence and can be continually updated as new information emerges. The goal of this process is twofold: to assess the strengths and weaknesses of any environment and to inform neurodivergent individuals about specific aspects of the environment they may need to use their own strategies to manage. Several steps can occur to help auditors objectively evaluate the environment:

- Auditors can review any survey feedback from or about neurodivergent visitors. One example of this is the comments option being available for each factor. The comments option can explain choices or circumstances surrounding the selection. In the case of the smell of the environment, an auditor might choose to comment on the presence of a dirty baby diaper, which they felt might be unusual for that setting, but undoubtedly impactful at the time of the audit.
- Auditors can search websites and social media posts for information on hours, special events, busy times, and other resources or events.
- Auditors can note their observations while visiting the space.
- Auditors can use objective smartphone applications (apps):

    ◦ A classroom noise level app is used in some circumstances, such as field trips.
    ◦ A decibels (dB) reader app measures overall and zone sound levels.
    ◦ An interior and exterior thermometer app measures overall and zone temperatures.
    ◦ A light meter app measures overall and zone lighting levels and intensity.

Apps are essential because they objectively describe conditions. There is a difference between saying something was very loud or saying ambient noise was 80 dB. With help, people can draw their conclusions from this objective reporting. An example can further their understanding. Knowing that garbage disposals have a noise level of 80 dB can be helpful in this process. Additionally, each auditor will have their own internal standards for comfort and measurement. What one person describes as loud may not be the same as what another person considers loud.

Table 13.1 provides a sample sensory audit form. This audit form features neutral statements about communication, sensory, and social factors that auditors can highly agree, agree, disagree, or highly disagree with. After completing the form, auditors can write a short report emphasizing three to five strengths and three to five action items based on factors they feel might hinder a quality visit. Comments and photos from auditors help. If more than five action items exist, auditors can complete a follow-up audit to determine their impact after making the first series of adjustments. Audits should be completed at the same time of day special events typically occur. Some auditors may prefer this form be converted into a digital form, and others may prefer a hard copy to write notes or sketch on.

Table 13.1. Autism- or Neurodiverse-Friendliness Audit Form

Auditor or audit team:
Audit location, date, and time:
Observations and contributing factors (such as weather, crowding, special events or exhibits):

Neutral Statements	Highly Agree	Agree	Disagree	Highly Disagree	Not Applicable
Directions to the venue are okay.					
Transportation to the venue is okay.					
Parking process (finding a spot, ease of payment) is okay.					
Parking area (like noise levels and safety) is okay.					
Getting from parking area or drop-off point to entrance is okay.					
Signage for entrance and exit is okay.					
Checking in and out (coatroom, bags, tickets, purchases) is okay.					
Layout and navigation are okay.					
Getting around (finding bathroom, café, shop, water fountain) is okay.					
People can find most everything they need on their own.					
Amount of floor or ground space to walk around is okay.					
Amount of crowding inside is okay.					
Amount of crowding outside is okay.					
There is a place for people to be alone or away from crowds if they need it.					
Temperature inside is okay.					
Temperature outside is okay.					
Smell of surroundings inside is okay.					
Smell of surroundings outside is okay.					
Smell of people is okay.					
Sound inside (such as music and people) is okay.					
Sound outside (such as traffic and planes) is okay.					
Visuals inside (signs and labels) are okay.					
Visuals outside (signs and labels) are okay.					

Neutral Statements	Highly Agree	Agree	Disagree	Highly Disagree	Not Applicable
Lighting inside (windows and lights) is okay.					
Lighting outside (such as on walkways) is okay.					
The place has a good feel to it.					
Using personal strategies (like stimming or pacing) is okay.					
This place feels safe.					
This place feels like it manages hygiene and cleanliness.					
Employees or volunteers are easy to identify.					
Employees or volunteers are approachable and seem okay.					
The number of people who can help others is okay.					
Employees or volunteers use appropriate language and verbiage.					
The number of different ways to communicate is okay.					
The process of purchasing items, food, or drinks is okay.					
This place seems like an okay environment for autistic or neurodivergent visitors.					
This place has strategies in place that can help autistic or neurodivergent visitors.					
This place has some barriers that might make it hard for autistic or neurodivergent visitors.					
Additional factors:					
Additional factors:					

Comments on strategies that help:

Comments on barriers that hinder:

General comments or other considerations:

Finishing the Audit Walk-Through

After the walk-through, auditors can share their thoughts and discuss collective results from the digital survey forms. Recording their conversation on a phone recording app, then transcribing it into a digital document using a transcription app such as Otter.ai can provide insightful information and verbatim comments that can be used to enrich the audit, especially if the report includes a suggested action plan. Audits can consist of the following information:

- Temperature inside and outside, and if applicable, by zones
- Smells inside and outside and of other people
- Noise levels from inside and outside the building and if applicable, by zones
- Clarity and usefulness of visuals, signs, and labels
- Lighting inside and outside the building and if applicable, by zones
- Crowding and crowd management
- Parking, including congestion, appropriate signage, painted curbs, speed bumps, and traffic buttons, pedestrian walkways, and adequate lighting
- Layout and organization of buildings and exterior spaces
- Signage for restrooms and entrances/exits
- Availability of people to help if needed, with people identifiable as employees
- Communication options when purchasing items or achieving venue or event goals
- Access to different types of communication including words and images, computer keyboards, and help buttons
- Space to move freely
- Options for comfortably using personal self-management strategies like finger flicking or pacing
- Safety factors including evacuation routes, surveillance, signage, identifiable personnel, store maps, and merchandise security
- Public health precautions like masks, policies, sanitization, and physical distancing

Writing the Reports

A *report for neurodivergent visitors* can include good-to-know factors; high-impact sensory, communication, and social aspects of the environment; feedback from neurodivergent individuals; and suggestions for preparing to attend the venue. The report for neurodivergent people can also include summative statements such as "We recommend visiting [museum] to other neurodivergent people." Follow this with the option for having planning statements such as, "We recommend visitors plan for noises in the 80 dB range (loudness of a garbage disposal)."

A *report for the community venue* can include sensory, communication, and social aspects that are well managed, factors that are not modifiable but people should be aware of, and possible recommendations. The report for the community venue can conclude with summative statements such as, "We think these are some of your environmentally friendly strengths, and these are some areas you may be able to improve. Please feel free to contact us with questions or for ideas or strategies."

Aiming for Usefulness and Consistency

Reports and templates for environmental audits can look very similar across different community venues. Creating a basic template that auditors can change, add, or remove text as necessary is helpful and creates consistency. Completing the comment section for each Google form item is also beneficial because these can provide valuable information, especially as trends form. If there are action items to consider, aim for realistic, attainable, and specific suggestions. With a bit of practice and coordination, cultural institutions can offer visits and suggestions for resources and strategies to one another. Textbox 13.1 shows some representative comments from neurodivergent auditors when visiting a coffee bar attached to a community venue. These auditors reacted to the layout of the space, the presence or absence of wayfinding signage, as well as the noise and light levels—most of which are factors that can be addressed by staff.

TEXTBOX 13.1.
COMMENTS FROM NEURODIVERGENT
AUDITORS IN A COFFEE SHOP

It has a large *open area where I can pace around a lot.*

I do wish there were some *pictures to go along with the menu.*

I would appreciate a *label out here before the hallway* to the restrooms rather than having to go into the hallway where it is.

Probably *earphones* would be a good idea.

They are *really loud,* the music, word conversation, but that's just me.

It's a lot *quieter in the back* than it is in the front.

(continued)

TEXTBOX 13.1.   *Continued*

I *like and don't like the spotlights,* personally; I have this new thing with my eyes where I can't really go from dark to light, dark to bright.

It's *not consistent lighting.* We have spotlights right here, so we have natural lights back there.

The *signage is clear,* yeah, they were black on white and a *good contrast.*

The coffee kind of comes with the territory—they have to make the coffee, right? But do they have to do the music? *That soundproofing foam here and there would work.*

It has really good acoustics, but it also *makes things reverberate.*

The restrooms were huge and very, very nice in there, but once you got in there, it was really good—but you had to do a little, little, teeny bit of searching . . . *the lock on the door needs oil.*[1]

NOTE

1. Anonymous comments from unpublished research.

As a tool to understand what a complete audit report might look for, the authors of this book have created a sample report for a fictional museum. Imagine that the Museum of Amazingness, or MOA, has invited a team of auditors to review the visitor experience from start to finish. Textbox 13.2 provides the results of this hypothetical audit.

TEXTBOX 13.2.
SAMPLE SENSORY AUDIT REPORT

Museum of Amazingness (MOA) Neurodiversity-Friendliness Audit

(Note: This is a faux museum and report created as a learning tool.)

Auditor or audit team: One museum employee and one autistic volunteer

Audit location, date, and time: Thursday, March 1, 6:00 pm

Observations and contributing factors (such as weather, crowding, special events or exhibits): Very rainy, a bicycle rally surrounded the museum, lots of police cars were assisting with traffic. Many visitors were in the museum, especially around restrooms and service areas.

Purpose

A museum educator partnered with an autistic volunteer who regularly visits the museum to complete an audit walk-through of the MOA. This small museum features exhibits and research options featuring flight and space experimentation. Average attendance is one thousand visitors per month, including children on fifth- and seventh-grade field trips and monthly home-school events. The MOA has become a favorite destination for autistic young adults and hosts 25–30 participants on Thursday date nights in conjunction with the local autism social center.

The auditor team paid special attention to sensory, communication, and social factors that might impact the experience of neurodivergent visitors with different abilities and skills, including autism and sensory processing disorders. Their goal was to assess the environment's strengths, inform individuals about specific aspects of the environment on the museum website accessibility page, and suggest to administrators potential modifications in programming or structure, especially in light of summer budgetary deadlines.

Audit Conditions

The museum contains three floors, with the main level being the 2nd floor. All three floors were audited. Due to rain, the exterior was not audited. There is one main entrance and exit at the front of the building. The Museum estimates 75% of activities occur on level 2. Stairs and an elevator can be utilized to get from floor to floor. The museum is transitioning between two major exhibits, so construction sounds were louder than typical. Auditors measured sound on phone apps and measured when construction equipment was silent.

Sensory, Communication, and Social Factors that Support Neurodivergent Visitors

- Exterior parking lot is easy to navigate.
- Layout is organized and intuitive, with graphic icons and signage in English and Spanish.
- There is ample space to move freely, plus various seating options, including study cubbies.
- Employees are available to help on each level and are identified by a name-tag and green polo shirt.

(*continued*)

TEXTBOX 13.2. *Continued*

Factors that Neurodivergent Visitors Should Be Aware Of

- Level of crowding and noise depends on the time of day and school events.
  - Least busy times are Saturday, Sunday, and weekdays after 3 p.m.
  - Most busy times are weekdays from 10 a.m.–3 p.m.
- Sound levels
  - The Main floor and upper floor range from 30–50 dB (sounds like a whisper or quiet conversation)
  - Lower floor ranges from 30–40 dB (sounds like a whisper)
  - Automatic entrance doors and café are at 68 dB (sounds like a washing machine)
  - Eco-friendly toilets are at 75–85 dB (sounds like a noisy office or busy street)
  - Hand dryers are at 95 dB (sounds like a motorcycle engine)
  - No music or audio input from speakers

INFORMATION FOR NEURODIVERGENT VISITORS

Significant Features:

- Lots of seating options, tables, computers, and study rooms
- 3 floors with open space on each floor
- Quiet environment overall but the noisy bathroom, café, and entrance doors

Good to Know:

- Staff wear polo shirts and name tags and are located at a central desk on each floor to answer questions.
- There is no sign on the front of the building, but the parking lot across the street has one.
- A children's area has its own section on level 1 with games, books, and a reading room.
- A calendar is displayed at the front by the entrance with daily activities posted by month.
- Rooms on the main level can be rented for events. Thursday date night happens here.
- Carpet keeps the noise down.

Comments from Autistic Auditor and an Autistic Visitor:

- "Be mindful of others and be respectful about your noise because it's a quiet place."
- "Felt it to be a safe space; it's very quiet if you don't use the bathroom and sit away from the automatic door."

How Visitors Can Prepare:

- Check the website for a photo of the MOA when planning the first visit.
- Look online at the posted navigation route and quiet times before coming.
- Visitors can call ahead to find out if field trips or home-school events might be happening.
- MOA encourages visitors to bring what they might need, including headphones and fidgets.

Overall: We rate this place as neurodiverse-friendly.

INFORMATION FOR MOA

Thank you for providing support for neurodivergent visitors. Our audit team found many strengths in your museum, such as clearly identified employees, great seating options, and plenty of room to move around. We have a few suggestions to make your place even more supportive. We are happy to offer you information about our suggestions. We also find that we prefer to use popular online vendors instead of medical supply houses when we order supplies and materials. This makes purchase options a little less intimidating for families or individuals who want to order their own things.

Manage the Noise:

- While in construction, you might let visitors know with web postings and signage. Offer visitors disposable earplugs. If you are concerned that some visitors might put the earplugs in their mouth, offer the corded ones.
- Your automatic door and bathrooms are relatively loud. Some things you can do are put objects that absorb sounds in these areas. You can check online options by putting "sound-absorbing plants for a workplace" in a search bar. You will find that a variety of tall and short plants can help. Bathroom options (if you can't replace your hand dryers and toilets!) include adding acoustical tiles to the ceiling, door, or under sink space, offering paper towels as an alternative to hand dryers, and wrapping pipes.
- Since your automatic door is loud, you might consider informing visitors of the quieter side door.

Communicate Even More:

- We really like your signs with the images. You might also look into what is known as "Plain English" as an additional communication support. Along with English and Spanish languages on signs, you might also get into the practice of including plain English or plain language text as a third option.

(continued)

TEXTBOX 13.2. *Continued*

Again, you can look this up on the Internet, but the gist of plain English is that you avoid any slang or jargon, use simple words, and focus on active voice. You will find that your non-English readers appreciate this too. An example of the difference between standard English and plain English is as follows, "Please deposit any paper trash in provided bins" versus "Put trash here."

• Post field trip and homeschool event times on the web so other visitors can plan accordingly.
• We hope you can install an MOA sign in front of your building.

Thank you again for offering such an approachable environment and events and allowing us to audit your place. Please don't hesitate to contact us if you want us to help you design signs or web supports.

Chapter Fourteen

Change Can Be Good

Accommodations and Modifications for Neurodiverse Visitors

In conjunction with their families, people who are neurodivergent usually spend some time working with special and mainstream educators and administrators to develop the best possible education plan for themselves. In the days of paper forms, it was commonplace for families to have entire filing cabinets devoted to educational plans. For families with a neurodivergent child, certain words become very familiar. Among these are the terms *accommodations* and *modifications*. While cultural institutions aren't schools, there is a logic to using the same terminology in both places. For one thing, there is less code-switching on the part of the family. It's one less new thing for them to learn, and if there is ever a time that a parent or neurodivergent person is asked to contribute to making plans with cultural educators, everyone speaks a common language. An additional benefit of making terminology uniform is that educational verbiage tends to be similar from state to state because many special education policies are set at the federal level and then interpreted at a state and local educational agency level. So what a teacher in Florida recommends will be understood by one of their peers in Hawaii if the family moves from one sunshine state to another.

In this chapter, you can expect to learn

- the purpose of *accommodations* and *modifications* and the difference between them;
- how accommodations may be applied to a program such as a student tour; and
- how cultural institutions may make environmental modifications to better suit the needs of neurodivergent visitors.

LEARN THE LANGUAGE

Operating under the assumption that uniform terminology is a good thing, certain working definitions will keep your operations consistent and understandable and make planning for classroom field trips easier, too. In educational settings, making accommodations and modifications is the process of using whatever it takes to help make a student with any kind of disability most able to access what is known as a *free and appropriate public education*, commonly referred to as FAPE.[1] FAPE essentially holds that on a child's third birthday, no matter when that day falls, they will have access to appropriate education at no cost to the family, regardless of any conditions or factors that may make their educational plans different from most—hence the term *special*. Under this law, students who require special education will have an individualized education program/plan, or IEP, created just for them that details any accommodations or modifications that are needed to support them in an educational setting.[2] In general, *accommodations* change how a child learns materials, while *modifications* change what they are taught. Accommodations are fairly simple to devise, especially for experienced teachers, while modifications are often in the form of curriculum adjustments that actually change what is required from the teacher and are subject to more external review and scrutiny. Teachers usually try making accommodations before they set their sights on making more challenging modifications.

To give an example set in a school, an *accommodation* for a neurodivergent student would be to present two or three math problems at a time (instead of twenty) for easier processing. A *modification* in the classroom environment might be changing the curriculum to teach reading at a second-grade level instead of a fifth-grade level. Modifications in the school system have a legal requirement connected to a student's IEP. In cultural institutions, legally required modifications are often related to ADA requirements. Thinking less formally for a cultural setting, an accommodation in a summer camp for children with autism could look like a portable sensory space that is made available for campers to take breaks, while a modification would be changing the standard camp curriculum to include a lesson on social skills.

CLASSIC ACCOMMODATIONS

Developing appropriate accommodations is a part of a student's IEP, which means doing whatever it takes to ensure that a student with disabilities, including those who are neurodivergent, can actively participate in their education. Additionally, some children with unique mental or physical needs may not need special education services but may still need some accommodations provided to them as a facet of Section 504 of the Rehabilitation Act of 1973.[3] Classic examples are students who use wheelchairs or other mobility devices to access the school environment, or students with attention deficits who need a seat close to the teacher in their learning environment. Ideally, accommodations will enable a student to fully participate in the school's general education curriculum and earn a diploma.

To make this happen, accommodations may be made to instructional methods and communication systems, the environment, and schedules, among other elements. Accommodation refers to the way a student is taught and learns from the materials. The curriculum standards aren't lowered for students; rather, they receive the instruction in the best way for them to be successful. Teachers who work with accommodations must be nimble and flexible in delivering instruction. In some ways, a teacher who accommodates many children's learning needs can evoke images of a one-room schoolhouse teacher in pioneer days—everyone seems to be doing something different. While this may appear to be the case on a surface level, the teacher often sees patterns in needed accommodations across many children's learning plans.

Many of these may also be the patterns that emerge in planning for groups of visitors to cultural institutions. Examples of classic accommodations that cultural educators might find useful in their setting include the following. For these examples, the term *visitor* refers to the neurodivergent visitor/student. Textbox 14.1 offers a scenario demonstrating how these methods can be applied to a student tour without singling out the student for whom the accommodations are being made.

Instructional Methods and Communication

- Develop a private signal for the visitor and educator to use when help is needed.
- Pair written and oral instructions and repeat when needed.
- Pair auditory and visual directions, demonstrations, and representations.
- Ensure visitors understand expected behavior.
- Use tactile and manipulative aids.
- Utilize visitors' areas of strength rather than try to develop new skills.
- Provide movement breaks several times each session.
- Simplify directions or break tasks into smaller parts.

TEXTBOX 14.1.
SCENARIO: ACCOMMODATIONS ON A MUSEUM TOUR

A teacher has let the museum know that one of the fifth-grade students com-
ing for a field trip has a sensory processing disorder. Luisa, a gallery educator,
communicates with the teacher in advance to better understand this student's
needs. At the beginning of the tour, after introducing herself, Luisa explains the
most important rules for students visiting the museum. While she does this, she
holds up a printout listing these rules in plain language, each paired with an
icon representing that rule. "If anyone wants to speak during the tour, please
raise your hand and I will call on you," she says, raising her own hand to dem-
onstrate. "Can everyone show me how you raise your hand?" The students
raise their hands and Luisa visually checks that they all understand. "If anyone
needs help or feels uncomfortable during the tour, please raise two fingers
in the air, like this." She holds up a hand with two fingers and again asks the
students to demonstrate the gesture.

"Now, we are going to walk through a gallery that has a sculpture that
makes sound. We won't stop at this sculpture, but if the noise bothers anyone
you can cover your ears or put on headphones. If it really bothers you, you
can raise two fingers and a chaperone will help you step out of the space." The
students follow Luisa through the gallery. Some cover their ears and one puts
on noise-canceling headphones.

Luisa seats the students on the floor in the adjoining gallery to discuss an
artwork. She shares that she will be asking the group questions, reminds
them that they should raise their hands to answer, and lets them know that
afterward, they will be building a sculpture with pipe cleaners. When the time
comes to build with pipe cleaners, Luisa holds up a printout with three-step
instructions and an image of a completed sculpture. She reads the instructions
out loud. After passing out supplies, she reads the instructions again and asks
for any questions. She tells the students they will have five minutes to work
on their sculptures.

Partway through the activity, a student raises two fingers. Luisa goes over
to the student and quietly asks if he needs to step away from the group. She
asks a chaperone to walk with the student to a nearby area until he is ready
to return.

After the students finish their pipe cleaner project and put away the sup-
plies, Luisa asks them to stand up. "Let's take a stretch break! Move your arms
and legs in a way that feels good for you and isn't harmful to the people and
art around you. Everybody raise your hand when you are ready to move on
to the next stop." When the students show they are ready, Luisa leads them on
to the rest of their tour.

Environment

- Consider whether background music will or will not enhance the experience. Use headphones or quiet zones for flexible offerings.
- Reduce visual and auditory distractions.
- Plan seating (noise, proximity to teachers or others, location in the room, etc.).

Schedules

- Give extra time to complete projects.
- Shorten work or instruction periods.
- Have predictable routines or offer information about the planned activities in advance.
- Alternate working time with breaks.

TIMING IS EVERYTHING FOR ACCOMMODATIONS

Several considerations can move the sessions forward when planning these classic accommodations. Some strategies, such as providing multimodal instructions, require advanced preparation *before* sessions occur. Some strategies, such as providing movement breaks, may require some help *during* the session. Others may require additional support *during* the first session, such as providing headphones to those who want them or settling on an agreed-upon background sound. Other accommodations, such as providing predictable routines, do not require additional support. Having a well-crafted planning session and proactively incorporating these accommodation strategies into plans can offer an optimal solution for making accommodations in programs and visits. You may also find that these strategies ultimately benefit many types of visitors and create a better experience for all participants in a group.

Of all these accommodations, meeting the environmental recommendation for reducing visual and auditory distractions may be the most difficult. While headphones may reduce auditory distractions, they also impact the ability of the visitor to benefit from social interactions with others or to receive instructions or information. One way to manage auditory input is to reduce sound distractions in the immediate area. When this is impossible, embed an image of headphones on the schedule suggesting when using headphones may promote success. Another way is to give the visitor more time to process verbal instructions and auditory input.

Using headphones in selected parts of the session might be adequate for eliminating noise when it gets distracting. Many neurodivergent visitors might find comfort in knowing if they tough out portions of their session when attending to auditory input is important, they can eliminate or reduce input with headphones during art activities or be allowed to take a break to relax with their headphones on. Informing visitors in advance of a sensory space that they may excuse themselves and visit if the sound becomes over-whelming is also a helpful strategy.

The recommendation to reduce visual distractions may seem counterintui-tive to a cultural institution like a museum emphasizing visual stimulation and input. When visual input is considered in a larger sense, it includes not only exhibitions but also lighting and other environmental features, people, decor, and signage. Suppose it is not possible to remove visual clutter from a program space. In that case, an alternative is to offer changes of scenery during the visit, alternating visually active with visually inactive or soothing areas, altering the number of visual elements present, changing lighting or other environmental features, or alternating natural and artificial lighting, oftentimes by moving from a room without windows to an outdoor space or a room that has natural light.

One of the best things about accommodations is that they are not set in stone. Oftentimes, as visitors adjust to their new surroundings, the tasks at hand, and the people they are with, they begin to relax and have an easier time processing more input. This can be a liberating experience for them and replace their worry and concern with a sense of pride and belonging. Keeping a list might help cultural educators quickly reference initial accom-modations and note when and which accommodations are being removed because they are no longer needed. This is an excellent way to demonstrate program success and provide families with healthy and encouraging com-munication in follow-up notes.

PRIME BEFORE YOU GO

As a facet of proactive planning, many aspects of accommodations might also be communicated to parents and neurodivergent people before their vis-its in the form of success stories (stories that describe ways to have a good visit) and schedules that can be posted on the institution's website. Involving neurodivergent visitors in making these supports to help others with similar concerns also increases their self-awareness and self-advocacy.

Accommodations are a moving target, and the good news for cultural educators is that there are numerous online examples. Certain considerations can help educators choose resources wisely. When searching for information about laws, rules, and regulations, it is a good practice to use the federal government, along with state education agency sites. State education sites are replete with information such as curriculum goals per grade level, behavior management strategies, how to support students who speak languages other than English, and considerations for navigating the tricky world of parent communication and privacy laws.

It is a major challenge to be a wise Internet consumer. Educators should focus on the resources that are needed rather than getting lost among the many, many choices that are offered. It is a good idea to cross-check all sources for how current and accurate they are, determine whether posted research reflects a higher level of evidence than testimonials and anecdotes, avoid being distracted by impressive infographics and amazing technology, and ignore clickbait that leads viewers off track. Navigating the Internet is complex and requires discipline but can also provide unlimited support.

EDUCATIONAL MODIFICATIONS

While accommodations for educational success can be easily envisioned in a cultural setting, making modifications is more complex. While accommodations *change the way* a student learns, modifications *change the content* a student is expected to learn. The following information details educational modifications that support learning and comprehension as well as environmental modifications that promote community participation for many with autism.

While educational accommodations can be referred to as whatever it takes to make a student successful in meeting curriculum goals, educational modifications manipulate or change aspects of the educational curriculum itself and are more procedural and subject to scrutiny. A common example of a curriculum modification is when a student cannot utilize a literature classic for whatever reason and can study an illustrated and shortened version of the classic as a substitute. Administrators and the IEP team must look at curriculum modification decisions in a broad and long-range sense to ensure it does not become an abused process and substitute or offset ineffective accommodations or teaching. For these reasons, teachers often create strategies for making curriculum modifications. In a cultural setting, modifications to teaching strategies may need to be applied to an entire group of visitors.

An example of how an art activity reflecting a historical period in art can have both accommodations and modifications can be seen in making linocuts. An accommodation to understanding the design and execution of linocuts could be to allow a student who lacks coordination, hand dexterity, attention span, or the ability to articulate safety precautions to use alternate materials such as foam blocks or Styrofoam food trays to create their block print. These materials are softer and require less effort on the part of the student to create a final product. An adjustment to the linocut assignment related to exploring the works of notable artists such as Picasso, Matisse, and Lichtenstein who used linocuts in their works could be to reproduce their style or work with a pencil and paper rendition. In this way, the material requirements have been modified. There is still a focus on style and execution, but two-dimensional renderings have replaced the requirement for carving and printing.

Table 14.1 presents a list of modifications with implementation strategies for a museum tour as an example of how these ideas may be applied in a cultural setting.

Table 14.1.   Sample Instructional Methods, Communication Accommodations, and Implementation Strategies

Instructional Methods and Communication Accommodations	Strategies for Implementation
Develop a private signal for visitors and educators to use when help is needed.	Demonstrate one-finger-up raised hand to group at beginning of program to signal for help.
Pair written and oral instructions, and repeat when needed.	Print handouts with written instructions for prompts.
Pair auditory and visual directions, demonstrations, and representations.	Print supporting images to show when speaking to a group.
Ensure visitors understand expected behavior.	Go over rules and expectations at the beginning of the program; hold up visual aid with text and icons.
Use tactile and manipulative aids.	Be prepared with fidgets or touch-friendly materials when beginning the program.
Utilize visitor's areas of strength rather than try to develop new skills.	Prepare prompts for discussion or response that offer multiple avenues of participation, including written, verbal, kinetic, or sketched.
Provide several movement breaks per session.	Plan kinetic activities such as stretches or poses between program stops or sections.
Simplify directions or break tasks into smaller parts.	Preplan prompts to offer both an overview of instructions and a step-by-step breakdown.

COMMUNITY PARTICIPATION MODIFICATIONS

Community participation goals for people who are neurodivergent are much broader and less specific than the federal and state laws that govern educational goals. In this case, people weigh in on matters of participation, and as a result, modifications vary by region, culture, and economics. While many program and curriculum modifications supporting participation are easy to make, others related to making environmental changes can involve money, labor, and extensive planning. This section describes examples of small to large modifications that contribute to neurodiverse-friendly participation planning efforts to stimulate creative thinking and discussions among cultural educators, planners, and administrators.

When neurodivergent visitors come to an institution, their experience will be impacted by social, cultural, and physical environments, along with their own communication, social, and self-regulation skills and sensory preferences. Across all these factors is the impact of a person's growth and development. For many neurodivergent individuals, their ability to communicate with others, plan, engage in social relationships, and manage their own sensory needs improves with age. This may be particularly evident in summer campers who may have had many challenges one year and, upon arrival, needed little support from others the next year. This may be because, between camp sessions, they matured and developed an internal awareness of what they needed in terms of self-management and communication and could provide for themselves. Growth and development aren't always a magic cure-all, but they help many people manage their social world and community outings in increasingly successful ways.

It is undoubtedly worth it to tough out the difficulties that might come up when people participate in community outings. People who are neurodivergent need to be around each other as much as their neurotypical peers, and the more often they are out in the community, the less likely they are to be segmented away from others.[4]

Simple to Complex Modifications to Community Participation Curricula

One factor that causes children with autism to struggle during the school day is the energy it takes them to refrain from engaging in potentially self-soothing or self-regulating activities. As a result, many of them are exhausted by the time they reach home. It is worth considering how assignments can be modified so that students can demonstrate their knowledge in different ways.

If other students are required to write a report of a community cultural arts experience, it is possible that offering a neurodivergent student a series of items in checklist formatting will enable them to report on their experience with less effort or frustration. Another way to modify the curriculum is to allow the student to take pictures of their visit as opposed to writing to describe their visit. By changing the workload and way they report on their community experience, the hope is the spirit of the lesson remains the same, but the content and learner outcomes are changed to align with student abilities. Photographing a community experience is not the same as writing about it, but the reality is that the curriculum modification allowed the student to complete the experience in the best way possible. Another curriculum modification falls under the umbrella of academic priming, or the practice of letting the student get a jump on the lesson by creating materials for the student to prepare in advance. In this case, the student has extra time and preparation allocated before the field trip ever happens. The teacher determines how much work they can do ahead of time, during the experience, and after it is over. If the student is more prepared, it is possible they may be able to produce a written report for their assignment because they could write part of it in advance and simply fill in the blanks during or after the experience.

More complex modifications can occur when students make cultural institution visits. Among these are the concept of providing an alternate but equivalent assignment. If a teacher can leverage the student's interest in certain preferred items, they are even more likely to fulfill the assignment requirements. An example might be a student with a strong interest in sculptures creating a replica of a sculpture from clay as opposed to writing an essay about the sculpture collection. The challenge behind this might be for the teacher to create a scoring system that is fair and equitable for all students.

Following are environmental modifications that may or may not find their way into learner outcomes. For some students, adjusting environmental supports, such as providing them an altered tour that bypasses noise and crowding, is a way to provide more relaxed engagement and attention to the assignment, and enables them to demonstrate more fully what they have learned because they are not frazzled. Cultural arts educators can check with teachers prior to student visits to see if their tours need to be modified to enable students to meet their learning goals. Other environmental modifications can help adjust a visitor experience.

Modify Lighting Options

Lighting is a complicated situation these days. With the advent of new technologies, many forms of lighting have yet to be systematically or formally researched regarding their impact on neurodivergent people. What is known is that in traditional classroom lighting, fluorescent bulbs or tubes provide a source of light and, unfortunately, sound. Many people do not hear this sound and fail to realize the impact of the incessant buzzing on others. This sound is often accompanied by subtle flickering or humming. Eliminating these tiny noxious sounds and flickering light displays can go a long way toward soothing frayed nerves.

A solution can be found in special filters for fluorescent lights. Autism light filters differ from typical fluorescent filters in that they aren't designed to scatter light more evenly but to reduce flickering and glare. Typically, they are made from heat- and flame-resistant materials that easily attach to a light source's metal frame with magnets. They can look like puffy cloud pillows, shower curtains, or parachute material. Common calming filter colors include blues and greens, and they can become part of a decorating scheme. People interested in the do-it-yourself method often use bleached or unbleached rice or mulberry papers to make interesting lampshades. However, these papers may be flammable and should be fused or attached to a nonflammable support surface in case they meet a lightbulb or tube that can heat up. One benefit of autism light filters is that they tend to relax everyone in the room in an unobtrusive way. With these special filters in place, many people may report having fewer headaches and less eye strain. A quick look at online sources affirms the popularity of autism light filters. Teacher customers comment that they could teach with their classroom lights on when using the filters, which improves everyone's ability to see their tasks. Librarians also weigh in on the benefits of these filters when creating a calm library.

Modify Environmental Triggers

Everyone is different, but certain triggers in the environment seem to impact most neurodivergent people—in both positive and negative ways. Generally speaking, there are two kinds of environments: the kind that can be altered to create a just-right combination of elements that stimulate without overwhelming and create a sense of calm without boring people, and the kind of environment that can't be changed. Typical environments can be modified in the home, school, or workplace. Other environments are often not modifiable because of the building's structure or mission. Sporting events are a great example of something that happens in an environment that can't be made quiet. While a child might love monster trucks, even if the environment were made to accommodate most sensory outbursts, being able to keep the noise level of many competing flashy monster trucks within comfortable limits might strain most peoples' ingenuity and budgets. A performing arts venue, however, can make meaningful modifications for neurodiverse audiences. Performances can be marketed as "judgment-free," and staff can be trained to make sure that holds true by being sensitive when audience members make noise or move from their seats. House lights can be set at a higher level and sound at a lower level, and resources such as headphones and fidgets can be made available to visitors.[5]

Modify by Priming and Practicing Before a Visit

When faced with unalterable environmental challenges, encouraging visitors to prime and *practice* before they visit a cultural institution is a good first start. A good priming session would be creating an advanced planning agenda, reviewing institution-provided materials, driving by the facility, and practicing what the visit might entail. A good practice session should simulate an envisioned real-life scenario as closely as possible with special attention given to noise level, crowding, and lighting conditions.[6] A great example of a practice session that helps is when airlines offer simulated flights just for neurodivergent people. Some airlines or flight museums will simulate the ticketing experience, allow visitors to board a plane, hear the preflight safety speech and demonstration, listen to flight attendants' preflight instructions on the public announcement system, then roll down the runway, before returning to the gate. Many other experiences, especially those that are very different from what most people experience in everyday life, can be practiced in a modified way or environment.[7] If a live session is not feasible, creating a resource in print, digital, or video format will help visitors work through their own practice scenarios and prepare for an in-person visit.

Determine the *amount of time* someone might expect to spend on different aspects of their visit. People in a stressful environment can often tough it out if other demands on them are lessened and they have some way of gauging how long they will be in the trying situation. In other words, if a neurodivergent person is challenging their executive function in a stressful environment such as a crowded concourse, noisy garage, or long queue, knowing how long the experience will last might give them the power to push through the difficulties.

Desensitize when possible, to create a long-term solution that will impact many settings. If a particular factor has been determined to be the difficult aspect of an environment, participating in a desensitization program can help people make it through their time in that place. The challenge with a desensitization program is that the environmental triggers must be accurately identified. It is often difficult to separate a variety of factors that occur together.

Think of a walk-through aviary at a zoo. A variety of environmental factors occur at once: many people may be present, unfamiliar odors fill the air, bird calls and shouting children contribute to a loud environment, and a variety of birds may be swooping or hopping unpredictably through the space. Is the stress caused by the crowding, smell, or noise? While it might be impossible to immerse a person in a complicated and unpredictable environment and gradually increase the exposure time to desensitize them, it is very likely that without identifying someone's primary trigger, even a five-minute exposure to this environment might seem impossible.

Cultural educators can help visitors prepare for navigating situations with offending or noxious environmental factors by offering tools and strategies to practice at home. An audio recording of the cacophony in the aviary might help someone with noise sensitivities decide whether they plan to visit the space and know what to expect if they do. Suggestions for less overwhelming experiences with birds, such as a visit to a duck pond, could help someone become accustomed to certain avian smells and mannerisms before they try the zoo enclosure. A prerecorded video available online and accompanied by a talk from a friendly zoo employee can also make the experience even more similar to the zoo event. The idea is to build tolerance by incrementally changing the experience until the actual experience does not seem difficult, or at the very least, can be tolerable for an agreed-on amount of time.

Alternate environments with triggers and environments that are pleasant to allow for a recharging or reorganizing period. One pleasant environment people might have out in the community is their car. It's possible that a trip into a stressful environment can be alternated with a break in the car, a lounge, or a pleasant zone. Again, identifying a rewarding environment is key to success with this kind of environmental experience. In many cases, behavioral supports or consequences aren't clearly identified and programs go awry.

A great example is the time-out chair. It's quite possible that having a moment to calm down in the time-out zone might be just what is needed, so an anticipated punishment is actually a reward. One nature museum allowed all their summer campers a daily ten-minute break that they could *spend* any time during the camp session. During their ten-minute break, campers could lay in a bean bag chair, check out their phones, listen to music, or watch trippy computer screen savers, then head back to camp activities after recharging their batteries. Camp facilitators noted that the break became more important as the week progressed, and the campers became more fatigued by the many new tasks, people, and places they were experiencing. A designated sensory space can serve this function at a cultural institution. In the case of the bird exhibits at the zoo, the negative experience of sitting close to the bird enclosure can be paired with a fun ride on the zoo monorail or some other agreed-upon pleasant environment within the zoo. If the child decides they are willing to try this strategy a few times, it may be that the negative experience is becoming, if not a positive experience, at least a neutral or tolerable one.

A classroom teacher can undoubtedly provide handy guidance on the ideas of modifications and accommodations. These features may require a lot of work upfront in the planning phases, but their benefits are immediately apparent once they are put into place. A bonus is that many children are already familiar with many of these benefits—it's just the cultural personnel who need to learn them. If cultural institutions work closely with certain classroom educators or have an advisory group, it is so helpful to ask for their expertise when designing modifications for programs or spaces.

NOTES

1. See IDEA, "Section 300.101 Free appropriate public education (FAPE)" at https://sites.ed.gov/idea/regs/b/b/300.101 for more information.
2. See IDEA, "Sec. 300.320 Definition of Individualized Education Program" at https://sites.ed.gov/idea/regs/b/d/300.320 for more information about IEPs and the IEP process.
3. See US Department of Education, "Protecting Students with Disabilities," at https://www2.ed.gov/about/offices/list/ocr/504faq.html for more information about Section 504.
4. The following article about environmental modifications provides ways to support community education: "Small Changes to Environment May Improve Care, Education of Children with Autism," *Infectious Diseases in Children*, June 14, 2018, https://www.healio.com/news/pediatrics/20180607/small-changes-to-environment-may-improve-care-education-of-children-with-autism/.
5. Taylor Woods (Board & Education Manager, Performing Arts Fort Worth) in discussion with Anna Smith, November 29, 2022.
6. See "Social Skills and Autism" at https://www.autismspeaks.org/social-skills-and-autism#:~:text=Social%20skills%20development%20for%20people,enhancing%20communication%20and%20sensory%20integration and "5 Ways to Help a Child with Autism Learn Social Skills" at https://health.clevelandclinic.org/5-ways-to-help-a-child-with-autism-learn-social-skills/ to learn more about the process of learning social skills. Practice is just one component of the process.
7. American Airlines provides a representative example of the programs they have developed for children with autism. See "It's Cool to Fly: American Airlines Programs Helps Kids with Autism Soar to New Heights" at https://news.aa.com/news/news-details/2019/Its-Cool-to-Fly-American-Airlines-program-helps-kids-with-autism-soar-to-new-heights/default.aspx.

Chapter Fifteen

There's a Place for Us

Sensory Spaces for Neurodiverse Visitors

In this chapter, we offer practical strategies that can be used to help people with sensory processing challenges enjoy their time in community events. Museums can help neurodivergent visitors optimize their behavioral state so they can adjust to or ignore various sensory inputs. A powerful strategy is to help neurodivergent visitors feel resilient, empowered, and able to tolerate things that might otherwise bother them.

This chapter is your guide to the ins and outs of sensory spaces, including

- steps that can be taken to make your entire space more comfortable for people with sensory differences;
- what should and should not be included in a designated sensory space; and
- how to create a portable pop-up sensory space.

EVERYWHERE A SENSORY SPACE

Our sensory world is rich and complex. Adjusting our spaces to help promote sensory regulation by supporting internal resilience and tolerance while alerting people to potential challenges and giving them the power to come up with solutions can make a significant difference in a visitor's staying power. Sometimes, thoughtful planning on the part of cultural educators can lessen the need for a trip to a designated sensory space. Your venue may be tranquil or chaotic by turns depending on when someone visits and how they approach the space when they do. Sharing this information with neurodivergent visitors and giving them the tools to plan according to their needs can make everything they experience at your institution more sensory-friendly.

Timing Is Everything

Some ways cultural institutions can contribute to a stress-free visit are to schedule events when commuting is free of rush-hour challenges. Some places refer to this as a relaxed opening time. Another is to offer a stress-free entrance and immediate orientation to the environment. Small welcoming gestures such as placing curtains that dampen sound and minimize light on entrance windows can significantly impact people when they are registering or signing in for the event. Directing visitors to the restrooms and water fountains and offering little bottles of water can also be a pause that provides refreshment and restoration. Providing visitors with small objects that can calm nervous hands can also be organizing and calming. These small touches can include Mardi Gras beads, tiny magnifying glasses, flip books of images related to the institution's collection or area of focus, and stretchy wristband coils. Visitors can choose to wear a red one to signal a preference to refrain from interacting with others or a green one to signal a readiness to socialize.

Mapping a Route

Creating sensory respites in the venue itself can be as simple as posting photos of headphones along a path or on a map. As a classic example, when visitors know that they are entering a *headphone zone* where ambient sound levels might call for the use of noise-canceling headphones, they may be more able to gain control as they decide whether the suggested sensory remedies are needed. Additional support can include offering guides to *sensory slow* routes—pathways through a space that provide limited sensory input—or directing visitors to sensory spaces or other quiet areas where they have an opportunity to collect themselves.[1] Consider infant nursing rooms as an example—they are simple, small, and calming.

CREATING A DESIGNATED SPACE

An effective strategy for offering sensory support is to provide a sensory space in which people may rest. These spaces can be a permanent part of your facility or a temporary structure for use at an event. They should be stocked with a few essential items that offer tactile, vestibular, and proprioceptive input. In most cases, a quick five-to-ten-minute visit to one of these spaces should be enough for people to recharge their batteries and soothe jangled nerves. After all, the goal is to be a part of the venue, not disappear into a sensory space.

Little cardboard houses, pop-up tents, art boxes, garden gazebos, and ice-fishing houses can provide a haven. They can be furnished quite simply by fold-up camping chairs equipped with hydraulic jacks to support rocking movements. These prevent the troublesome traveling or scooting that rocking can lead to, and with their sling-style seats and backs, they provide a helpful tight-squeeze feeling. To provide deep pressure touch, spaces can also contain weighted gel-based lap weights that are easily cleaned and stored. Additional features include visual displays and white noise or music makers. Sensory toys do not need to be expensive or complicated. See textbox 15.1 and figure 15.1 for instructions on how to make a low- or no-cost sensory bottle using recycled materials.

TEXTBOX 15.1.
TIP SHEET: HOW TO MAKE A SENSORY BOTTLE

Sensory bottles, sometimes called sensory tubes or calm-down bottles, are easy and budget-friendly tools for sensory self-regulation. Sensory bottles can be made with recycled materials or things you may already have in your cupboard.

Sensory bottles can be made in advance of events by staff and kept in the sensory room, or they can be made by program participants or parents and caregivers as a sensory toy to make and take home.

The following instructions create one type of sensory bottle, but the variations are endless. Small plastic toys and beads can be added to the bottles to give more visual interest. Eye-spy sensory bottles can be made using dry material like rice and fun objects to search for by shaking the bottle, such as pennies, pom poms, googly eyes, seashells, and buttons. Figure 15.1 shows the materials needed for this project.

Materials

- Empty 8 oz. water bottle or plastic jar, with labels removed
- 6 oz. bottle of glitter glue
- Glitter (fine glitter is preferred)
- Strong, water resistant adhesive like super glue or E600 epoxy
- Warm water
- Food coloring (optional)

Instructions

1. Squeeze about half (three ounces) of the glitter glue into the empty container. You may want to use slightly more or less depending on the size of your container.
2. Leaving about an inch of space at the top, fill your container with warm water.
3. Add as much glitter and food coloring as you like and close the bottle.
4. Shake the bottle until everything is combined.
5. Carefully unscrew the lid and add a few dots of a strong adhesive to the inside of the bottle's lid. Screw the lid back on and allow the adhesive to dry completely before use.

Figure 15.1. Supplies needed to make sensory bottle.
Emily Wiskera

Visitors to sensory spaces seem most calm and collected when the areas offer them a choice. In this case, offering sensory space visitors a sense of control over their environment by providing them with remote controls that power the sound and light displays is popular and validating, as are opportunities to enter and exit the space at will. Figure 15.2 shows a sensory space on a museum landscape. Figure 15.3 shows a sensory space interior. And figure 15.4 shows how portable a sensory space can be.

Figure 15.2.   Sensory space in a museum landscape.
Tina Fletcher

Figure 15.3.   Sensory space interior.
Photo by Jake Dockins, courtesy Dallas Museum of Art

Figure 15.4.   Sensory spaces can be highly portable and easily stored between events.
Tina Fletcher

KEEPING THINGS SAFE

To ensure safety in sensory spaces, staff can remove items that may pose a safety risk or could be used as a projectile and focus on promoting calmness and opportunities to self-regulate. In our COVID-influenced world, all surfaces should be cleanable, so cozy blankets should be replaced with washable or wipeable lap pads with textural or weighted features. One last safety consideration is ensuring easy physical access to sensory spaces and using any items inside. A decision point in selecting an ice-fishing house for a sensory space is whether they have door thresholds. Many tents and covered spaces have thresholds as a matter of structural integrity, especially in windy areas. Structures without thresholds offer immediate access to the interior space, whether by walking in or using a wheelchair or other wheeled mobility device.

BUILDING YOUR SENSORY SPACE

When you are ready to create a sensory space at your institution, refer to table 15.1. This table is a planning tool for creating a portable sensory space contained within a 70" × 70" ice-fishing tent. We suggest choosing the items from each section that best fit your needs and storage capacity. Please note that prices are estimated and may vary.

Table 15.1.   Budget for Portable Sensory Space

Item	$ Price Range	Justification
Structure and Furnishings		
Portable ice-fishing shelter	150–450	Portable sensory space without flooring
Outdoor camping chair with hydraulic rocker jacks (Child and adult sizes)	50–100	Rocks without moving around on floor
Outdoor folding beach chair (Child and adult sizes)	20–60	Provides stable seating for those who don't want to rock
2' foam interlocking flooring	50–100	Provides a clean and portable surface for outside use
Foam tile storage bags	20	Stores foam floor blocks
Electrical and Lighting		
LED night-light/star projector with Bluetooth and remote	25–50	Remote offers a sense of control, noise can mask outside sounds, has soothing effects
LED fiber-optic cable lights	100–150	Light displays that can be handled

Item	$ Price Range	Justification
220W portable power station	100–200	Enables set-up anywhere
25 ft extension cord, three outlets	15–30	Can be used for lights
Power strip	10–20	Can be used for lights
Transportation and Climate Control		
Double-decker folding wagon	125–150	Stores, transports, folds
45-gallon wheeled tote	25–50	Stores, transports, stacks
Evaporative air cooler	150–200	Moves and cools air
Cooling fans	20–30	Moves and vents air
Blankets and Small Items		
Minky lap pad or crib blanket	25–50	Textural sensory input and neutral warmth for laps or when laying on the space floor
5 lb. weighted lap pad	25–50	Deep pressure input for laps or when laying on the space floor
Tag security blanket	10–25	Lightweight textural variation for fidgeting
Weighted gel lap pad	25–50	Easily cleaned deep pressure input for lap
Marble fidget toys pack	15–25	Give away fidgets
Green and red wristbands pack	10	Indicates preference for interacting with others
Mini flashlights pack	10–20	Provides a sense of control – turned in when done
Noise-canceling headphones	15–30	Controls auditory input – turned in when done
Maintenance		
Laundry bag	10	Stores used weighted blankets and pads for cleaning
Laundry soap and spray cleaner	10	For washing and wipe down

NOTE

1. See the following for information about sensory guides: Tina S. Fletcher, Amanda B. Blake, and Kathleen E. Shelffo, "Can Sensory Gallery Guides for Children with Sensory Processing Challenges Improve Their Museum Experience?" *Journal of Museum Education* 43, no. 1 (2018): 66–77, https://doi.org/10.1080/1059 8650.2017.1407915.

Part 5

DEVELOPING PROGRAMMING AND BUILDING COMMUNITY CONNECTIONS

Chapter Sixteen

Better Together
Forming Healthy Partnerships

The research for best practices is well under way, your focus group has expressed interest, and you have the green light from your administration. You are ready to start the planning process! But your head is still swirling with questions: What kind of programs will you offer? What kind of resources or equipment are needed first? What wayfinding tools should you have in place for a successful launch? What will you do if things don't go as planned?

It can be overwhelming when you feel like you're not enough of an expert to get started. But it is not about *what* you know; it is about *who* you know. The answers to planning questions can be informed by local colleagues and community constituents who have had years of experience with neurodiverse audiences. Developing partnerships with colleagues in your community can make all the difference. Partnerships are different from consultants or advisors whom you might call at specific moments for their expertise and experience to inform decisions. Partnerships are beneficial to both parties beyond receiving payment in exchange for services. Joining forces with community partners cultivates a sense of shared ownership and creates stronger, more nuanced programs and offerings that are informed by a variety of perspectives.

In this chapter, we will present strategies for identifying partners in your community with whom you can nurture a mutually beneficial relationship. These include

- determining if a partner is a good match;
- thinking through partnerships based on what each partner can contribute; and
- developing a formalized partnership, using the model of the Dallas Sensory Consortium.

FINDING (AND KEEPING) THE PERFECT PARTNER

In some ways, professional partnerships are a lot like romantic relationships. They are built on a foundation of trust, both parties share important values and goals, and they demonstrate a dedication to one another. But how do you know if you've found "the one?" And once you've found them, how do you keep them? Unlike romantic relationships that have been endlessly explored through rom-coms and have dedicated bookshelves at libraries and bookstores, professional relationships do not have the same level of attention, reflection, and guidance. But don't despair! By examining our past partnerships, both successful and not, we've outlined the key qualities of a successful partnership and action steps you can take to nurture its continued growth. Table 16.1 lays out some characteristics of successful partnerships and the actions that help them to thrive.

How can you determine if a potential partner shares your values and goals? If you have worked with a focus group on program development, talk to them about their experiences with a potential partner. Read online reviews by community constituents to learn more about public perception of an institution or organization you plan to work with. Go to their website, read their mission statement, and see how they describe neurodiversity or autism. Does their message reflect an openness? Do they want to strengthen neurodiverse learning methods and reduce barriers to participation? Do they view neurodiversity through a strength-based lens, or do they see autism as a condition that needs to be cured? If your institutions share similar values and goals, consider forming a partnership. If the answers to the above questions reveal that your missions and messages to the community are not aligned, it's okay to politely stay independent. Co-author Emily Wiskera recalls an experience where a partner was not a good match.

> When first starting neurodiverse programming at the Dallas Museum of Art (DMA), we invited a well-known autism research organization to host an information table at our events. After hearing from program attendees that they found the mission of the organization to be offensive, we cut ties, worked hard to rebuild trust with community constituents, and were much more cautious when selecting partners in the future.

DIFFERENT LEVELS OF PARTNERSHIP

Think about the friends in your life. There are the friends who, although you care for them, you only see occasionally. And then there are the friends with whom you share a much deeper bond. It's likely that you are more actively

Table 16.1. Characteristics of Successful Partnerships and Actions That Promote Success

Characteristics	Actions
Mutually beneficial	Research the organization's mission and values. How does it align with yours? How does working with this organization advance the mission of your institution?
	Be clear and upfront about your goals, values, and scope of your work.
Dependable and organized	Systematize a planning process to follow with all partners (i.e., planning meeting, issuing a memorandum of understanding [MOU] with roles and responsibilities, confirming dates, evaluating the program, and debriefing when it's over).
	Each party is reliable and responsive.
Synchronized expectations and shared responsibilities	Articulate and agree on the roles and responsibilities of each party in a written agreement.
	While you may follow a systematized planning process, the specific goals will vary from partner to partner. Success will look different from site to site.
Features clear boundaries	How can partners hold each other accountable?
	Partnerships should stretch each party, but not overextend them.
Features open communication and collaborative problem solving	Each party is responsive and listens to the other.
	Take a collaborative approach to decision making and conflict resolution. How might we . . . ?
Is a positive learning experience for both parties	Conclude each partnership with a debrief, where you can discuss lessons learned and how to move forward. Should the partnership continue as is, evolve, or come to a conclusion?

engaged in each other's lives. Professional partnerships, like friendships, have varying levels of commitment. Some partnerships, while still being fruitful, are not as consistently active or deeply involved. In this section, we will explore the partnership of the Dallas Sensory Consortium, its collaboration with outside partners, and how the varying levels of partnerships have been beneficial to our institutions, programs, and communities.

In 2017, the DMA, Nasher Sculpture Center, Dallas Zoo, and Texas Woman's University (TWU) officially formed a partnership called the Dallas Sensory Consortium. The formation of this partnership happened organically—the arts and cultural institutions had been hosting similarly structured sensory-friendly family days for several years. They informally collaborated, sharing advice, spreading the word about programs, and occasionally hosting an activity table at each other's events. Another unifying factor was a partnership with Tina Fletcher, who supported each institution's specialized autism programming since its inception.

As an expert in the field of autism, Dr. Fletcher consulted in the development of these specialized programs and continues to inform best practices as the programs evolve. She also leads annual training sessions for staff and volunteers, focused on improving visitor experience for neurodiverse populations. Under the guidance of Dr. Fletcher, occupational therapy students at Texas Woman's University develop activities and help to conduct sensory-friendly programming at the DMA, Nasher Sculpture Center, and Dallas Zoo. Their participation in Sensory Days is built into their course curriculum and allows students to apply their studies in hands-on ways. The involvement of the TWU students has been critical to support the growing number of participants in each event. Approximately eighteen to thirty students support each event, which welcomes between five hundred and a thousand participants.

With similarly structured programs, shared values, and a mutual partner, a union between the Dallas Zoo, the Nasher, and DMA is obvious in retrospect. The institutions wanted to support each other and see their neighbor's programs succeed. But by not partnering, they were inadvertently competing. This became obvious when, due to not scheduling their events in dialogue, all three institutions planned a sensory-friendly family day during April, Autism Awareness month. Families voiced frustration that events were not spread out throughout the year, and too much was being asked of TWU students who were staffing an event every weekend in April. Something had to change.

Soon thereafter, staff from the zoo, sculpture center, art museum, and university met to discuss a plan. In this meeting, the idea for a formal partnership arose. Each representative wrote a challenge that they were facing, a unique asset of their institution, and a goal of their autism programming on big sticky notes around the meeting room. Upon reading the responses, participants realized that one institution's assets could solve another's challenges, and those shared issues could be solved by working together. Moreover, attendees of the meeting were struck by the cohesiveness of their goals and values. In the following days, the Sensory Consortium officially formed when representatives excitedly drafted and agreed upon the following shared goals:

- Making our institutions an inclusive place, where activities are designed to engage learners across the spectrum of modalities and skill levels
- Making our institutions a welcoming place, where families can access the resources they need to navigate the space and choose the activities that fit their interests
- Making our institutions a safe place, where guests can explore the environment with knowledgeable staff who make accommodations that result in a more enjoyable and accessible visit

Members of the consortium drafted a memorandum of understanding (MOU) that detailed the institutional commitment to participating in the Sensory Consortium. Members agreed to schedule their events together, take turns hosting and supporting each other's events, and maintain a shared website under the domain *sensorydaysdallas.com,* which would consolidate all Sensory Day event listings and partner resources in one place. The MOU not only ensured that all members understood their individual commitment, but it also secured a certain level of institutional buy-in. Knowing that specialized programs were often staff passion projects and in danger of disbandment in the situation of staff turnover, a member of leadership was required to sign off on the agreement. Textbox 16.1 is a sample partner agreement for a Sensory Consortium.

Through the partnership, consortium partners also learn about innovative equipment and best practices modeled at other locations. For example, an ice-fishing house was discovered by one partner who adapted it for a sensory haven. It resembles a domed, floorless tent with a black interior that can be outfitted with small constellation-like lights to calm a child. Sharing large pieces like this can be an advantage where budgets and storage of equipment may be difficult to accommodate.

Meetings are planned quarterly to review the upcoming calendar of events, confirm the theme and which partners will be participating, and brainstorm activity stations. When providing an activity at a partner institution, verbal and pictured nonverbal tip sheets are prepared and sent in advance to the host. Meant to guide the visitor through the activity, it also informs the institution what materials and utilities (water, electrical outlets) will be used so they can plan accordingly. Knowing whether it's an active or passive sensory activity also helps to determine its position on the host institution's event map, to ensure sensory seekers and avoiders have a zone nearby to go to. Whether over virtual platforms or in person, having regular meetings keeps partners connected and energized by recently discovered resources and research. Updating posts to the website keeps the public visiting the site for the latest programs and encourages crossover attendance to new partner locations.

TEXTBOX 16.1.
SAMPLE SENSORY CONSORTIUM PARTNER AGREEMENT

This document affirms an agreement made between (institution names). By signing below, we agree to be a participating institutional member of the "(_____) Sensory Consortium." It is the stated intent of each of these institutions to

- collaborate to offer sensory-friendly programming; and
- maintain the shared website (URL name) as a centralized resource for families in (state or region) to learn about our events and resources.

The goal of the Sensory Consortium is to improve access to community cultural and recreational venues for visitors with autism and sensory challenges.

The Sensory Consortium offers sensory-friendly programming as a way to remove barriers to participation. During these events, families can enjoy sensory-friendly activities at each of our venues, with modifications such as sound adjustments, previsit materials, and designated sensory spaces.

Sensory Consortium partners are dedicated to continual learning and development of best practices, through program evaluation, focus groups, and research.

Sensory Consortium Collective Mission:

- Provide centralized resources for families in (state or region) to learn about sensory-friendly events.
- Partner with other community organizations to promote events for families who have children with autism or sensory challenges.
- Coordinate events at times of the year that are mindful of other institutions offering sensory-friendly programming.
- Learn from program participants and community partners about best practices in serving children with autism and sensory needs.
- Share knowledge and experience with others, such as other interested institutions and staff of one's own institution. This may take the form of, but is not limited to, training, workshops, resources on shared website, and writing of journal articles.

Institutional Inclusion Goals:

- Making our institutions an inclusive place, where activities are designed to engage learners across the spectrum of modalities and skill levels.
- Making our institutions a welcoming place, where families can access resources they need to navigate the space and choose the activities that fit their interests.

- Making our institutions a safe place, where guests can explore the environment with knowledgeable staff who make accommodations that result in a more enjoyable and accessible visit.

Benefits to Sensory Consortium Partners:

- The opportunity to host or support one or more sensory programs per year, in which other Sensory Consortium partners will provide an activity or support in the form of volunteer staffing.
- Equal use of and access to shared domain (include URL) to promote sensory-friendly programs and resources from your institution.
- Equal use of and access to a shared database of contacts through email sign-up via shared domain.

Sensory Consortium Partner Commitments:

- For partners with an institutional venue: to host a Sensory Day event at their institution or provide an activity at a sensory program hosted at other participating institutions.
- For university partners: to support sensory programming at host institutions as a component of coursework under the direction of (university contact). This takes the form of on-site staffing and activity design for sensory programs.
- Partners will participate in at least [specify number] Sensory Consortium planning meetings on an annual basis.
- Each partner will be responsible for updating the shared website with sensory events and registration links, and other information related to sensory-friendly resources.
- Partners should give notice to the Sensory Consortium when major changes are made to the shared website. Login information should not be changed without prior notice and consent from the Sensory Consortium.
- (_____) absorbs the cost of maintaining the shared website services and domain name hosting.
- Partners must provide written notice to the Sensory Consortium if their organization can no longer participate as an active member.

Institution Name:

_____

Representative Name and Title:

_____

Signature: _____

Date: _____

A side benefit of the partnership is this cross-pollination of audiences, introducing new people to your institution, either through the shared website or attendance at other partners' events. Having fliers on the table enables your institution to promote the upcoming sensory event in your space and makes you known to the families. They can ask you questions and become familiar with your staff and the kind of experience they can expect.

Since the Dallas Sensory Consortium's inception, other institutions have joined the partnership. The Dallas Public Library and Frontiers of Flight have proven to be invaluable members. While the Dallas Public Library does not host the same type of sensory-friendly family days as other members of the Sensory Consortium, they participate in other meaningful ways. Librarians from Dallas Public Library attend the sensory-friendly events, facilitating story time for participants. At the library, consortium members set up temporary sensory spaces for their public events. With a growing circle of partners, the consortium has expanded its network with other institutions and professional organizations with whom they have collegial associations. Realizing the neurodiverse community has a wide spectrum of interests, the consortium hopes to welcome institutions with varied collections to offer the public a suite of different experiences to be enjoyed throughout the year. There is strength in having a diversity of partners.

The consortium partnership is different from other contractual relationships. The Nasher Sculpture Center and the Dallas Zoo are certified Kulture-City™ locations. To complete certification, the majority of front-of-house staff must successfully complete training modules to understand the needs of neurodivergent visitors. A modest membership fee is paid annually by affiliated institutions to KultureCity and they agree to maintain their visitor resources, such as signage, success stories, and sensory bags containing supports such as fidgets and headphones. Unlike other members of the Sensory Consortium, the Dallas Museum of Art was unable to form a relationship with KultureCity because of its large number of contract staff who would be unable to complete training requirements.

Members of the Sensory Consortium have also formed their own independent partnerships within the community. At the Dallas Museum of Art (DMA), one such partnership was formed through continued engagement with a contractual guest artist group, Chiptunes 4 Autism. This nonprofit organization is a collective formed by musicians who all identify as having autism. The DMA first engaged with this group at a Sensory Day where they were hired to play a low-sensory music set. The musicians went above and beyond, inviting children to try playing their electronic instruments and teaching parents how to make their own musical toys for sensory self-regulation at home, as seen in figure 16.1. Finding that the DMA and Chiptunes

Figure 16.1.   Chiptunes 4 Autism performs at a Dallas Museum of Art event.
Photo courtesy of the Dallas Museum of Art

4 Autism shared goals and values, their relationship quickly moved from a one-off contractual encounter to an ongoing symbiotic partnership. When Chiptunes 4 Autism needed a family-friendly venue for their annual musical showcase, the DMA eagerly volunteered their space. When the DMA hosts family festivals, Chiptunes 4 Autism performs musical sets for both sensory avoiders and sensory seekers. Both organizations promote each other to the community and benefit tremendously from this partnership. While the DMA would highly recommend this organization to others, shared partnership is not a requirement for the core partners of the Sensory Consortium.

Parent groups and community constituents are another valuable form of partnership, serving in an advisory capacity and giving useful insights.

Co-creating programs with them is a win–win. Having their voices in the planning process ensures the interests and needs of neurodivergent children are given priority. Factors that may not otherwise have been considered are brought to light and solutions are found together.

In addition to knowing the various levels of partnerships and being able to judge if a partnership is mutually beneficial, there are a few practical matters to consider when forming and working with partners. Textbox 16.2 lists some major things to ensure a smooth relationship with a potential partner.

TEXTBOX 16.2.
PRACTICAL ADVICE FOR FORMING PARTNERSHIPS

- *When it comes to forming a partnership, size matters.* For core partnerships, it is important that you have a big enough team to support your operations, but not so big as to impede scheduling and decision-making. Think about the sizes of committees of which you have been a member. When did the number become so large that your individual contribution to its operation wasn't necessary? You want your group to remain effective and action-oriented, so select a few valuable partners that will stay engaged.
- *One size doesn't fit all.* Synchronous events (those that take place at a set time for all participants) at partner institutions will not look the same. Expect them to reflect their collections and to attract different audiences. Some partner institutions may choose only to have *asynchronous* events (programs where participants can drop by at their own pace at any time) at their site but will come and support other partner locations when they host. Be open to alternative ways that partners support neurodiverse programming at their sites.
- *When planning the calendar of events with partners, consider what months are best for the comfort of your guests.* The South is hot and humid in the summer, so events outside are best kept to the spring and fall. In the North, snow and chilly temperatures are restrictive in the winter, but temperate summers make for an optimal outdoor event. Indoor events are more flexible, so give scheduling preference to partners whose venues don't have that option.
- *You don't have to be the expert in all things, but you are responsible for partnering with experts.* You are not required to have professional degrees or special certifications to work with neurodiverse audiences, but you should know and be informed by people who have that level of expertise. Seek out those who are well-regarded in the field to inform best practices for your institution. By building relationships with local experts, trusted advice will be just a phone call away.

WHAT MAKES US DIFFERENT

When reflecting on the partnership model of the Dallas Sensory Consortium, we are struck by a few things: we are not aware of another collective like ours, and we couldn't do it without each other. While this book is intended to provide a basic framework, true success will come when you make it your own. When setting forth to nurture your own partnerships consider the following: What makes your city special? Which organizations or individuals are beloved by your community? Who are the little guys with big dreams? Who should be at the table to make your partnership representative of your specific community? By joining forces, you can not only accomplish your own goals but help others to reach theirs, too. Success is best when shared.

Chapter Seventeen

Set Yourself Up for Success

Logistics for Sensory-Friendly Events

When deciding what your programs or resources will look like, it is crucial to consider the particularities of your institution, staff, and community. Whether choosing the synchronous or asynchronous route, the following factors should be carefully considered to ensure you have sufficient support and resources. Additionally, we humbly include a list of lessons we learned the hard way and thoughts on what we would do differently.

Among these lessons, we will share

- considerations for how your staff can handle programming;
- a timeline for planning a sensory-friendly event;
- tips for budgeting for events; and
- examples of what has and has not worked at our own institutions.

FACTOR ONE: STAFF CAPACITY

What are your staffing capacities for an event? Will other colleagues be available to support your event? That answer will determine if a synchronous or asynchronous program format is best for your institution and if you need to limit event attendance. Depending on the scope of the event plan, your institution may require many willing, trained people to staff it.

So how do you know how much staffing is appropriate? Parents may accompany their children everywhere in the space, but it is still helpful to have teams of two greeting attendees at the entrance, stationed at each activity table, and at least two seasoned staff members or volunteers in each space who are ready to assist a family if needs arise. With two or more stationed at each activity table, one person can turn their attention to prepping materials and keeping the area well-stocked and clean, while the other greets attendees and helps them engage in the activity. If the table is busy, two staff or volunteers are more capable than one to address the varied needs and questions of participants. Depending on the number of registrants and the number of activities offered, the number of tables and personnel can be adjusted to accommodate the scope of the event.

FACTOR TWO: STAFF CAPABILITIES AND COMFORT LEVEL

Does your institution offer sensory training for all front-of-house employees, including security, as part of their onboarding procedure? Recognizing the signs of someone needing a quiet place and knowing how to approach that visitor with sensitivity is very important. As mentioned in the previous chapter, the Nasher Sculpture Center opted for online training and certification through KultureCity since security and employees are added throughout the year. Other approaches like bringing in consultants for all-staff training are also highly beneficial.

FACTOR THREE: WHEN SHOULD I START PLANNING?

Thoughtful planning is key to feeling confident and prepared to host an event. But when should you start planning? And do you have enough time to check all the tasks off your to-do list?

The checklist below provides a handy rundown of tasks to consider when planning a large-scale synchronous event. Table 17.1 outlines when the big tasks need to take place over the course of a calendar year, using a recurring,

Table 17.1.   Example Program Planning Cycle for Sensory-Friendly Event Occurring Three Times Per Year

January	February	March	April	May	June
Set dates and themes for upcoming year	Create schedule, order supplies, write contracts for guests	Registration opens	Event takes place	Process evaluation	Create schedule, order supplies, write contracts for guests
July	*August*	*September*	*October*	*November*	*December*
Registration opens	Event takes place	Process evaluation	Create schedule, order supplies, write contracts for guests	Registration opens	Event takes place

synchronous, large-scale event as an example. This timeline can and should be adjusted to fit the particular needs of your institution and aligned with event timing that responds to the availability of your community.

Example To-Do List for a Sensory-Friendly Event

Four to Six Months before the Event

- Set dates and themes for the upcoming year.
- Add dates to the institutional calendar and communicate dates to security and event support staff.
- Communicate dates to partners and volunteers.
- Add dates to your website.

Two to Three Months before the Event

- Ask partners about their participation, activity, and needs (electrical, water, etc.).
- Create event schedule, success story, and map with universal icons.
- Translate event schedule, success story, signage, and other guest resources into additional languages used by your institution.
- Order supplies for activity stations.
- Write verbal and nonverbal tip sheets for activities.
- Write contracts for any guest artists, performers, and contract specialists.
- Recruit and confirm volunteers.
- Request promotion of event by your marketing team to social media channels.
- Develop evaluation instruments to be used at the event.

One Month before the Event

- Open registration to participants (include consent permissions on the form).
- Submit facility requests within your institution for any temporary building modifications (such as dimming lights), furniture that needs to be placed, or areas that will need deep cleaning.
- Create volunteer schedule and descriptions of volunteer placements.
- Train staff and volunteers for event.
- Prepare supplies.

Week of the Event

- Send event reminder to participants with additional resources attached, including parking information, schedule of events, and success story.
- Make a contingency plan if forecasted weather will affect activity locations.

- Confirm with the facilities manager that no loud construction or landscaping work will take place during the event.
- Hold an internal run-of-show.
- Send internal event reminder to support staff, security, and operations.

Day before the Event

- Set up activity stations, check-in table, and sensory spaces.
- Print copies of event schedule, success stories, and map.
- Print signage specific to the event.

Day of the Event

- Have carts available to load in equipment for partners, guest artists, and performers.
- Meet with volunteers, guest artists, performers, and contract specialists and place them in their respective stations at the event.
- Confirm that stanchions, signage, and security are in place.
- Set up evaluation stations.
- Take photos to document event.
- Write down verbal feedback from participants along with staff observations.
- Deliver payments to any contract staff.
- Have fun!
- Clean up and reset after the event concludes.

Weeks Following the Event

- If applicable, send out an additional questionnaire to attendees.
- Process evaluation that was conducted at the event.
- Summarize the results of survey and evaluation.
- Archive visitor feedback and photos from the event, as well as attendance numbers and any other statistics that will be useful when applying for grant support.
- Meet with staff and core partners to reflect on successes and challenges.

FACTOR FOUR: WHAT'S IT GOING TO COST?

Each institution knows what works best for them logistically and financially. Many institutions are nonprofit or municipally owned. As such, funding for new programs is dependent on grants, donations, or approval by the city.

Budget cycles may require planning your first program further out. Costs that should be factored into your request are security expenses for gallery coverage if your event happens before or after public hours, honoraria for focus group consultants and staff training, translation fees for written materials, printing, marketing promotion, supplies, and valet parking (if your institution doesn't have a nearby garage).

FACTOR FIVE: ALL STAFF AND PARTNERS SHOULD KNOW THEIR PART OF THE PLAN

A *run-of-show* meeting should be scheduled for all staff and partners involved to remove the element of the unknown. Representatives from the security and facilities departments should be present to answer any questions about where guards should be positioned or where tables, chairs, and electrical cords are needed. If the event will be held outdoors, the group can make a weather contingency plan. During the run-of-show, staff can distribute maps with locations of activities and sensory spaces as well as the logistics of when and where partners will arrive to unload their supplies and park. This is a good time to review behaviors common to neurodivergent people and share strategies for approaching and helping a visitor who is experiencing sensory overload. It is our experience that a one-page handout featuring the event map and another that highlights how to interact with event guests are the most welcomed takeaways.[1]

LESSONS LEARNED

If in-person programming for neurodivergent visitors is in your plan, we have some general guidance to offer based on our own experiences. The following are field-tested suggestions for what you should and should not do when hosting a sensory event.

Facilitating Smooth Transitions

- *Be mindful when naming your event so it is respectful of the group you are inviting.* A decade ago, "autism awareness family celebration" was considered the standard. The term for the past few years has been "sensory-friendly," but now "neurodiversity" is being used more frequently. Ask your focus group how they would like to be identified.
- *Engage your guest from start to finish beginning at the curb.* Place an information table at the entrance to your institution so that guests can easily

see where to check in and get the event map, activity checklist, gift fidget, and recyclable bag to store all their creations. If you opt for valet parking to mitigate transition issues from a parking garage, convert the entrance table to an activity table near the valet stand toward the end of the event. Because there is often a line at pickup, having an activity that families can enjoy at the tables or take with them to complete at home creates a wonderful parting memory. You want parents to know that you have considered their families' needs from beginning to end.

- *Make parking simple and accessible.* Making a smooth transition from your attendees' homes to where they will park and how they will enter your building is essential. Some families attending events at the Nasher and Dallas Museum of Art (DMA) have driven an hour or more to get to an event and found it necessary to turn around because the distance from their parking spot to the entrance created so much stress. Based upon their feedback, the Nasher now offers free valet parking for events in a nearby garage. Each museum also offers a success story that includes directions to the garage and other parking locations nearby so they can prepare for their visit.
- *Give time warnings.* Nobody likes the experience of suddenly being told, "Party's over! Everyone out!" When an activity is ending, use sand timers, adjusted lighting, and verbal announcements to give fifteen-, ten-, and five-minute warnings.

Showing the Way

- *Prepare signage with universal design icons in spaces where basic services like bathrooms, water fountains, quiet rooms, ramps, and elevators can be found.* Signs indicating where headphones are advised for loud ambient sounds are also helpful for visitors who wish to proactively avoid sensory triggers. If there are items in your space that are off-limits, place icon-based signage informing visitors what may or may not be touched.
- *Develop a handout with your institution's success story on one side and a map with the locations and times of activities on the other.* Make a checklist for the activities, so visitors can self-select and record their completed favorites.

Designing Successful Sensory Spaces

- *Choose the location of your sensory spaces carefully.* At an autism family day at the zoo, staff made the mistake of placing the sensory space far away from the action of the event. The reasoning was that the space needed to be in the quietest location. But when overstimulated attendees left the loud and echoey monkey house, their priority was getting to a quiet space quickly. On the verge of a meltdown, they needed the space to be close, not perfectly quiet. Think of your spaces as being as necessary as public restrooms for your attendees. During a larger event or if your space has a bigger footprint, your institution may offer several locations dedicated to sensory self-regulation.

- *Don't make your sensory space too much fun.* Attendees won't want to leave what is intended to be a temporary recovery space. Parents usually want their child to socialize with other children and explore the event as a family. Once, the DMA made a sensory room along a campout theme, complete with tents and stars that glowed. It was so much fun that the "campers" who came to the room to find calm didn't want to rejoin the group activities. Parents expressed that one of their main objectives for coming to events is to provide opportunities for their kids to interact with other children. Although the objective of sensory spaces to reduce stressors was achieved, the family's goal was missed.
- *Be mindful of projectiles.* While large exercise balls may be common in occupational therapy spaces, leave them out of your sensory room. Instead of being used for seating, stability balls can quickly become airborne, like the largest and most perilous game of dodgeball.
- *Leave out the scents in a sensory space.* Aromatherapy with calming scents like lavender may seem like a good idea, but trust us on this one . . . it's not. Scented rooms can commonly cause allergies, headaches, and (recalling an event we'd rather forget) a room full of vomit.
- *Share sensory space ideas with visitors.* One of the most common questions from parents and caregivers is how to set up their own sensory space at home. At your event or if you have a permanent sensory space at your institution, provide a handout that explains the features of the room and where these items can be purchased.

Making Activities Accessible to Everyone

- *Tip sheets are a helpful resource for visitors.* On your activity tables, use a Plexiglass stand to display a user-friendly tip sheet containing step-by-step instructions. Offer verbal and nonverbal directions, with images for each step.
- *When planning activities, remember that everyone learns differently.* Offer a mix of activities so both sensory seekers and sensory avoiders can find their spots to enjoy. Open-ended activities make everyone feel successful. Avoid projects that have one set outcome.

- *Art activities can be made more accessible through simple and cost-effective means.* A tennis ball with a hole cut through each side can be used as a paintbrush or pencil grip for participants with less hand dexterity. Don't be afraid of your solutions looking handmade—it models easy solutions that can be replicated at home.
- *Reduce your attendee's fear factor by continually giving previews of what is to be expected throughout your event.* Outside of the DMA Art Studio, staff place signage that reads, "In this room, I can . . ." and shows pictures of each activity.
- *It doesn't have to be complicated or expensive to be effective.* Some of our most popular table and engaging activities at sensory-friendly events have also been the simplest. Themed sensory bins full of objects to touch and explore can keep kids engaged and happily playing with others. An ocean-themed sensory bin might contain water beads and plastic sea animals. Shallow trays filled with kinetic sand are always a hit among attendees.

Preventing Physical and Emotional Harm

- *Make sure your activities aren't dangerous.* Don't offer materials that can easily be thrown, exploded, or swallowed. (Yes, all of these have happened in our museum spaces!) Avoid materials such as balloons, stress balls, or fidgets containing glitter or slime.
- *Be aware of sound as a major cause of a sensory meltdown.* In the restrooms, offer paper towels instead of hand dryers. A simple sign or cover for the hand dryers during the event will politely inform attendees not to use them.
- *Be sensitive to possible allergies of your guests if you offer snacks or tactile materials.* Many neurodivergent children experience allergies and digestive health issues. Avoid items with gluten or nuts. If you offer modeling dough at an activity station, make sure that it is gluten-free, and include signage for parents to let them know that the material is safe for their child.

Asking for Feedback

- *Gather information in multiple ways.* Wanting visitors' last word on the experience means getting creative with questionnaires. We have many methods to capture feedback but have found that using two different instruments (one for the child and one for the parent) allows everyone's voice to be understood. We have used fun stickers or paint daubers for children to identify their favorite activity stations, and while they are making their choices, we are listening to the parent's conversation with the child and taking mental notes of their exchange. For the parents, we have used a simple half sheet of paper that asks no more than five questions or a Quick Response (QR) code if they don't have time to answer the questions at the moment.

- *Distill your questionnaire to the essence of what your department and grant funders want to know.* Parents are in a multitasking mode as you approach them, so making the questionnaire quick and uncomplicated is your best chance of learning what matters most.

  A recent questionnaire included these questions:

  ○ What activity did your family enjoy most?
  ○ What was most difficult?
  ○ What can we offer to enhance your family's experience?
  ○ What days are best for your family to visit the museum?
  ○ More comments:

- *Eliminate language barriers.* As with the flier, map, success story, activity guide, and any other information communicated, the questionnaire should be written in the languages commonly used in your area. The Nasher and DMA offer all materials in both English and Spanish.

What we have gleaned from years of offering sensory programming is that what benefits some people, benefits everyone. Neurodivergent visitors learn best when multiple senses and strategies are employed. But doesn't everyone have mixed needs and strengths and therefore different ways we learn best? Who among us doesn't enjoy a variety of approaches to understanding concepts? By utilizing best practices in neurodiverse programming, we have seen the benefits at those specific events and have implemented multisensory programming across our educational platforms.

NOTE

1. See textbox 11.1 for a tip sheet on interacting with neurodivergent visitors.

Chapter Eighteen

Spreading the Word

Reaching and Involving Audiences

You've planned your event, you've trained your staff, and you've prepped your supplies. Now what? At this stage in the process, it can feel like you've planned a party and you are waiting by the door for your first guest to arrive. It can be anxiety-inducing to wonder if people will actually attend and if all of your hard work will pay off. The good news, however, is that there are many strategies to spread the word and ensure that your event is attended and enjoyed by many.

This chapter is focused on marketing your program, a task that often falls to educators and other program staff even in institutions with a formal marketing department. As such, we will share

- grassroots strategies that may help you make direct connections with the people who are most likely to appreciate and benefit from what you have to offer;
- the types of businesses and organizations you might successfully market your program to; and
- suggestions for connecting with area schools.

SPECIAL INTEREST GROUPS

One of the wonderful things about technology is that it is easier than ever to find and connect with others who share an interest or aspect of their identity. Among the many communities that use web forums and social media to meet, ask questions, and share information are those with disabilities. Many people with disabilities, including those who are neurodivergent, appreciate

Internet-based platforms for their more flexible and relaxed modes of communication and reduced barriers to participation.

If you are looking to spread the word about your event or resources, the Internet can be a great place to start. A cursory search on Facebook can reveal local groups of neurodivergent individuals or their family members who use the platform to connect and share resources. You can use search terms like *the name of your city or region* and *autism* or *neurodiversity*. Broaden your reach by more generally searching for local parent groups in which members share events and resources for children and adolescents. Given the prevalence of autism and neurodivergence, all interest groups for parents and caregivers are likely to contain members who would be interested to know what your institution has to offer. If allowed within the rules of the group, posting information about your event can help you to directly reach potential constituents.

Another great way to spread the word about your offerings is to identify any web-based or printed publications for parents and caregivers. Most cities or regions have at least one magazine that addresses the concerns and needs of families. In Dallas, *DFWChild* is the go-to resource to easily find out about upcoming events for children of all ages and interests. Even more specialized is their offshoot publication, *DFWChild Special Needs*, which is dedicated to sharing resources and promoting acceptance for children with disabilities. Both publications were delighted to include our events on their calendar and help spread the word, without the cost that would traditionally come with advertising.

LOCAL BUSINESSES

When trying to spread the word about your events or resources, it can be helpful to look to other businesses in the community that already engage with neurodiverse populations. Are there any businesses that sell toys or adaptive resources for individuals with disabilities? Are there local businesses that offer sensory-friendly times for their patrons? Many cultural institutions, including theater centers and concert halls, have begun offering specialized performances to meet the sensory needs of their patrons. In addition to nonprofit organizations, many movie theaters, arcades, and restaurants now cater to neurodiverse communities through special events for individuals with sensory-based needs.

A great way to spread the word about your event is to make contact with these businesses and organizations. Take a printed flier that has a quick response (QR) code directed to your website or a stack of fliers that patrons can pick up and take with them and go visit these businesses during times when they are not busy or hosting a specialized event. Talk to the manager or business owner about your institutional offerings and see if they would be amenable to posting your flier or making them available at the cash register. Instead of just asking for this directly, it can be helpful to first explain your knowledge of their programs and offerings and how they engage with neuro-diverse communities. Ask the manager or owner if they have printed informa-tion that you could share with attendees of your event, or if they would like to come to your event and host a resource table. In turn, many businesses will happily help you spread the word about your own events and resources.

MEDICAL PRACTITIONERS

Go to any city and you will find hospitals, doctor's offices, and centers for behavioral or occupational therapy. Medical practitioners are a staple of any community and a great source for reaching your target audience. A web search can help you identify which medical practitioners specialize in family medicine or pediatric care, and even those who specialize in autism or other neurodivergent conditions. Find an email address for each medical office and send them an introductory email. Explain the services and resources that your institution provides and attach a flier to the email. Most medical practitioners will be interested to know about your offerings and may even ask for printed materials that they can provide to their patients. In partnering with local doc-tors, therapists, and hospital staff, they have all expressed a shared interest in informing their patients about resources beyond medical care. Especially at the point of diagnosis, parents are often comforted to know there are fun events and resources in the community designed with their child in mind.

SCHOOLS AND THEIR STAFF

You have reached out to your patrons and potential visitors through your website, fliers, and social media. You have connected with local businesses and cultural institutions that provide specialized events of their own. Now you are wondering what else can be done to reach those who would gladly utilize the space and specialized programs you have created. As prevalent as they are in every state, one other entity that may not be on your mind is the school district. But if you are looking for a line of contact to neurodivergent children and their families, look no further than their biggest champion—school district faculty and staff.

In the school setting, many positions work in collaboration to teach and sup-port the success of students who are neurodivergent or autistic. This includes school psychologists, autism specialists, behavior specialists, speech patholo-gists, occupational therapists, and general education and special education teachers who work together in the generalization of skills across settings. Staff want to ensure that their students are not only successful in the school setting but that their acquired skills and resulting success extends beyond the campus and into every aspect of the student's life. In support of this goal, staff often think about the student's life holistically and create resources that are familiar to students from their use in the school setting but can be integrated into daily life. Resources may include visual communication supports, social-emotional strategies, and behavioral plans that students can apply in the informal learn-ing environment that is the whole wide world around them.

By making contact with school faculty, you can express your interest in welcoming their students to your cultural institution. School faculty are likely to understand the value of your institution as a place where students can practice and continue to develop the skills they have learned on campus. Col-laboration with school faculty can be as simple as dropping off event fliers to be included in student take-home folders, or faculty may even create tailored resources to help their students prepare. In Dallas, local teachers and school staff have not only helped to spread the word about our events and resources but have spent time with their students practicing "the museum rules" and creating visual communication cards to accompany the schedule of events.

But no matter the number of resources created for students, staff are aware that there is another group that requires support—parents and caregivers. Typi-cally, through consultation, staff ensure that parents and caregivers are aware and making use of the resources available to them. It cannot be assumed that the parents will be cognizant of all that is available to them, in the community and in the school setting. Parents may be focused on their child's needs in the school setting and not consider additional resources they can gain access to from school staff, particularly those working in school psychology. School psychologists are well-practiced at considering and understanding the stu-dent's and the parent's needs in all settings and identifying relevant resources.

School psychologists are a great conduit for sharing information with stu-dents and families. Start by contacting local school psychologists and share what events and resources your institution provides, as well as your intent and intended audience. Cultural institutions benefit greatly from this collabo-ration, as school staff can give more detailed information about the specific needs of students and families. Discussing potential barriers to participation with school staff often leads to jointly supported solutions. For instance, if many families experience a transportation barrier due to low socioeconomic status, schools and cultural institutions may work together to organize school buses to transport students and their families to your location.

Depending on the level of collaboration, school psychologists may serve as consultants to your institution, spread the word about your resources to other school staff, or facilitate presentations to families of students who are neurodivergent. Methods of dissemination to the families within school districts may start with presentations to families in the school setting. Typically, parents may request training by the school districts on how to support their neurodivergent children at home, ranging from creating a structure that would benefit their child or developing a reinforcement system to work on positive behaviors in the home setting.

School districts regularly offer such training sessions on their campus or office. Collaboration between cultural institutions and school staff to host a training session is an excellent way to showcase the program, alleviate concerns by personally answering questions from parents, and cultivate excitement around your offerings. With the ubiquity of virtual meetings, these presentations can even be done from the comfort of your home or office! With the school district as a collaborator, the holistic experience of the neurodivergent person may be supported through community entities working in partnership with school district staff and, of course, family members. Through this collaboration, students and their families can utilize the world, beyond campus, as an environment for learning and personal growth. Once the cooperation is established, regardless of the ebb and flow of individual staff members, the institutional relationship can be warm, growing, fluid, and most important, ongoing to serve the whole community.

IF YOU BUILD IT . . .

As the saying goes in the 1989 film *Field of Dreams*, "If you build it, they will come." Any event or resource, built with dedication and belief in its value, is likely to eventually find success. But in the beginning, it is often necessary to springboard your success with a little legwork and connect with others who can amplify your message. Local businesses, schools, medical offices, media outlets, and online communities are all great avenues for reaching your target demographic. However, this list is not exhaustive. Think creatively about how to spread the word about your institutional offerings. What places are frequented and what resources are utilized by neurodivergent individuals in your community? Start with these connections to ensure lively participation as you debut or grow your events and resources. As your offerings and participant pool grow, you will find that marketing takes less of your time and effort. The most effective form of marketing, word of mouth, will gradually and continually spread the message for you.

Chapter Nineteen

Lessons Learned

Stories of Community Success

In this chapter, we detail the various types of programs and resources created by the Dallas Sensory Consortium to engage neurodiverse audiences and share how these offerings have evolved over our nearly fifteen years of experience. If you are ready to dive in and want a fast track to success, we provide advice based on what has worked for us and share our sometimes-difficult lessons learned along the way. However, this advice comes with the caution that there is no one-size-fits-all solution. To be truly successful, arts and cultural institutions must respond to their unique community and work within the resources and limitations of their institution. We hope that this chapter will provide you with a framework that can be tailored to your specific needs and allow you to learn from our mistakes and growing pains.

Within this chapter, you will find

- a discussion of *synchronous* and *asynchronous* programming models;
- stories of how synchronous programming for neurodiverse audiences has evolved at the Dallas Museum of Art; and
- an example of an asynchronous resource, the Sensory Tote, used at Nasher Sculpture Center.

CHOOSING THE RIGHT TYPE OF EVENT: SYNCHRONOUS VERSUS ASYNCHRONOUS

Synchronous events take place on a set day and during a limited time frame. Synchronous events typically have multiple activities or event offerings occurring simultaneously and often take place outside of public hours to create a more welcoming environment and to minimize noise distractions. Working with institutional partners to conduct synchronous events alleviates the need to involve as many of your staff coming in early or staying late to support. If your synchronous event takes place outside of public hours, you may need to consider securing additional funds in your budget to cover the cost of security and other front-of-house staff who will support your event. Attendees of synchronous events routinely report that the structure promotes socialization with other children and that they want their child to experience side-by-side peer interaction. Families also appreciate the hands-on support from trained staff during the event.

Asynchronous programs have a drop-in nature, where visitors come during regular business hours and receive tailored resources to support a dynamic and successful visit. As in the following example, this could take the form of a sensory tote bag with activities and aids designed with neurodivergent visitors in mind. These anytime resources can include, among other things, earplugs or noise-reducing headphones, a fidget, communication cards, a scavenger hunt or other activities to promote engagement, a success story, and a map of your institution. The map should note the location of low-sensory spaces, as well as important safety and access accommodations. Participants of asynchronous resources commonly say that they favor the flexibility of schedule and autonomy of experience that this structure provides.

Sometimes available space may be difficult to locate, but with some creativity and administrative support, a room can be outfitted with tools and toys for sensory self-regulation and made permanently available for visitors. At the Nasher Sculpture Center, our sensory space was previously a seldom-used "pop-up" bartender's room near the auditorium. It now features low lights, soft chairs, washable weighted blankets, and engaging toys that are safe for all ages.

STORY: DEVELOPING SYNCHRONOUS EVENTS AT THE DALLAS MUSEUM OF ART

Conscious of the prevalence of autism in the community, but aware that this population seldom participated in their programs, education staff from the Dallas Museum of Art (DMA) started to wonder how they could remove barriers to participation and increase access to the experiences of their museum. In discussions with families who have children on the spectrum, parents reported a hesitance to participate in events due to the social challenges of crowds and trepidation around how a new environment with unknown stimuli might cause their child to react (and others to look on with judgment). The unfortunate outcome is that these families avoided public events and became more isolated, not due to a lack of interest, but because of existing institutional and societal barriers.

Before attempting to create programs for neurodiverse populations, the DMA sought the advice of professionals, experts, children with autism, and their parents to address potential participants' individualized desires and needs. Through discussions with the community, the museum received feedback that demonstrated interest in programs that provided a comfortable learning environment where participants could engage with one another while informally developing social and communication skills. The expressed interest of these community members prompted our staff to consider what, as an art museum, we could uniquely offer and what specific constraints we needed to consider.

Researching online, museum staff gathered preliminary information about learning differences through articles written by experts on the subject. We contacted nonprofit organizations and foundations specific to autism to cultivate resources and models of best practices: tips on how to prepare, welcome, and inform visitors to our museum with success stories and signage; modes for developing engaging activities with both sensory seekers and avoiders in mind; and resources for creating a private, quiet space for families to unwind. Most important, we formed a partnership with Tina Fletcher, professor of occupational therapy at Texas Woman's University. With a shared goal of increasing access to arts and cultural institutions for neurodivergent populations within the metroplex, Dr. Fletcher welcomed our questions, met with our team, and consistently supported each step in our institutional and program development.

Six months of conversation with community constituents, staff learning from Dr. Fletcher, and internal program planning culminated in April 2009 with our first autism-specific event, which we promoted as the Autism Awareness Family Celebration. While the name of the event has changed (now simply called Sensory Day), the basic structure of the event has remained the same. Held four times per year, the DMA opens its doors two hours early with free admission for children with autism and their family members. Welcoming neurodivergent children and their families into a museum during private hours was not an attempt to separate this population from the rest of the community, but rather to provide a time of individualized support by adapting or removing barriers that would otherwise hinder their museum experience. This private time provides an opportunity for neurodivergent children and their families to socialize and explore the museum in an understanding and supportive environment. While the Autism Awareness Family Celebration started out with a small and dedicated number of attendees, the event quickly grew through word of mouth within the community. To reduce sensory overload, it became necessary after our first year of programming to limit attendance to the first five hundred registrants. It is our continued hope that this specialized program will open the museum experience to neurodiverse populations, help attendees become more familiar and comfortable in the museum space, and even encourage integration into daily museum programming.

Knowing that participants of the event can be sensitive to various stimuli, the DMA offers an immersive, low-sensory space staffed by occupational therapy students. This space is distinguished by low lighting, comfortable seating, and therapy tools such as washable weighted blankets. Event-specific narratives and images about visiting the DMA are sent to families before each event so participants can become acquainted with the museum and its scheduled activities prior to their visit. Several parents have reported that they print and laminate the event schedule and use it as a placemat for their child in the days leading up to the event or read the success story before bed to help prepare their child for a new environment.

During the event, families choose from a variety of activities in the DMA's Center for Creative Connections, an interactive and experimental gallery space. At the event, families explore at their own pace, taking part in sensory experiments and art-making activities in the studio, playing games in the sculpture garden, and enjoying an interactive musical performance led by a local music therapist. Families can also explore the museum's galleries through staff-led experiences, such as story time or teen tours.

Activities at each event are tied to a specific theme, suggested by the community, and chosen in collaboration with Tina Fletcher and Texas Woman's University (TWU) occupational therapy students. Past themes have included Rockin' Robots, Sculpt-o-rama, Weird Science, and Space Explorers. The art-making activities, games, performances, and sensory experiments all tie back to the event's theme. One of our most successful events was themed Fun at the Fair, suggested by parents who wanted to take their child to the state fair but knew that the overwhelming sensory stimuli would make the visit impossible. At our museum state fair, attendees could try their hand at carnival games in the outdoor courtyard, play with animal puppets in a circus tent, and even participate in so-called butter sculpting, using yellow foam clay as a sensory-friendly alternative.

The DMA often brings in special guests to take part in the event, including collaborating with the Dallas Symphony Orchestra (DSO) during a music-themed event. Former DSO music director Jaap van Zweden spoke to children about movement in music and used a colorful streamer to show how he conducts. Following van Zweden's instruction, participants joined him in conducting while the DSO performed; van Zweden's wife, Aaltje van Zweden–van Buuren, talked to parents and caregivers about her family's experience using music therapy with their neurodivergent son. In addition to the DSO, the DMA has also collaborated with other local organizations that offer autism programming, such as the Dallas Children's Theater, which hosts informational tables at each event to share its resources with the community.

While event activities are primarily designed around the goal of fun and socialization, their greater impact continuously surprises our staff. After a young attendee had participated in van Zweden's demonstration of how to conduct the symphony using ribbon streamers, his mother excitedly approached museum staff with tears in her eyes. The colorful demonstration had inspired her son, who previously only drew using graphite pencils, to draw a picture with color for the first time.

After years of hosting the sensory-friendly event, the biggest change to the program took place with the formation of the Dallas Sensory Consortium. In 2017, the DMA, Nasher Sculpture Center, Dallas Zoo, and TWU officially formed the Dallas Sensory Consortium, although they had been participating as guests of each other's sensory-friendly events for several years. With the formation of the consortium, the structure of Sensory Day shifted. Instead of being held quarterly at the DMA, all participating institutions took turns hosting the event, with other members providing activities and staff support to the events when they were not hosting. During times of budget cuts and staff reduction, this shift allowed the DMA to continue providing the program when it otherwise may not have had the resources.

Additionally, the formation of the consortium had many unforeseen benefits. Scheduling the events in dialogue with other members provides more consistent opportunities for families to engage throughout the year. Shared sensory room supplies provide a sense of consistency and comfort for attendees. Each institution cultivates new audiences through the cross-institutional promotion of events, and participation in the consortium and its activities provides staff with valuable opportunities for cross-institutional learning.

STORY: DEVELOPING ASYNCHRONOUS EVENTS AT THE NASHER SCULPTURE CENTER

Nasher Sculpture Center has organized large-scale, synchronous sensory-friendly events that are publicized through social media to parent groups, schools, and families. Since the Nasher has nearly two acres devoted to a sculpture garden, many of its event themes have related to the outdoors with titles like It's a Material World, Camp Nasher, Sculpture Rocks, and Art and Nature.

In conjunction with these events, the Nasher Sculpture Center has also partnered with KultureCity™, a nonprofit which offers staff training and sensory-inclusive accreditation, to offer sensory bags for asynchronous or drop-in visitors. As a certified location, the Nasher checks out KultureCity sensory bags to drop-in visitors who want helpful tools like headphones, fidgets, and communication tools. Becoming a KultureCity partner involves the successful online training of front-of-house staff, having a success story on your website, and offering branded sensory bags and signage throughout the institution's spaces. It is a flexible, budget-friendly way for a nonprofit institution to educate its staff since training can occur during each employee's onboarding, and the certification fees are affordable in comparison to other training options.

In 2020 with the advent of COVID-19, synchronous events were temporarily suspended to prioritize public health. Suddenly it wasn't safe for hundreds of people to be in close proximity to one another or to have children share materials and tools while enjoying activities, story times, and games. That meant that every commonly used museum surface and resource would have to be sanitized. With CDC protocols as their guide, the Nasher recognized they would also need to temporarily pause the use of KultureCity backpacks and shift to issuing paperless or one-time usage packets. The museum still wanted families to come and explore but knew the materials handed out had to reflect the global reality.

Starting in the fall of 2020, the Nasher collaborated with members of the Dallas Sensory Consortium to adapt previous sensory-friendly family day programming into the format of a Sensory Tote, with self-directed activities and wayfinding resources. In adherence to COVID-19 sanitization protocols, the visiting child and family used and kept the totes. Totes were available to reserve and pick up, free of charge, at consortium locations throughout the community.

People who used the totes confirmed that these asynchronous resources allowed for more flexibility and autonomy in their visit. Totes debuted at the Nasher shortly after the center reopened, allowing a limited number of admissions each hour. This safety measure enabled families to reserve tickets and a tote for a specific date and time, with the assurance that congested spaces and ambient noises would also be lessened. The Nasher offered free admission to encourage neurodivergent families to venture out again and discover this asynchronous resource that was launched with its consortium colleagues.

Totes were designed in collaboration with the School of Occupational Therapy at TWU and continue to be used by consortium members. They contain resources to improve guest experience, including lanyard ear plugs for on-demand noise reduction, communication cards to nonverbally communicate frequent museum rules, and red or green colored wrist coils to convey the visitor's comfort level to institutional staff. Toy binoculars are included

Figure 19.1. Single-use sensory tote with its contents.
Anna Smith

to promote close-looking activities as they focus the user's attention. Small sand-filled hourglasses have been ideal for creating structured, timed activities. Figure 19.1 shows an example of a Sensory Tote and its contents.

In addition to shared resources, totes contain a folder specific to each member of the Sensory Consortium (Dallas Museum of Art, Nasher Sculpture Center, Dallas Public Library, Dallas Zoo, Frontiers of Flight Museum). Within each folder, participants can find materials that encourage a visit to the other participating locations, including a map, success story, and activities for engagement. While a detailed online success story enables families to be well-prepared, a one-page version in the tote highlights suggestions for a successful family visit. Parent tip sheets in the tote can inspire fun challenges between siblings or move an activity sequentially along in an ordered, predictable manner. For some children, this opportunity to virtually repeat or restart activities over a period of days greatly reduces the anxiety or frustration that can occur during the compressed time of a traditional synchronous experience and may build family confidence for a return visit.

At the Nasher, activities like scavenger hunts, proprioceptive prompts, and sketching are featured in the tote. The center's map uses icons to show where the sensory room, water fountains, and bathrooms are located, as well as zones where headphones are recommended for those sensitive to sound. A one-page success story provides a quick review of the longer online version that parents may have shared with their children to prepare. If parents prefer to access information and family activities with their phones, quick response (QR) codes are printed on the corner of information sheets to link visitors to the center's website. This open-ended approach enables guardians and children to select what method, time, activities, and flow are best for them through the museum's spaces.

Perhaps the most versatile information sheets in the Sensory Totes are those developed by occupational therapists. TWU created practical, everyday activities for families to engage in that promote sensory-friendly lifestyles, including healthy ways to practice sensory self-regulation and strategies for environmental and personal adjustments that can be made when sensory input is not regulated or is unpredictable. Table 19.1 lists typical tote contents.

While the Sensory Totes, as a self-guided resource, provide benefits like a flexible schedule and visitor autonomy, this asynchronous offering also comes with its challenges. As numbers resumed to prepandemic levels, and guests using the bags began visiting during busier public hours, specially trained staff cannot always be situated where escalations occur to mitigate environmental challenges. Staff at the Nasher Sculpture Center have found it extremely important to proactively anticipate and plan for the complete guest experience.

For other institutions implementing similar resources, the following suggestions may be helpful. Beginning with helpful information on the website, visitors should be able to map out transportation details like their driving route and parking options online. Once on-site, the tote should aid the visitor with essential wayfinding information and contain engaging activities and tools to make it a memorable outing. Whether you provide a map with universal icons in the tote or position easy-to-see signage throughout your space, areas with sensory challenges should be clearly communicated. Recognizing that every institution has different constraints, and building layouts, these sensory tips should be tailored to fit your specific location and feedback from your community.

Lessons Learned: Know Your Guests and Your Spaces

With the Nasher's large outdoor garden, children can walk on the grass or walkways comfortably, engaging with nature and art. Downtown traffic noises are somewhat muffled by the travertine walls, allowing children to react to their surroundings in a safe, semi-private space. Some factors like the sound and visual activity of the water fountains can have a dual effect: they can prompt a child to run to the water's edge, jump in (something guests are not allowed to do), or provide a soothing backdrop. Nasher staff hoped

Table 19.1.   Sensory Tote Contents

Success story for each institution	Success stories can help neurodivergent individuals and their family members plan for a visit. The information is presented in a concrete, step-by-step way and illustrates what to expect and what behaviors are appropriate. This helps prepare the visitor for the experience at a cultural institution and assists with the change in routine that many individuals with autism find difficult or distressing.
Map for each institution	Maps for each participating organization are included within their institutional folder. Maps clearly note accessible routes, safety features, and sensory spaces.
I'm feeling . . . hook and loop chart	Some people on the spectrum are very chatty, others are shy, and others are nonverbal. To encourage dialogue and comfort, pictures are used to illustrate and communicate different feelings.
I need . . . card	This card features images of available resources within the tote bag. Nonverbal visitors may find it helpful for communicating their needs.
Communication cards on ring	This ring contains directives and associated pictograms to communicate frequent museum rules.
Stress ball fidget	Some people with autism find that fidget toys offer the tactile sensory input and repetitive motor movements that are needed to help them with self-regulation.
Sand timer	A sand timer is a helpful tool for giving time warnings. Sand timers can be used to visually communicate when an individual needs to move to the next activity, or can even be used for in-gallery timed sketching or "I spy" games.
Sunglasses	Sunglasses may be helpful for visitors who are sensitive to the various levels of lighting that may be found within a space.
Earplugs on a lanyard	Noise-reducing earplugs can help visitors with autism by reducing overstimulation from loud, unexpected noises and crowded galleries.
Folding binoculars	Binoculars are a helpful tool for focusing attention and visual stimulation. Binoculars can additionally be used for in-gallery "I spy" games.
Colored pencils	A small pack of colored pencils is included within the tote bag, to be used with drawing and writing activities within each institutional folder.

(continued)

Table 19.1. *Continued*

Red and green wrist coils	Wrist coils are included to signal a guest's comfort level to our staff. If guests are comfortable and would like our staff to share fun facts and initiate conversation, they can wear the green wrist coil. If not, they can wear the red wrist coil. Wrist coils can also be used as a fidget.
Activities for engagement	Each institutional folder contains activities for engagement, using shared tote bag materials like binoculars, colored pencils, and sand timers. Activities are designed to engage with a wide range of ages and learning strengths.
Tote bag for extended engagement	After the visit, the tote bag itself becomes an opportunity for extended engagement. Users can color, decorate, and personalize the bag using permanent markers or fabric markers from the comfort of their homes.

to prepare neurodivergent visitors for these environmental features in such a way that parents would consider this a safe and welcoming place for both sensory seekers and sensory avoiders.

The first step in this process included a survey of potential sensory triggers in the museum environment. Areas that were crowded or noisy, or those that had echoes or water features, would need to be indicated in a success story, which would be posted online to guide families from the moment they parked their car in the museum parking lot to the time they left the building. The Nasher's success stories have included everything from how to purchase a ticket at the front desk, what the guards look like, the activities visitors can enjoy, a wayfinding map, and areas to avoid if crowds, smells, or certain sounds are problematic.

In contrast to synchronous events where attendees can find pop-up sensory spaces throughout the galleries and garden, Nasher staff needed to designate and refashion a dedicated sensory space for times when sensory factors become overwhelming. In true can-do fashion, education staff outfitted a seldom-used bartending room near the downstairs auditorium as the museum's new Quiet Room. While smaller than the multifamily sensory spaces found at synchronous events, the permanent sensory space is notable for offering the same features: low lighting, weighted lap pads, soft seating, and a variety of fidget toys.

After the initial due diligence of researching best practices and preparing the museum with basic resources for an asynchronous visit, staff needed to test the efficacy of these practices with a focus group. Informed by neighboring colleagues, staff members first contacted parents who had previously inquired about our offerings. Participant forms that were filled out at large-scale synchronous events generated additional names.

Conducting a focus group and developing a survey to capture the experience of these individuals was essential in knowing if our expected outcomes were realistic and what preparations needed to be changed or expanded to meet mission objectives. Staff members observed the focus group as they traveled throughout the museum and took notes about how the group engaged in activities, what tools were used, and what additional resources were requested. Focus group participants responded with what activities they enjoyed the most, but also with what they found most challenging, and if they would return as a family. Parents gave us helpful feedback about the needs of their children and how to reach other families in the neurodiverse network.

The Sensory Totes were designed and introduced during the pandemic as a way to continue offering young visitors a multimodal, sensory-rich experience. Even though health conditions prompted this change, the benefits of this present model have encouraged the Nasher to maintain the resource, even as health conditions improve. Offering this self-paced mode of engagement has enabled families much-appreciated flexibility; they can come and enjoy the museum safely and at a time that works best with their schedules. In contrast to a one-time event, Sensory Totes afford families multiple experiences over time. The totes contain activities designed to engage visitors across the spectrum in ways compatible with their interests and sensitivities. While on the surface the shift from synchronous to asynchronous events may appear to be a drastic change, the fundamental goals and elements of the program have remained the same. See table 19.2 for a comparison between synchronous and asynchronous-adapted offerings.

Co-author Lynda Wilbur shares a cautionary tale with a happy ending for cultural institutions hoping to offer asynchronous resources or events.

A large, colorful artwork by Judy Chicago called *Rearrangeable Rainbow Blocks* (1965) was on view in the galleries. What could possibly go wrong with an artwork resembling giant toy blocks graced with an enticing title? As you might imagine, the colors, scale, and playful nature of the work attracted visitors who wanted to move the large pieces around. Additionally, turnover and shortages in gallery attendant staffing due to decreased visitor numbers during the pandemic created a situation where museum staff were not prepared to protect this artwork in a thoughtful way. After an incident where someone tried to, well, rearrange the rainbow blocks, education staff had to work together with front-of-house and curatorial staff to head off future incidents before they could happen.

The takeaway is to consider items that visitors may find irresistible to touch and work with security and other relevant team members to develop a precautionary plan. As staff welcome families to your space, communicate areas on the map with parents that their child may find of interest, but where special attention is needed to enjoy them safely. At the Nasher, once precautionary measures were in place, no visitors or rainbow blocks were harmed.

Table 19.2. Synchronous Events and Asynchronous-Adapted Offerings

	Synchronous	Asynchronous
Sensory accommodations	Multiperson sensory space: controlled space with minimal sound and lighting, ice-fishing houses, tents and cardboard houses, weighted blankets, rocking furniture, tiny flashlights, and reduced overhead lighting throughout interior event spaces	Permanent single family-sized sensory space with reduced lighting, weighted blanket, soft furniture Sensory tote: earplugs, communication cards, and colored wristbands to signal participant's level of desired engagement with staff and others
Sensory-based and imaginative play activities	Kinetic textural sand, sensory bins, sound-mixing station, puppet theater, costume trunk	Sensory tote: sensory poem prompt, self-guides with pretend play prompts, creative storytelling, drawing or writing, binoculars with "I spy" looking prompts
Strategy to extend engagement	Event-based scavenger hunt Temporary multifamily sensory space, activities such as story times, sequencing, scale or compare-and-contrast prompts	Sensory tote: collection-based scavenger hunt, sand timers Permanent single family-sized sensory space. Prerecorded story times and "art stops" with activities
Fine- and gross-motor activities	Real-time activities indoors and outdoors facilitated by venue or occupational therapy student helpers: arts and crafts stations, obstacle course, outdoor kinesthetic games	Sensory tote: self-guides with movement-based prompts, in-gallery art-making activities Virtual activities prompted by the website
Resources for structure and setting expectations	Previsit success story, timed event schedule, maps of the venue, directions for parking	Sensory tote: previsit success stories and maps for each participating institution, sand timers for activities and giving time warnings, communication cards, websites offering additional resources
Crowding adjustments	Limited attendance over one two-hour period and begin before regular hours Wayfinding signage: touch-friendly, quiet zone, and headphone zones posted	Limited attendance over a one-week period due to number of visitors admitted per hour Wayfinding signage: quiet zone and headphone zones posted
Facilitators	Large numbers of family members, education staff, occupational therapy students, attendants	Small numbers of family members, education staff, occupational therapy students, attendants

Part 6

SECURING FUNDING AND CONDUCTING RESEARCH AND EVALUATION

Chapter Twenty

Ask Away

Conducting Formal and Informal Program Evaluation

The science of program evaluation is exploding thanks to the many types of technology and ease of communication we all enjoy. Stacks of data that used to take hours of meticulous counting and time spent slaving away over an adding machine have mercifully given way to sleek, accurate, and compact ways of collecting information from visitors, observing their behavior, and compiling statistics about them. As a result, we can quickly and efficiently analyze data to provide answers to a variety of questions related to visitor satisfaction, interests, actions, and behavior. The only catch is that there are so many things to measure that it is easy to go down the wrong path, asking questions that are not helpful or applicable, overcomplicating the process, and creating more uncertainty, frustration, or problems than the effort is worth. Program evaluations have many purposes, such as gaining insights on the effectiveness of format and content, identifying areas needing improvement, and learning what impact the experience has on participants. These are all important considerations and may result in evaluators using various strategies to get to the heart of the matter. Sometimes, just developing questions can become a major challenge.

This chapter covers many facets of program evaluation, including

- finding the right type of evaluation for what you hope to learn;
- purposes of and strategies for informal evaluation methods;
- standards and tools for formal evaluation; and
- when and where to look for external support.

WHO, HOW, WHAT: BUILDING AN
EVALUATION STRATEGY AROUND YOUR NEEDS

Determining what you want to know and how that information will serve neurodivergent visitors is the first step in an effective evaluation strategy. First, consider *who* the stakeholders in your program are and *how* your findings will be shared. Will they be shared internally among program staff, institutional executive staff or board members, program funders, or more broadly through publications and presentations? Understanding who will have access to your results can help to determine the focus and method of your data collection, the formality of your evaluation, and the extent of your ethical responsibilities, which include protecting privacy and doing no harm to the program or people involved. This chapter will refer to *informal evaluations* designed to address largely practical questions about program effectiveness for a limited audience of institutional staff and program funders. *Formal evaluations* will be those that may be more research-oriented and are published or shared with a wider audience of professional colleagues or the general public. The latter should be undertaken with a clear understanding of research ethics—such as minimizing the impact of any unintentional harms like time loss, unanticipated expenses, performance anxiety, or reputation damage that may occur as a result of the research—and may require the support of a university or research agency as detailed later in this chapter to offset any of these and other pitfalls.

What you want to learn through your evaluation should be driven by your program goals and the intended audience for your results. Informal evaluations may be focused on collecting and analyzing data that will help future events run more smoothly, connect more deeply with participants, and serve a broader audience. Formal evaluations are more likely to be geared toward producing findings that will contribute new knowledge to the field and support others who have similar goals. Remember that no matter the evaluation type, goals should be specific, measurable, attainable, relevant, and timely so their structure should help define your questions. Reporting requirements for program funding are also an essential consideration when deciding what information to collect. Most grant funders will want to know basic demographic information about your audiences, such as the age of participants and zip code. These data are most easily attained at the point of event registration, which will clear more space to collect other quantitative and qualitative data during the event.

How you gather this information will also be determined by what you plan to do with it. Informal inquiries may offer opportunities for unorthodox tactics, while formal evaluations require adherence to time-tested research methodology for their results to be replicated and generalized when appropriate; meaning, other people can reproduce your study methods with their population and the results others gained from their research might help other visitors, too—including yours. As you plan your process, be mindful of how you will put your findings to use. The most insightful evaluation in the world is meaningless if no one reads it or acts upon its results. Be intentional about revisiting your findings and incorporating important insights into future programming instances.

PRACTICAL MAGIC:
STRATEGIES FOR INFORMAL EVALUATION

Drop-in or open registration sensory-friendly events offered by many cultural institutions present a common set of logistical challenges. These may be large-capacity events with limited staff, making dedicated evaluators few and far between. Young visitors may come with family or school groups whose chaperones could find completing an evaluation challenging. Program participants may include a range of neurodivergent people along with various relatives or companions, making it difficult to parse who responds to questions. And finally, with a suite of on-site activities designed to be fun and engaging, why would anyone want to devote their energy to filling out a questionnaire or giving an interview? If your purpose is to assess program elements from a practical standpoint with the overall goal of improving attendance and visitor satisfaction, it's okay to be creative.

Approach your data collection instrument from the perspective of your audience. A two-track approach, with questions and format appropriate to young or intellectually challenged participants and their caregivers, can offer a broader view of the response to your program. It may be most helpful, for instance, to learn about the experience from the child but to hear about the logistics, such as registration, communication, and wayfinding from the adult.

A long questionnaire or interview might be impractical for a nonverbal program attendee or a caregiver whose attention must be elsewhere. The results produced from these data collection methods will skew toward the responses of communicative visitors with ample time on their hands. If you opt to use these methods, consider limiting yourself to three of your most important questions. Think also of when and where you present your survey or interview questions. Are there moments in the flow of your event where participants have a moment to pause, such as at a snack or beverage station or as they are waiting their turn? Is something available to occupy children if your questions are aimed at their caregivers? You could offer a coloring sheet, quick activity, or an incentive such as a small toy from a toybox at your evaluation table. To capture the undivided attention of an adult participant or caregiver, a postevent questionnaire sent via an anonymous platform such as Google Forms or SurveyMonkey may be more convenient, especially when delivered within three days of the event. Digital questionnaire completion may be incentivized through a raffle for a prize, a sponsoring vendor gift, a membership, or a code for free tickets.

You can also collect data from participants using nontraditional instruments. A one-question evaluation such as "Is this your first time visiting our institution?" can be answered by placing a pom-pom or other colorful object in one of two containers representing yes and no responses, as seen in figure 20.1. Figure 20.2 shows how educators at Nasher Sculpture Center assessed the popularity of activities at a sensory-friendly event by creating a tabletop grid chart listing each activity station along with an identifying visual icon, inviting participants to stamp their favorites with a bingo marker as they left the event. You can build upon the theme of your event and the nature of the information you hope to capture as you develop your creative ideas.

LEARNING BASIC STANDARDS
FOR FORMAL EVALUATION

Cultural institutions tend to have a lot of balls in the air and many of them can be evaluated. This includes the experience, environment, programs, content, personnel, climate control (yes, there are studies published on this factor alone), visitor satisfaction, and infrastructure. Collecting data and analyzing it in systematic, reproducible, and reportable ways can lead to improvements in institutional practices and ultimately to the development of beneficial policies, guidelines, and practices. This in turn can bring about larger contributions to the field of cultural education. For our purposes, we will focus on the neurodivergent visitor experience.[1]

Let's revisit our original ideas related to setting up a good program evaluation system and begin to consider how we will collect data in the form of written or verbal communications from some of our exceptional visitors. Identifying an easy-to-use framework for program evaluation is a strong beginning. Initial considerations should surround what will be evaluated, how evaluations will occur, and if the results will answer the program evaluation questions. Components of program evaluation should include defining who stakeholders are, developing an accurate and understandable description of the program, detailing how the evaluation will be conducted, the types of data that will be collected, what kinds of conclusions could be drawn, and whether or not the results answer the original questions.

Figure 20.1. Physical survey instrument using pom-poms in labeled bins.
Anna Smith

Figure 20.2. Physical survey instrument using a tabletop chart and bingo stampers.
Anna Smith

In the case of neurodivergent visitors, evaluators should provide ways to collect data from neurodivergent or other vulnerable populations and their companions. If the neurodivergent visitors are children, in the spirit of honoring the United Nations Convention on the Rights of the Child,[2] individual children and groups of children have a right to express their opinions and thoughts about things that directly impact them. In this process, children need to be provided with an environment where they can freely do so without fear of reprisal or worries about deviating from the group norm. Like adults, children have the right to express their opinion privately, and their responses should take into consideration their age and level of maturity. Similarly, it is often argued that because neurodivergent people may have communication difficulties, others can speak for them. Still, a more equitable way of collecting data would be to offer neurotypical visitors and their companions an opportunity to express their opinions using methods of communication they are comfortable with.

It is tempting to think of smiley face rating systems, or smiley face Likert scales (SFLs) as an appealing way to collect information from children. Still, researchers Hall, Hume, and Tazzyman[3] cautioned that children have a documented tendency toward selecting faces that smile rather than faces that are neutral or unhappy, no matter what their true feelings about the questions are. The researchers further determined that if five versions of only a happy face (a Five Degrees of Happiness SFL) are presented, all five of the faces will be selected. While this might be confusing to evaluators who don't have the bandwidth to create their versions of a Five Degrees of Happiness SFL, the takeaway message is that using multiple ways to collect data from children or people with differing maturity or intellectual capacity might be a more accurate way to fairly represent their opinions or beliefs.

CREATING AND USING
BASIC DATA COLLECTION TOOLS

There are many ways to collect information about programs, and many of them involve asking questions in either survey, interview, or focus group format. Because questioning is at the root of many evaluations, this chapter focuses on developing good questions. Chapter 21 will revisit asking questions as a part of creating research designs. Interestingly, an excellent overview of developing surveys can be found in the publication *Anesthesiology*, where a physician and researcher detail their experiences in designing surveys research to gain patient feedback.[4] In their work, they provide readers with the essential elements of good survey design, including ensuring the survey instrument was pilot tested, has a grounding in statistical methodology, has been reviewed for any ethical concerns, and like we have previously discussed, whether the questions provide data that will actually answer the question or aim of the survey. Under the assumption that less than half of survey instruments distributed will be answered, survey designers need to ask themselves a few things about their goals. Will there be enough responses to justify statistical analysis, and if not, will the text or verbal responses to interview-style questions be enough to provide needed information?

Let's assume a decision has been made to go with a simple survey that won't need statistical analysis. Questions must be written in a specific way to lend themselves to whatever type of analysis is desired. Some responses can be tallied to provide what are known as *frequency counts*. Frequency counts can be used when information falls into separate categories, such as whether visitors drive a car or ride a train to get to their destination. Evaluators can count these numbers themselves without a statistician's help. These responses can be represented by either actual numbers or percentages, such as "Thirty-three out of a hundred survey respondents report using a train to get to the symphony" or "Thirty percent of survey respondents use a train to get to the symphony." When illustrating this information, a frequency table, pie chart, or bar graph can be used to illustrate findings because these figures represent parts of a whole.

A more advanced step is to determine what is known as information about *central tendencies* or *summary statistics.* These methods typically provide three measures: a mean, median, and mode. *Mean* refers to the average and is familiar to many people. It is usually calculated using continuous data such as height, weight, and temperature, but can be used with discrete data that has clear spaces between each number. Means are helpful ways to understand central tendencies unless a few scores are very different from most of the others. These types of scores are sometimes referred to as outliers. An outlier can throw a mean way off, rendering it useless. In this case, a *median* score is often more helpful. A median score is a middle score where half the scores are above it, and half are below it. The final central tendency score is the *mode.* A mode is the most commonly selected score. As an example, applying the concept of mode instead of the mean can help a cultural institution to understand the popularity of activities. Let's say there are three activities: one for children, one for teenagers, and one for adults. Evaluators obtain the ages (in years) of people participating in their age-related activities. When visitors' ages are averaged to get the mean, this score gives general information about the audience but may not reflect which is the most popular activity. Instead, the mode score would reveal which activity was attended most frequently.

LANGUAGE AND PHRASING FOR SURVEY QUESTIONS

We have tinkered with some basic math, and now it is time to move into designing well-written questions. While some words, such as yes or no, can be converted into numerical values like one and two, others will require deeper analysis and more effort on the part of evaluators, so questions should be brief, specific, and free from any biases. While this sounds easy, it takes some practice to get questions right. Let's take a look at how to achieve this goal.

First, keeping things *brief* means two things. The questionnaire itself should be brief and limit the burden placed on the respondent. Many people do not like participating in surveys because they are time-consuming. One way to offset this is to tell people how many items or how long a questionnaire will be while they are considering whether or not they want to participate. A great way to advertise a digital survey with low user burden is to offer up a QR code along with text saying something like, "Help us with your feedback. Take a three-item (or one-minute) survey about your experience." A familiar example of a quick survey is the "Please rate our bathroom" button seen in some public restrooms. People push a number value or red, yellow, or green light to indicate their perceptions of the bathroom experience. In reality, participants have provided two types of data every time a button is pushed; their bathroom evaluation score and the time of day the button is pushed. With these two bits of data, statisticians may be able to track the frequency of use and perceptions of bathroom quality related to the time of day, day of the week, or when the bathroom was last cleaned. On the downside, this information is only provided by people tall enough to reach the buttons or who choose to do so.

The second *keep it brief* directive is related to the survey questions themselves. Language that is simple and focused will provide the most accurate responses. Consider the difference between these two statements, "We know your time is valuable, and we appreciate your efforts to continually improve at this venue. Please tell us if you found the temperature in the auditorium to be what you would define as comfortable" as opposed to "What do you think of the auditorium temperature?" or, "The temperature was comfortable—agree or disagree" In the first example, a busy visitor juggling a neurodivergent child in a stroller, service dog on a leash, and one other child in tow might see the words *valuable, effort, improvement* instead of *comfortable temperature*. They may miss the point of the question or answer it incorrectly. Short questions on a short questionnaire are important.

Now let's look at what the concept of *specific* means in reference to survey questions. Back to our comfortable temperature question, it is possible that survey respondents may be thrown off by the term *comfortable* and that the term itself needs adjustment. A quick search on the Internet provides alternate language and concrete examples of a comfortable indoor temperature. It might be a statement, "We keep our indoor temperature from 68 to 72 degrees. Please tell us if you felt this auditorium temperature was comfortable." Another example of the term *specific* means only one thing is being evaluated. A question that asks for two responses is known as a double-barreled question. Here is an example; "We keep our indoor auditorium temperature between 68 and 72 degrees and let Mother Nature determine the outdoor amphitheater temperatures. Please tell us if you felt the temperatures were comfortable." It's quite possible the participant was satisfied with the indoor temperature but not the outdoor one, but only one response was available.

The third survey guideline related to *freedom from biases* can be challenging. Here are some examples of wording that imply something needs changing and may introduce bias in the respondent's thinking: "Help us improve your museum experience," "Your feedback will enhance future exhibitions," and "We want to meet your needs." When using language that asserts improvement is needed or a goal, an institution implies that its services are not up to par or as good as they could be. In reality, they may be. Other factors that may invoke bias are where and when surveys or other feedback tools are offered to visitors. Asking visitors to rate your services while they are stuck in a line may be a way to keep them busy, but it also may bias their responses toward the institution needing to improve services. Conversely, when visitors are offered a survey option right after a successful experience, positive contact, or an exciting program, they may be biased toward rating things highly to reward the institution for their efforts. While this can be complementary, it may not provide the desired information.

Once you have devised your questionnaire using suggested guidelines, run it past a few sets of eyes. Ask colleagues to review what you have written to ensure that it is bias-free and unlikely to cause confusion or prompt unhelpful responses. Regional Education Laboratory West, part of the Institute of Education Sciences, offers a clear, contemporary guide to survey design with helpful examples of problematic questions and how to fix them, as well as guidelines for using inclusive language in survey instruments.[5]

Because creating surveys for people on the autism spectrum is even more complicated, the Academic Autism Spectrum Partnership in Research and Education teamed with the Partnering with People with Developmental Disabilities to Address Violence Consortium to develop an approach that can be used to modify existing survey instruments to the needs of autistic adults. They recommend that neurotypical and autistic stakeholders review surveys to adapt and consider the following recommendations:

1. To effectively co-create this collaboration, make sure all partners understand the background, terminology, and processes used in survey research.
2. Collaboratively select what to measure with the survey.
3. Discuss all constructs to ensure alignment among all parties.
4. Identify existing instruments used to measure this construct.
5. Choose from existing instruments.
6. Make needed modifications, including adaptations, modified response options, added hotlinks for terminology, and newly created measures when needed.
7. Consider appropriateness of created proxy report versions of adapted measures.
8. Determine the adapted tool's psychometric properties. Will they work?[6]

USING EXTERNAL SUPPORT TO GET THE JOB DONE

Program evaluation can seem like a tall order. Sometimes there isn't enough time to get things done, or there are not enough people to complete the evaluation. While this might sound like putting the cart before the horse, one thing an institution can do when seeking funding to complete an evaluation is to build the cost of hiring an external evaluator into the budget. To identify sources of external support, cultural institution staff may find the American Evaluation Association to be a helpful resource or may have luck seeking a partner on the forum of a relevant professional organization, such as the American Alliance of Museums. Using a research center can be effective and efficient and may provide powerful results in a surprisingly short time. Institutions can select another option: partnering with a university to achieve several of their goals, ranging from research to program development. Each entity brings something different to the plate, and all can be welcome additions.

In sum, conducting a program evaluation can be challenging but provides plenty of rewards. It can be a tool for internal reflection and improvement or a way to connect more deeply with the needs of your community. In addition, a well-designed program evaluation can make your institution seem like a safe bet for funders, which is always good news.

NOTES

1. See the American Museum of Natural History's clear explanation of program evaluation as a component of their research agenda at https://www.amnh.org/learn
-teach/evaluation-research-and-policy. Their work is reported in *Curator: The Museum Journal*; Karen Hammerness, Anna MacPherson, and Preeti Gupta, "Develop-

ing a Research Agenda Aimed at Understanding the Teaching and Learning of Science at a Natural History Museum," *Curator: The Museum Journal* 59, no. 4 (2016): 353–67, https://doi.org/10.1111/cura.12178.

2. Laura Lundy, "'Voice' Is Not Enough: Conceptualising Article 12 of the United Nations Convention on the Rights of the Child," *British Educational Research Journal* 33, no. 6 (2007): 927–42, https://doi.org/10.1080/01411920701657033.

3. Lynne Hall, Colette Hume, and Sarah Tazzyman, "The 15th International Conference on Interaction Design and Children (IDC '16)," in *Proceedings of the 15th International Conference on Interaction Design and Children (IDC '16)*, 311–21 (New York: Association for Computing Machinery, 2016), https://doi.org/10.1145/2930674.2930719.

4. D. A. Story and A. R. Tait, "Readers Toolbox: Understanding Research Methods," *American Society of Anaesthetics* 130, no. 2 (2019): 192–202.

5. Region 15 Comprehensive Center; Regional Educational Laboratory West (ED/IES); WestEd, "Creating Effective Surveys: Best Practices in Survey Design. Evidence Use in Education," 2021, https://files.eric.ed.gov/fulltext/ED619797.pdf.

6. Christina Nicolaidis, Dora M. Raymaker, Katherine E. McDonald, Emily M. Lund, Sandra Leotti, Steven K. Kapp, Marsha Katz, et al., "Creating Accessible Survey Instruments for Use with Autistic Adults and People with Intellectual Disability: Lessons Learned and Recommendations," *Autism in Adulthood* 2, no. 1 (2020): 61–76.

Chapter Twenty-One

Beyond Evaluation

Research Practices and Ethics

While you probably have little intention of being a professional researcher, knowing what research practices are available for you to improve your programs is important. You may be asked to participate in designing a study or collecting data at your institution or you may need a more in-depth understanding of the impact of what you offer to neurodiverse visitors. Nobody knows the culture and logistics of your place and consumer base like you do, and contributing valuable information about them will become more effective if you have an idea about research design and the responsibilities that go along with it.

When conducting formalized research, as opposed to basic program evaluation, you will likely want to work in collaboration with a research institution, such as a university, which will have the tools you need to ensure you are working within ethical codes and research standards. Even so, it is helpful to be well-versed in research design before designing or implementing a study.

The goal of the chapter is to provide readers with some practical considerations related to pairing the realities of their institutional settings with the constraints and anticipated outcomes of different types of research designs. Topics we will cover include

- an overview of research designs;
- a discussion of quantitative and qualitative methods; and
- ethical standards when working with autistic research collaborators and participants.

INTRODUCTION TO RESEARCH DESIGNS
USED FOR PROGRAM EVALUATION

At its most basic level, a research design is a lot like a recipe. All research designs have common elements that must be addressed, and once the basic considerations are met, researchers can make informed decisions about how the design can be adjusted to account for the types of research questions being explored, factors related to the institution itself, and considerations such as time frames or manpower hours needed to make the research a reality. Revisiting the concept at a basic level, all research designs must address the following ingredients: a discussion of the aim and purpose of the research, the research questions that will be asked, the methods used to answer the research questions, and how data will be gathered and analyzed. Program evaluation is a type of research, and many administrators may see the parallels in this formula.

Many factors affect how different types of research methods can help advance the way you understand your institution. For example, there is a difference between learning *what* people believe is important to incorporate into mission statements versus *who* reads them and *why* they do so. There are many realities surrounding the types of research questions that can be asked, such as the number of people needed to participate in the study so the researcher can derive useful information from what people say or do. Believe it or not, there are also some important distinctions between when the researcher does their legwork (collecting the data) versus their headwork (analyzing the data and interpreting how the outcomes answer the research questions) in different research designs. You can help make these plans if you know something about research designs.

QUANTITATIVE AND QUALITATIVE
RESEARCH OVERVIEW

Almost all research designs fall under the umbrella of quantitative or qualitative research—or both. *Quantitative research* is based on data that can be counted, measured, or quantified. An example of a quantitative study might be understanding the relationship between the ages of participants and how much they enjoy sensory-friendly programs. *Qualitative research* seeks to understand subjective components, often through words or narratives. Qualitative data related to why participants enjoy sensory-friendly programs might be gathered via interviews.

Mixed methods research, which combines aspects of quantitative and qualitative research, can be conducted sequentially, as in explanatory or exploratory research, where quantitative and qualitative research studies predictably follow each other, or happen simultaneously, as in the case of analyzing complex surveys to gain quantitative and qualitative information with the same instrument. A classic example is a survey that features numerical scales or multiple-choice questions along with open-ended or fill-in-the-blank type questions. For the purposes of this chapter, we will call those types of research designs mixed methods research. Many online resources, such as Harvard University, provide helpful descriptions of conducting mixed methods research in community settings.[1]

Qualitative and Quantitative Research Are Partners and Equals

Quantitative and qualitative research methods are equal partners in the research world. One is not better or more manageable than the other; they are counterparts. Each methodology uses different types of research questions to examine topics of interest and importance. Each has procedures in place to ensure that participants are treated ethically and respectfully and that the study design is an appropriate way to ask the research questions, also known as *validity*. For example, a survey designed to explore enjoyment but which actually measures attendance would not be considered valid. The research designer's responsibility is to ensure that research questions are relevant for finding out what they need to know and that the logistics of the situation at hand align with what the method requires. (You have probably already gleaned that research vocabulary permeates this chapter. To learn more, see the research glossary published by Research Collections or other online sources.[2])

GUIDELINES FOR INCLUDING AUTISTIC PEOPLE IN PROGRAM EVALUATION AND OTHER RESEARCH

There is a growing interest in what is known as participatory autism research; meaning, people with autism are directly involved in many phases of research.[3] In the case of the program evaluation process, there are instances of museums throughout the country involving autistic visitors as key stakeholders in the process. One such example is the Madison (Wisconsin) Children's Museum. Their efforts to explore the needs of families with children on the autism spectrum or with other sensory processing differences led to a group effort of over forty community members, including parents of children with autism, to create a customizable evaluation toolkit, and while the children with autism were not specifically mentioned as research collaborators, their actions and preferences were documented in the Toolkit to Increase Accessibility and Inclusion for Children on the Autism Spectrum and with Sensory Processing Differences in Cultural Institutions. They also noted that collaborations between autistic individuals and other stakeholders in initiatives like this are usually small in scope and project specific.[4] This may be in part due to hesitancy regarding involving autistic children more directly in the research process.

The state of California took a more formal step toward involving autistic shareholders in program evaluation. In this case, the Sacramento Employment and Training Agency involved nearly thirty autistic young adults in the evaluation of training resources and offered them a structured way to participate in an overhaul of elements of the program that they deemed insufficient for the facility and to develop new programs to meet their stated goals. The institutional report reflected that all parties benefited from collaborations, including enhancing public speaking skills, improving general communication and leadership skills, and a closer alignment between autistic and neurotypical stakeholders. Their executive summary clearly demonstrates that many of the strategies posed by AASPIRE guidelines are echoed throughout their evaluative progress, and that cultural institutions can do the same.[5]

To date, there is no single overarching set of guidelines governing the best ways to conduct the research. This section details the Academic Autism Spectrum Partnership in Research and Education (AASPIRE) guidelines, a representative set of well-known autism research principles. Many other guidelines are available and can be found online, in databases such as PubMed, university research centers, and the National Institutes of Health. The frequently-cited AASPIRE guidelines provide an example of evidence-based guidelines for neurotypical researchers when they collaborate with autistic partners who collaborate on research activities, including either designing and conducting research, or serving as participants who provide data.[6]

AASPIRE guidelines focus on adults with autism and emphasize practicality, which is useful in an institutional setting that is not geared toward research. If you stretch your thinking, you can see that even when research questions focus on children with autism, adults who serve on a research team can provide unique autism-specific insights. For example, an autistic research partner working with co-author Tina Fletcher emphasized how he could make a unique contribution when they told her an autistic person could read an autistic person. On another occasion, an autistic teenager told Fletcher that her personal goals for sensory-friendly programming would be to have "quiet, with a place to rest."

AASPIRE Guidelines

One of the distinct features of AASPIRE guidelines is that they have a flexible starting point that can vary from one context to another. AASPIRE guidelines clearly define the roles and responsibilities of researchers and participants with autism. They detail how to work with both autistic co-researchers and participants, so once a researcher reviews the guidelines, they can understand and address the two roles that people with autism may have in this research, which we will now explore.

Neurodivergent Co-Researchers

AASPIRE has seven guidelines for when neurodiverse people serve as *co-researchers,* meaning they help with components of research design and implementation. This is particularly valuable if they have insights about the location being researched, the potential participants who may become involved in data collection, or in interpreting how the collected data are analyzed to answer the research questions. There are seven co-researcher guidelines:

1. Have transparency about partnership goals.
2. Clearly define all partner roles.
3. Ensure effective communication and power-sharing.
4. Build and maintain trust.
5. Collaboratively get research findings out to stakeholders.
6. Fairly compensate all for their work.
7. Actively encourage opportunities for people with autism to become more educated, participate in internships, and serve as research staff.

At first glance, these guidelines may seem clear and easy to meet. However, meeting all of these guidelines is not as easy as it may sound. This is why an action plan that clearly establishes how these guidelines will be addressed is an important starting point for a fledgling research collaboration between neurotypical and neurodiverse research partners. In particular, it can be challenging to share power, especially for people with autism who have spent a lifetime being cared for by others. In some cases, they may not want to be the center of attention or vocal about their opinions. People with autism may need encouragement and help setting boundaries with team members when in a co-researcher's role. When the expectations related to their contribution are made clear from the beginning, many awkward exchanges can be circumvented later in the research process. Examples of potentially tricky situations that can benefit from frank up-front conversations can include how participants will be recruited, how data will be collected from participants, and what the responsibilities are for each team member as to writing up or presenting the research results. Small matters such as who will be listed as an author on a professional paper, or who will lead a speaking team at a conference, can take on looming proportions if they are not discussed at the beginning of the research. This is not coddling people with autism, but empowering and respecting them.

Co-author Tina Fletcher recalls some of the challenges of conducting research:

> It doesn't matter if you are an autistic or neurotypical researcher when it comes to managing some of the challenges of conducting research. One of the biggest frustrations happens when you've designed a nice study to evaluate program effectiveness and you need a certain number of participants to give you significant results—and for whatever reason, people don't respond to your recruitment efforts. It is very hard to refrain from begging people to participate, and it can easily happen without you even intending to do it. I really have to coach co-researchers to respect people's decisions not to participate, or even worse, their right to pull out of a study right in the middle of things. But when participants signed on to be a part of the evaluation process, that's what we said they could do, and we all have to respect their decision.
>
> Another frequent challenge for co-researchers is fulfilling promises to get research findings such as program evaluations out to various stakeholders. It's important to have frank conversations about how the research team intends to do this. If it includes conference presentations, some team members may develop stage fright when it's time to present to a crowd. If you can address this well in advance—including practicing your presentations with each other, or picking other team members to present in case nerves and anxiety really limit someone's ability to speak in front of others—the research and program evaluation obligations will be met without causing a lot of distress or embarrassment. All these details may seem manageable when they are on paper, but helping co-researchers plan for the realities of the research process is an important obligation of the principal investigator.

Neurodiverse Participants

If neurodiverse people are slated to provide data instead of collaborate in the research process, then they are *participants*, formerly referred to as subjects. Participant guidelines can help them through this unique process. Many people express a mixture of pride and worry when discussing their experiences of being interviewed, completing surveys, or participating in focus groups. Participants may even worry about the legibility of their handwriting when completing open-ended survey questions. For some, the experience can involve anticipatory anxiety before data collection ever begins, perfor-

TEXTBOX 21.1.
COMMENTS FROM NEURODIVERSE RESEARCH
PARTICIPANTS ABOUT BEING INTERVIEWED

"It was just so hard to stay focused. Someone will be talking about science, and I want to be talking about something else."

"I also have a little bit of hearing loss. And then sometimes I won't be able, I wouldn't be able to hear someone say my name."

"When someone keeps telling me to do something and my mind still has to process the information slowly, and then, and that could make myself quite frustrated."

"Question, yes, I mean, what does hiding your identity, what does that mean, what we were talking about?"[1]

NOTE

1. Anonymous comments from unpublished research.

mance anxiety during data collection procedures, or worries related to how their input affects outcomes and findings during the data analysis phase. It is common for participants to voice concerns regarding whether they have completed tasks correctly or given the right answers in interviews or focus groups, despite assurances that there are no right or wrong answers. Textbox 21.1 shows examples of what neurodiverse individuals have to say about their experiences participating in research.

When people with autism serve as participants, AASPIRE guidelines work to ensure they are treated as fairly and ethically as possible. As a result, the six guidelines researchers must put in place for their interactions with autistic participants are quite different from those related to working with co-researchers with autism. These guidelines include the following:

1. Promote the person's autonomy by avoiding influence or exploitation by researchers.
2. Make the consent process user-friendly.
3. Offer many ways for a person with autism to participate in the research.
4. Avoid assumptions that data collection instruments are valid when used with neurodiverse populations.

5. Create accessible interview guides.
6. Use skilled helpers to support communication when needed, especially in cases when individuals rely on assistive technology such as an augmentative and alternative communication device to communicate.

In particular, the guideline related to making the consent process user-friendly is worth emphasizing. Nothing is scarier than trying to read and understand, much less sign, a detailed informed consent form. When an institutional review board committee conducts an ethical review of any study, they scrutinize the actual words on consent forms. One of the main goals of consent forms is to ensure that procedural safeguards are systematically addressed using very specific and consistent language. Consent forms are always comprehensive and, as a result, can be intimidating. It is fairly common for a potential participant, whether they have autism or not, to pull out of a research study simply because providing informed consent seems daunting.

Examples of factors detailed on informed consent forms include listing any potentially harmful side effects resulting from participating in the research, no matter how small the risk of them occurring. These can include the participant's time loss related to how much time they spend participating in the study, the loss of confidentiality that can occur if the participant's contact or other personal information is leaked, experiencing performance anxiety related to being interviewed individually or in groups, and feeling distress when recalling events related to the topic being explored.

Table 21.1 provides potential challenges and actions that might occur when AASPIRE guidelines are being utilized. It may become evident when looking at the challenges and actions on the table that communication, multimodal communication, and clear expectations summarize the spirit of AASPIRE guidelines.

DON'T SKIP THE ETHICAL REVIEW

Involving ethics reviewers ensures that research conducted on or with neurodivergent people respects their privacy, is respectful, and the classic research ethics mantra "Do no harm," clearly echoes throughout the process. This includes knowing when expert help is needed, being aware of guidelines for including neurodivergent people in research, and understanding how Institutional Review Boards (IRBs) ensure research participants are treated fairly, respectfully, and ethically. Because autism and neurodiversity are often accompanied by conditions such as intellectual disability, using guidelines to inform research practices becomes even more essential. While it may seem

Table 21.1   AASPIRE Guidelines

AASPIRE Guidelines	Potential Challenges	Potential Actions
For Co-Researchers or Evaluators		
1. Have transparency about partnership goals	Partners are not clear on individual and group goals.	Create multimodal documents (text and graphic) of overall research or evaluation design with each person's role labeled prior to starting research.
2. Clearly define all partner roles.	People overstep boundaries or underperform in research or evaluation roles, especially if they are implied or assumed.	Provide all team members with definitions of research roles prior to starting research or evaluation.
3. Ensure effective communication and power-sharing.	There is no clear chain of command or communication system, and people do not communicate with their team or "go rogue."	Develop a schedule of meeting times and who will moderate each meeting prior to starting the research or evaluation process.
4. Build and maintain trust.	Team members do not trust other members to do their own work and take on others' responsibilities.	Create a check-off schedule that can be shared on a drive. As tasks are completed, members check them off.
5. Collaboratively get research or evaluation findings out to stakeholders.	Team members may not fully consider all options for disseminating work, and resist or be unable to participate in traditional podium talks.	Provide each member with a variety of options for disseminating research that is developmentally and physically appropriate for each team member, including using assistive technology devices or photo documentation.
6. Fairly compensate all for their work.	People who work in conjunction with an autism center may not be able to accept cash payment for their work.	Explore types of compensation that are non-monetary, such as service credit points, gas vouchers, meal cards, courtesy admissions or memberships prior to starting research.

(continued)

Table 21.1 *Continued*

AASPIRE Guidelines	Potential Challenges	Potential Actions
7. Actively encourage opportunities for people with autism to become more educated, participate in internships, and serve as research or evaluation staff.	People who work in conjunction with an autism center or school may not be released from their program to participate in research.	Break tasks down and find educational or curriculum equivalencies that need to be met at the center or school. Provide documentation regarding how their participation in research meets these criteria.
Guidelines for Conducting Research with Autistic Participants		
1. Promote the person's autonomy by avoiding influence or exploitation by researchers.	People may not participate in research for personal reasons, and research team members overcommunicate with them or try to coax them into participating.	Review all inclusion and exclusion criteria and line items on the consent form, including deciding not to participate or withdrawing from participation with no penalty with all team members prior to recruitment.
2. Make the consent process user-friendly.	Participant does not sign and return the consent form even if they say they will.	Plan for multiple modes of confidential transfer of consent form, obtain consent in person, or provide alternate methods such as secured email. Make sure all modes are approved by ethics reviewers.
3. Offer many ways for a person with autism to participate in the research or evaluation process.	Participant who is being interviewed has trouble expressing themselves.	Prior to the interview, tell participant the communication options they might use during data collection. Make sure all are approved by ethics reviewers. Options include PowerPoint images to accompany interview questions, having a trained person function as a neutral helper, and increase response time, such as one day after interview questions were delivered.

AASPIRE Guidelines	Potential Challenges	Potential Actions
4. Avoid assumptions that data collection instruments are valid when used with neurodiverse populations.	Participant seems to function poorly on a standardized measure, either related to administration procedures or content.	Provide multiple methods of collecting data to offset the flawed instrumentation. Note the instrumentation limitations in reporting.
5. Create accessible interview guides.	Participant seems to underperform in the interview or does not answer questions.	Provide multimodal questions, involve a trained neutral helper in questioning.
6. Use skilled helpers to support communication when needed.	Participant seems to take an extra-long time using their assistive technology device in the interview. Answers seem limited.	Provide participant with opportunities to practice with and without a neutral helper.

easiest just to opt out of doing research with neurodivergent people, having experts and guidelines available is something that helps instead of hinders the process. When researchers take advantage of them, the risk of harming participants shrinks, and the possibility of producing high-quality work grows.

BUDGETING FOR RESEARCH

Planning upfront for research costs will enable you to anticipate how you can meet potential grant requirements related to collecting and analyzing data in rigorous, trustworthy ways. Studies designed with professional research teams are more likely to be published in scholarly peer-reviewed, high-impact publications. These costs, outlined in table 21.2 are intended to offer an estimate of what you might expect to spend, and will vary based upon the scope of your research and the specifics of collaboration with a research institution.

Table 21.2. Budget for Research

Service	Typical Hours	Hourly Price Range in $	Justification
Developing research questions, aims, and goals	5–10	90–150	Professional services will increase the likelihood that research questions, aims, and goals are aligned and attainable.
Recruitment	5–15	45–100	Professional recruitment increases the front chances of reaching optimal numbers, controlling for biases, and improving retention.
Project design and logistics	10–25	90-150	Professional research design increases the chances a study will be robust and trustworthy.
Interviews and focus groups	Per session	75–100	Professional interviewers ensure data collection is optimal, controls for bias, and increases rigor in the study.
Survey collection	5–15	45–100	Professional researchers can perform more complex data analysis methods and produce more complex findings beyond the typical frequency counts.
Basic data analysis	15–25	90–150	Qualitative and quantitative data analysis can be performed using sophisticated software unavailable to most community venues.
Results presentation and reports	10–25	75–135	Professional researchers will format visual findings in the most useful ways and create reports that directly answer research questions, aims, and goals.
Editing	Per documents	50–75	Professional editing will ensure that research findings will be more likely to be published, which is often a requirement of the grant.

NOTES

1. See "Community Engagement Program" at https://catalyst.harvard.edu/community-engagement/mmr/.

2. For a deeper dive into research terminology, see "Child Care & Early Education Research Glossary" at https://www.researchconnections.org/research-tools/research-glossary.

3. For more information about participatory autism research see Hannah Pickard, Elizabeth Pellicano, Jacquiline den Houting, and Laura Crane, "Participatory Autism Research: Early Career and Established Researchers' Views and Experiences," *Autism* 26, no. 1 (2022): 75–87.

4. Libby Hladik, Robin Meyer, Scott Allen, Sandra Bonnici, Nicole A. Froelke, Holly Romaniak, Yasmeena Ougayour et al., "Accessibility and Inclusion for Families with Children with Autism Spectrum Disorders in Cultural Institutions," *Curator: The Museum Journal* 65, no. 2 (2022): 435–49.

5. Leela Hebbar, Caleb van Docto, Miguel Gasca, and Caitlin Grey, "Evaluation of the Transformative Autism Program," Social Policy Research Associates, prepared for the Sacramento Employment and Training Agency, June 2021.

6. Christina Nicolaidis, Dora Raymaker, Steven K. Kapp, Amelia Baggs, Elesia Ashkenazy, Katherine McDonald, Michael Weiner, Joelle Maslak, Morrigan Hunter, and Andrea Joyce, "The AASPIRE Practice-Based Guidelines for the Inclusion of Autistic Adults in Research as Co-Researchers and Study Participants," *Autism* 23, no. 8 (2019): 2007–19, https://doi.org/10.1177/1362361319830523.

Chapter Twenty-Two

Find the Money to Make It Work

Fundraising for Sensory-Friendly Programming

Everything is in place, and you're ready to go, but one small detail looms large: finding the money needed for the event to happen. This chapter provides essential information that demystifies the art of grant writing:

- finding funding sources;
- writing a purpose statement;
- formulating goals and objectives; and
- setting a budget.

In a way, grants are a gift that keeps on giving, and the more you share your successes and failures with others, the greater the payback is to the organization that funded you.

For anyone who has worked in the nonprofit sector, the end of the book may seem like a funny place to address fundraising. In practice, funding generally comes first while program details come later. Unless you are fortunate enough to have a generous budget from the get-go, producing resources, setting up special spaces, buying supplies, and paying contract staff are simply not possible. Building your budget and reaching out to funders—probably multiple funders—to determine what you can and can't afford to do is a critical part of early planning.

Who leads the grant writing process will vary based on an institution's staff size and structure. At smaller cultural institutions, educators or even highly committed volunteers may be responsible for seeking program funds. At larger venues, educators will need to work closely with development or advancement staff to formulate a funding plan. This chapter is designed to be a resource for staff members who may not work primarily in the fundraising arena, or for professional fundraisers who are less experienced in seeking support for education and access programs. As a learning tool, the chapter will provide opportunities to practice writing a grant proposal using your institution's resources, plans, goals, and proposed strategies for evaluating program effectiveness.

LOOKING FOR FUNDS IN ALL THE RIGHT PLACES

Seeking the right funder for your program can be a bit like making a new friend. You should know what qualities you are looking for, whether their interests match your own, how they will support your needs, and what they will ask for in return. You might face rejection and need to develop a thick skin. But take heart, there are plenty of others who might be a better fit. With some preliminary research and an understanding of the types of funders out there, you can find one that's right for you.[1]

Types of Funders

Broadly speaking, program funders are likely to fall into one of four categories: government, corporate, foundation, or individual. To decide which is right for your initiative, it can be helpful to think about why each one might be motivated to give you money. In essence, government agencies purchase services from nonprofits when they give to a program. As such, they may be much more likely to ask for detailed information and supporting documentation to explain how you will be spending taxpayer money. This process may take additional time, so factor that into your submission timeline. Similarly, corporate donors may expect a more transactional relationship and will be motivated by how your program promotes its image in the community. These funders may be highly driven by reach and attendance numbers. Foundations come in all shapes and sizes, from small family foundations with a kitchen table–style operation to larger organizations that may have many employees and a large board. Mission alignment can be key for foundation grants, and some may ask for letters of intent, site visits, and documentation to ensure that what you implement will reflect well on the charitable work they do. Finally, individual donors are a wildcard. They may have idiosyncratic reasons for giving related to their own life experiences, and they typically require more cultivation, in-person contact, and relationship-building. However, individuals passionate about your work may become loyal donors and support your cause year after year.

Finding a Match

If you are starting from scratch, it can be tough to know where to look for financial support. One entry point is to research other programs that are similar in scope and purpose to your own and find out who funds them. Cast a wide net. If you work for a theater, search for funders aligned with education and access to the performing arts. Look into programs that broadly promote cultural or social engagement for people with disabilities. If you work at a smaller cultural institution, seek regionally focused foundations that offer right-sized support with less competition for funds. When considering a larger foundation, a review of their publicly accessible 990 tax documents can help you to discover the average size of grants given—so you can apply for an appropriate amount of money—and what types of programs they favor.[2] If you work at an art museum and are looking into a foundation that mostly supports symphonies, you might be barking up the wrong tree.

Setting Boundaries

While you may be excited about the prospect of getting money to implement your program, make sure not to overpromise what you'll be able to deliver. Co-author Anna Smith recalls an instance where museum staff promised a corporate funder name inclusion in every education program and a working relationship with specific schools partnered with the corporation.

> The results were messy, to say the least. Program listings were clunky with titles like "Corporation Teacher Workshop" and "Corporation School Tours." To cap it off, the administration of the selected schools had no idea that the corporation had identified them as partner organizations and was unwilling to work with the museum. The situation became a painful lesson on standing one's ground and setting realistic expectations when courting a sponsor.

A best practice to avoid situations like this is to develop a list of wills and won'ts before you begin pursuing funding, so you and your grantor start on the same page. If unforeseeable circumstances like COVID-19 occur in the course of the grant-funded year, it is important to keep the grantor aware of steps you are taking to meet the terms of the grant and how the details of your program may change.

APPLYING FOR FUNDS

Once you have identified the funding entities you want to approach, you'll need to ensure your grant application gives the best impression possible. To do this, you'll want to make sure you have a good handle on your timeline, key information about your institution, and a clear vision for your program. You'll also want to be prepared to mold this information to fit multiple proposals—remember, rejections will happen!

Timing Is Everything

In a perfect world, some kind soul would see the incredible potential of your program and send you the money to start next week, no questions asked. In reality, careful planning and a lot of waiting are inherent to the process of raising money. You can think of a grant deadline as a center point in a timeline that includes internal work time on one end and turnaround time for being awarded funds on the other.

No cultural worker is an island, and you will need the support of other institutional departments to contribute budgets, legal documentation, and other items to meet application requirements. Find out how much lead time these staff members will need to produce a given document or data set and build this into your timeline. Be respectful of your colleagues' workloads and allow a generous margin. Also, consider the time you will need to adapt supporting documentation to the format required by the grant application. Be kind to yourself and build in enough lead time to avoid a last-minute scramble. Expect a wait time between submitting your application and receiving notification of whether you will be awarded funds. The exact length varies from funder to funder and their individual processes for reviewing submissions. Still, you might imagine a quick turnaround being in the three to six month time frame, with more extended waiting periods taking up to nine or even twelve months—research what to expect before leaping ahead with program implementation. Make your deadline a week before content is due, and ensure all your letters of support and reporting documents are in hand and ready to submit.

Gathering Documentation

Be prepared to produce certain commonly requested documents, facts, and figures before you start an application process. Funders may ask for your institution's Form 990, annual budgets, financial audits, mission statements, biosketches,[3] and executive leadership and program staff résumés. Prepare a general description of your program in several lengths to suit different word count requirements. If your project proposal involves collaborating with outside partners, they may also need to write a letter of support stating their commitment and understood responsibilities. Statistics such as annual attendance and demographics of people served by your institution are also commonly included in applications. In most cases, quantitative information is more valuable than qualitative statements, but remember, you can shape a story that suits the nature of the grant by choosing how you present quantitative information and what aspects of the data you emphasize. Many grants will let you submit supplementary documents that can give more qualitative information, like letters of support from participating families, quotes from participants that show the need or impact of your programs, photos of past events, and newspaper articles about your offerings.

Writing a Compelling Application

The key to a narrative that will capture the attention of a grant reviewer is relevance. Based upon the call for submissions, what is the grantor looking for? What else can you discover about their priorities by searching through their mission statement, press releases, and list of organizations they have previously funded? Now, how can you make it clear that your project aligns perfectly with their objectives?

Try to address the standard who, what, when, where, how, and why of your program, but don't get too caught up in *why* your work is needed. Assuming you've found a compatible funder, they already know that cultural programming for neurodivergent learners is valuable—that's why they're dedicating money to the cause! Dedicate space to the specifics of your idea: who will it serve, and how many participants do you expect? What partners, performers, or teaching artists will you work with? If you haven't identified them yet, what will your criteria be when choosing whom to invite?

A simple step that can't be overstated is ensuring you have followed the funder's submission instructions. Cross-check your application to ensure it meets all criteria they set out. Review what you have written and make sure that it specifically answers the question or questions laid out in the application materials. You can begin your grant statement by restating and answering the question in the call for submissions. Grantors often have a rubric to see if an applicant's request aligns with their objectives. By beginning your essay with what matters most to them, you have just checked off their first box! If the application portal allows for it, use formatting such as headings, bullets, and bolding, so the information you want reviewers to notice is easily visible. The person who reads what you have written may have countless applications to sift through, and putting the best face on your proposal can make an impact.

Juggling Multiple Applications

Depending upon the scale of your program, there may be opportunities to build a portfolio of multiple supporters in order to ensure you are fully funded. Read through a funder's call for submissions carefully to determine if there is any reason they would prohibit additional sources of income for the program. Some grants specify that they will only cover a certain percentage of expenses and ask for documentation of how the remaining funds will be obtained. In this case, additional leads on financial support are helpful to have. Other types of grants may only contribute to certain aspects of a program, such as supplies or transportation costs. In this situation, finding a way to support additional expenses like marketing costs or staff time, will be useful.

When applying for multiple funding opportunities, being organized is the best thing you can do for yourself. Create a grant calendar that includes application and reporting dates, and work backward to set deadlines for receiving supporting information from internal sources, finalizing drafts, and reviewing your submission. You can find many software solutions for organizing a calendar that will allow you to easily visualize information, set reminders, and loop in other contributors. Services designed for project management are good options, such as Microsoft Planner, Trello, Asana, or Monday.com. Avoid using a spreadsheet or personal calendar, and seek something more functional. Keep clearly marked files with up-to-date supporting documents, evaluation results, statistics, and previous grant applications that can be adapted to new requests.

PREPARING A BUDGET

When applying for a grant, it is essential to understand the actual costs of your programs and to prepare a budget that considers all expenses. While some expenses, like art-making supplies or sensory room materials, may be obvious, other less apparent costs are equally crucial to your event's success. What is the collective cost, including staff time, marketing efforts, supplies, and even building maintenance? Are you applying for a grant covering a single event or a specific duration of programming? Are you asking for the full expense or a percentage of your operating cost? Is the grant amount you are pursuing accurate while still being realistic and attainable?

Broadly speaking, you might think of your program budget in terms of direct and indirect costs. Direct costs may include expenses that are, as you might guess, directly necessary to the function of an event or resource, such as supplies or equipment, contract staff honoraria, printing, food and beverage, or transportation. Indirect costs, while often critical to a program's existence, are not directly tied to the implementation of an event or resource. These could include staff time, training fees, equipment maintenance, market-

Table 22.1. Budget for Sensory-Friendly Event Engaging up to Five Hundred People

Honorarium for autism specialist	$200
Honorarium for music therapist	$200
Supplies (nonreplenishable)	$100
Supplies (replenishable)	$180
Total for single event	$680
Total for four quarterly events	$2,720

ing, and security or facility costs. Almost all funders will support direct costs, but some will not give money toward indirect costs. Make certain you know which type you are dealing with before you begin an application.

When budgeting for direct costs, you might start by considering projected attendance and program frequency. Then, focus on what resources you need and what will be spent supporting a single event. Table 22.1 is a real budget showing the amount allocated for various expenses for a two-hour sensory-friendly event at the Dallas Museum of Art (DMA), engaging up to five hundred people.

If requesting support for one year of programming, and this event takes place quarterly, the most basic budget (from the sample expenses outlined above) would equal $2,720. Note that the sample budget includes a line for nonreplenishable supplies, covering items such as reusable fidgets, sensory room furniture, or art-making tools like paintbrushes. Surprisingly, most government-funded grants do not allow you to include nonreplenishable supplies in your budget. If an item is intended to last longer than the duration of the program, it may need to be funded by a different type of grantor. This projected budget for sensory-friendly programming does not include expenses beyond the program's hours, namely, staff time.

For education programs, the greatest expense often comes from the indirect cost of staffing. Supplies for an art project or touch table might have a modest price tag, but the qualified people who plan and implement programming have a greater value. How many paid staff will support the planning and implementation of the event? What percentage of their time will be spent creating sensory-friendly programming, and what does this translate to in terms of their salary? Don't forget to include preparation time for the event, including meetings with your community advisory group or hours preparing supplies. Your anticipated expenses may also include the cost of the security and front-of-house staff required to support the event if it takes place outside of standard operating hours. Table 22.2 is a sample budget that includes estimated staff time to plan and implement quarterly sensory-friendly programming at the DMA. These estimates are based on a program that staff would spend 5 percent of their annual time planning and implementing. Looking at the sums of

Table 22.2.   Estimated Staff Time Sample for Sensory-Friendly Programming

Staff Member(s)	Percentage of Annual Time	Total to Include in Budget
Manager of Access Programs	5% of $50k salary	$2,500
Teaching Specialist	5% of $40k salary	$2,000
Paid Intern	Endowed position, not included in expense estimate	$0
Event support staff: Five Gallery Attendants	$15 per hour for a two-hour event, four times per year	$600
Total		$5,100

tables 22.1 and 22.2, when we add staff time to our basic budget of $2,720, the resulting cost to support one year of sensory-friendly programming is $7,820.

Other Expenses

While the sample budget is already very robust after considering staff time, a few related expenses still need to be included. Will you need to pay for outside marketing opportunities or engage the time of your in-house marketing staff? Will you hire a photographer for the event or utilize the time of a staff photographer? Does your institution have an evaluator on staff who will gather participant feedback at the event or help you design an evaluation protocol? Does your institution typically provide free parking on-site, or would you consider reducing parking expenses for attendees by renting a nearby lot or contracting a valet for the duration of the event? While you want to request a reasonable amount when applying for grants, these other expenses can demonstrate your institutional commitment to the event by comparing the total expenditure (and what the institution will cover) to the funder's requested amount.

Get It Together

Now that you have the basic gist related to grant applications, there is nothing like putting it all together. Use this template to formulate your thinking. You may be skilled at developing a solid and compelling narrative but need more finesse in developing a budget that makes sense to you and your reviewers. It's easy to get bogged down in writing a grant. People tend to stay within their comfort zone and disregard the portions that don't appeal to or make sense to them. You can use this format as a diagnostic tool. It can help you see where your strengths—and weaknesses—lie and where you might need a little push or assistance from others. Textbox 22.1 offers a sample template for a grant application.

TEXTBOX 22.1.
GRANT APPLICATION TEMPLATE

APPLICANT INFORMATION

Applicant:
  Applicant Role:
  Applicant Contact Information:

Collaborator (person who adds expertise to the project without serving a role significant enough to be considered an applicant and does not receive direct funds):
  Collaborator Organization:
  Collaborator Role:
  Collaborator Contact Information:

Consultant (person who can receive direct funds to provide a specific service):
  Consultant Organization:
  Consultant Role:
  Consultant Contact Information:

PROJECT INFORMATION

Title of Project:
Human Subjects Research, Ethics, and Compliance Training (if indicated):

ABSTRACT (150 WORDS)

A succinct and accurate description of the proposed work when separated from the application, including broad, long-term objectives, specific aims, the target population, and methods for achieving goals.

NARRATIVE (500 WORDS)

- Program concept and opportunity provided (include a concise review of literature, statement of need, the rationale for the project, and description of the target population).
- Objectives and aims of the project.
- Methodology or implementation strategies (data collection, statistical analysis, and soundness of data collection instruments).
- A timeline describing when you will accomplish aims and objectives during the project.

(continued)

TEXTBOX 22.1. *Continued*

- If the project conducts research with human participants, detail how you will ensure safety and protect their rights.
- Consultant support. Describe the applicant's ability to conduct this project and include the other people with skills who can ensure it happens.
- Significance of this project to the specific site or professional field.
- The evaluation plan to determine the success of the objectives and aims.
- Future anticipated external funding opportunities.
- Proposed methods of presenting results and findings.

BUDGET

Salary support, project assistants, salary and fringe benefits, and maintenance and operations (M&O) expenses such as postage, telephone calls, paper, computer software, and equipment. Funds requesting consultants must be well-justified in the proposal narrative. Provide budget justifications.

SUPPORT

Listing of all current and pending funding sources for this project, including the funding agency, amount, date of application, and application status. When appropriate, provide the funding critique or score for the submitted proposals not (yet) funded.

PUBLICATIONS, PRESENTATIONS, AND AWARDS RESULTING FROM PAST SUPPORT

For each person, a listing of all outcomes for the past five years resulting from past program grants.

CURRICULUM VITAE FOR EACH APPLICANT

These need to be up to date, formatted according to requirements, and emphasize how each person meets the needs you detailed in your narrative.

OTHER ATTACHMENTS

As an appendix, a copy of any evaluation tools, project surveys, questionnaires, a copy of any human subject's review approval (or indication of a pending application), a letter from any colleagues who will collaborate on the project, a letter from an administrator of the facility stating that the project may be conducted there, and an endorsement or support from the grant.

NEXT STEPS

With thorough planning and practice, you can make a strong case for funding your program. From there, it is in the hands of prospective funders. The next chapter offers insight into the grant review process. It explores what will be expected of you when your program is chosen for funding, as well as how to manage unexpected situations that may prevent you from meeting the terms of your agreement.

NOTES

1. Information in this section contributed by Vanessa Hadox (director of Institutional Giving, Nasher Sculpture Center) and Cale Peterson (manager of Institutional Giving, Nasher Sculpture Center) in discussion with Anna Smith, November 30, 2022.

2. Form 990 records can be found through online search engines such as the one offered by ProPublica at https://projects.propublica.org/nonprofits/search.

3. To learn more about biosketches and miniature versions of curriculum vitae and how to write them, see National Institutes of Health Grants & Funding at https://grants.nih.gov/grants/forms/biosketch.htm.

Chapter Twenty-Three

Funding Follow-Through

Reviewing and Reporting on Grants

You have amazing ideas, found a funding opportunity, and just typed the last period in your grant proposal. Now what? Without a doubt, knowing how to review an application will help you strengthen your own grant writing skills. This chapter details grant reviewing considerations including

- objectively evaluating the proposed significance, approach, planned use of preexisting resources, and budgetary information for your application;
- how to put together an effective grant report; and
- what to do if you are unable to fulfill the terms of the grant.

STEP INTO THE REVIEWER'S SHOES

You may wonder what happens when you fire off your grant application in the first place. There are many similarities between applying for a grant and submitting a manuscript for publication review. Typically, like a publication editor, a grant reviewer studies the application, then decides whether it meets the minimum criteria needed to advance it to an expanded formal review. A committee then examines the proposal, determines how well it meets established standards, and decides to either reject, recommend revisions, or fully accept the application. While you won't send off the practice application provided in this book, it's a good idea to find a colleague willing to serve as an informal grant officer or peer reviewer and look at your application. We will revisit that idea later in the chapter when we go over what it takes to be a good reviewer.

One of the best ways to create a solid application is to begin with the end in mind. Spend some time thinking about the best ways to preach to the choir by anticipating a reviewer's thoughts, questions, and feelings. A helpful way to do this is to engage in the process of review. It's a good idea to step away from your application and then give it a go-over with a grant review checklist. In 2020, researchers led by Steiner Davis[1] found that being an effective grant reviewer takes some skill. In particular, they learned that reviewers' most highly valued competencies are impartiality, openness to novel ideas, and objectivity.

The takeaway here is that it is essential to address the issue of neutrality by refraining from statements that might be prejudicial, reflect your bias, or jump-start theirs. Tackling bias is always challenging, and when people develop proposals and seek money for these proposals, they almost always have an inclination that their project will improve something. Even if it does, it's essential to refrain from making a grant application sound like a used car pitch. Be honest. If you aren't sure how some things will go, that's normal. It's crucial to provide your reviewer with a balanced view that is grounded in what you have found in the literature and what you and your team of experts believe is the next step in that journey.

Steiner Davis's team also found that subject matter expertise is a highly valued attribute, but the grant review team may not be experts in what you are proposing, especially if it is a novel idea. Help them out. Spell out your vision, provide supporting documentation, and don't make the reviewers work too hard to figure out your plan, or they will move on to the next application.

Run your idea by a colleague or another cultural educator. Then, after taking a few days away from your application, use this provided evaluation form to see how well your application might fare. Try hard to avoid falling into the compliments and praise routine with your peer reviewers. While it's nice to get a pat on the back, it won't improve your application. Table 23.1 offers a template for grant application peer review.

GRANT REPORTING

Almost all funders will require a grant report after you have spent the money and implemented a grant-supported project. The funder believed in your project enough to give you financial support, but they will want to know how their money was spent and if you met the goals stated in your application. A grant report details how funds were utilized, the impact a project had on the community, and what challenges or changes took place. While it might seem like prematurely counting your chickens to think about grant reporting before you have submitted your application, this is the perfect time to consider if the goals in your proposal are measurable (and can be reported) and just how you will gather that information during your project implementation timeline.

Table 23.1. Grant Application Peer-Review

Application Title:			
Applicant:			
Evaluator:			

Score each criterion on a nine-point scale, with 1 being exceptional and 9 being poor. Average the scores for an overall score which reflects how well the program could benefit the community and field.

Influence/ Impact	Score	Descriptor	Additional Information
High	1	Exceptional	Exceptionally strong with no weaknesses
	2	Outstanding	Extremely strong with negligible weaknesses
	3	Excellent	Very strong with minor weaknesses
Medium	4	Very Good	Strong with at least one minor weakness
	5	Good	Strong with several minor weaknesses
	6	Satisfactory	Some strengths but also some minor weaknesses
Low	7	Fair	Some strengths but with at least one significant weakness
	8	Marginal	A few strengths and a few significant weaknesses
	9	Poor	Very few strengths and numerous significant weaknesses

Criteria	Score (1–9)
Importance • Does the program address a significant problem or barrier to progress in the field? • If applicants achieve program aims, how will program knowledge, technical capability, or institutional practices be improved? • How will successful program completion change concepts, methods, technologies, services, or practices in the field? • Will the applicant get data for future work, publish or present results, and pursue more significant funding due to the proposed program?	
Applicants • Are the applicant, collaborators, and consultants suited to the program? • Have they demonstrated accomplishments that advance their fields? • If the program is collaborative, do applicants have complementary expertise? • If students or volunteers are participating, do applicants have supervisory experience?	
Innovation • Will the program challenge or shift current practice with approaches? • Will applicants follow a sequence of procedures? • Did applicants propose a refinement, improvement, or new application of approaches?	

(continued)

Table 23.1.   *Continued*

Criteria	Score (1–9)
Approach • Is the strategy, method, and analysis plan appropriate to program aims? • Did applicants address potential problems, alternative strategies, and benchmarks for success? • Are plans to manage difficult aspects addressed? • If the program involves research, are plans for the protection of human subjects, including minorities, both sexes/genders, and minors justified? • Is the time frame realistic?	
Resources • Has the applicant identified the location and setting? Is this space adequate? Are letters of support in place? • Are the equipment, trained personnel, and other physical resources already in place, and are they adequate? • Will the program benefit from unique environmental features, visitor populations, or collaborative arrangements?	
OVERALL SCORE: CRITERIA AVERAGE: Highly recommend for funding (score 1–3) Recommend for funding (score 4–6) Do not recommend for funding (score 7–9)	
Comments/Explanations/Justifications/Recommendations: 	

Most grant funders are happy to provide their grant reporting template at the time of application, or at least tell you what information will be required if you ask. The grant application itself also provides excellent clues as to what types of information are of interest to the funder. Does the funder ask for visitor demographic information? If so, this question will likely be repeated in the grant report. Knowing what to expect early on allows institutions to ensure that they have a process for capturing this information from participants before they implement the project.

Many grant reports also require grantees to provide receipts or an expense log of purchases related to the project. This information helps the funding organization or individual feel confident that their money was allocated as described in the grant application. To save yourself some time during the reporting period, you can highlight expense lines related to the grant in your ledger as costs are incurred. Create an organized process for tracking expenses at the outset of the project and stick with it to make life easier for you and your accounting department.

Likewise, it is extremely important to consider the process for measuring the goals you present in the application. Do you have enough staff and a process in place to collect this information? Compelling goals are typically written with quantitative outcomes in mind. Instead of stating that your goal is "to create sensory-friendly programming to help increase social interaction," try to write a measurable goal, such as "75 percent of participants of sensory-friendly programming who responded to a written survey will report an increase in social connections." Building goals that are not just attainable, but measurable, will simplify your reporting process when the time comes.

While funders are interested in measurable outcomes, qualitative information helps paint a richer picture of the impact of the initiative and strengthens the bond between institution and funder. Photos from programs, quotes from participants, and anecdotes from events are the types of feel-good information that can supplement your measurable goals. Funders can easily share this information with others to help spread awareness about their activity and impact in the community. In turn, this not only helps to improve your relationship with the funder but also helps them to raise more money to support programs like yours.

Capturing Meaningful Data

Getting good data about your program in the heat of the moment can be a challenge. Whether it is quantitative metrics or qualitative survey comments, make sure you research what elements are required in advance by your funder so you can include them somewhere in your information capture. There are many ways to connect with your participants and learn more about their experiences. Quantitative or aggregate data comprise demographic information such as participant age and zip codes, or metrics like attendance numbers or time spent at the event. Qualitative information reveals individual perspectives—impactful personal accounts of how a visitor felt welcome or what activities they enjoyed most and least, as well as suggestions for event improvement. Institutional funders request metrics more often than impact stories. Knowing your funder's report priorities and your institution's information wish list helps you design those essentials into your forms and interactions with participants.

In addition to general demographics for your city or community, many funders also want to know about the staff members who will be designing and facilitating the proposed project, including their demographic information, résumés, and annual salaries. They may also request your institution's profit and loss (P & L) statements and balance sheets. All of these items should be gathered together a week or more before the submission deadline in order to provide a buffer for polishing the application and to allow for an unexpected illness or vacation of another department staff member.

COPING WITH UNEXPECTED CIRCUMSTANCES

While it would be nice to have a crystal ball to see the future of your project, many types of unforeseen circumstances may thwart your plans after you have been awarded a grant. So what happens when your project is disrupted by something that is out of your control? When planning events, most cultural workers imagine common issues that could arise and develop contingency plans for rain and other inconveniences. But some things happen in real time that you cannot anticipate—flooding, tornado warnings, marathons, police motorcades, or severe accidents that block your downtown traffic grid. In such cases, participants can be cautioned not to come by sending out a timely event cancellation notice, and sometimes with a little advance notice, a newly scheduled date can be sent out. But when nothing can be done to salvage a planned and paid-for program, what is the best course of action? This section offers some case examples of working through challenging circumstances to maintain relationships with program funders.

Case Example: Programming in a Pandemic

In the early months of COVID-19, many cultural institutions closed their doors for long periods of time. When they reopened, new guidelines had been set by the CDC to protect the public's health. In many cases, what was promised the year before to foundations in the grant-writing process could no longer be fulfilled in the manner that was promised. In a situation like this, it is the grant recipient's responsibility to communicate the need for modification to the funder and to get their approval for a revised plan.

Such was the case at the Nasher Sculpture Center when, in March 2020, staff members were poised to offer their annual sensory-friendly program, but the museum closed the week before the scheduled event out of concern for public health. Anyone who experienced the pandemic may have an idea where this story is going. The museum closure was only supposed to last for two weeks, but as the situation progressed it became clear that no large-scale syn-chronous public program would be possible within the time frame of the grant that funded it. Nasher staff pivoted to offer an asynchronous program featuring single-use activity totes meant to keep germ-sharing to a minimum. In addi-tion, the museum offered virtual activities for neurodivergent visitors designed by the Texas Woman's University occupational therapy students who had been planning to support the in-person event. The museum's funders understood the challenges staff were facing and accepted the changes to the initial proposal.

Case Example: When a Partner Disappears

Another lesson learned by Nasher Sculpture Center staff came from a grant meant to fund programming with a specific partner organization. Partnerships with community groups can be a wonderful way to realize mutual goals with another nonprofit, but even established multiyear programs can be capsized by turnover in staff. This was the case with a national organization the Nasher had partnered with for years on an after-school program. Both institutions took a summer hiatus, and in the fall, Nasher staff reached out with calls and emails to schedule the next year's program dates. When the emails bounced back, museum staff discovered that the partner organization had undergone a complete change in leadership and no one on their new team had ever heard of the Nasher or the after-school program. The partner didn't wish to take on what they thought was a new program, leaving Nasher staff unable to fulfill their grant's stipulations. Fortunately, by working with the funder, the mu-seum was able to renegotiate the terms and create programming for another community organization with a similar mission.

Case Example: Making Yourself Heard

Not long ago, co-author Tina Fletcher received a large state-funded com-munity participation grant for neurodivergent citizens. In all honesty, she felt intimidated by the award and had some worries about sounding worthy of the funding when communicating with her grant officer at the state capitol. The every-six-weeks reporting schedule turned out to be a key to her communi cation success. After she submitted a few reports and her funders sent only perfunctory "thank you for the timely submission of your report" messages, she got a little bolder and sent additional messages, emphasizing good news and interesting information. One evening, she was shocked to receive a call from her grant officer, who sought her advice.

The officer expressed frustration with her own challenges related to keep-ing state officials interested in funding neurodiversity research. She asked for insights on how to make the reports engaging instead of repetitive and, well, boring. Together, they developed some strategies for keeping the higher-ups interested in what would happen next. After this, Tina made an extra effort to communicate openly and honestly about how the grant activities moved forward. Even after the funding cycle ended, she continued to credit her funders for their support, shared any information about publications and presentations that came from the work, and to ensure full transparency and adherence to copyright restrictions, she made sure to receive permission from journal editors to share copies of publications with her funders.

KEEPING IT FLUID

The key takeaway from these stories is the importance of keeping communication with a grantor fluid. It is not enough to tell them why something is not going to happen; you should also have an alternate strategy to share. When things change, develop a modified plan that still aligns with the priorities of the grant. If you don't know all of the who, what, when, and where details yet, explain the steps you are taking to work through the decision process. Be as clear and detailed as possible. If your grantor knows you are nimble and actively working to fit your revised project's function with their missional goals, you are building trust between your organizations. By developing a positive grant history with them, you may also increase your chances for future renewals, creating lasting outcomes for the community you both seek to serve.

NOTE

1. Miriam L. E. Steiner Davis, Tiffani R. Conner, Kate Miller-Bains, and Leslie Shapard. "What Makes an Effective Grants Peer Reviewer? An Exploratory Study of the Necessary Skills," *PloS One* 15, no. 5 (2020): e0232327, accessed December 1, 2022, https://doi.org/10.1371/journal.pone.0232327.

Chapter Twenty-Four

Adding Your Voice to the Chorus
Publishing and Presenting

The life cycle of a great idea begins with a spark, then comes implementation, then refinement, and finally dissemination—when the idea can ignite new sparks. Your program or initiative may be humming along smoothly, connecting with neurodiverse learners in your community, and fulfilling your institution's mission, but there may be others who could benefit from your expertise. The museum down the street, the zoo the next town over, or a children's theater on the other side of the country might be struggling with a situation you've already overcome or even mastered. While there may be limits to what you can offer your community through your own institutional resources, you have the power to help these colleagues build and improve upon what they offer to their communities. By sharing your experience and knowledge, your impact can go further.

This chapter offers insights on spreading the word to professional colleagues about how you engage neurodiverse visitors. These include

- how to find out if the topic of your presentation or publication will be a unique addition to the field;
- suggestions for presenting at professional conferences;
- where to look for a publication that will be a fit; and
- preparing and submitting an article for publication.

WHAT'S GOING ON OUT THERE?
DATABASES AND WHERE TO FIND THEM

Before you set out to share your story with the world, you will want to know how similar it is to what others have already published. This section details how to determine what's going on in your field and where to find the information to support what you intend to write or present. A search of this nature may have been a straightforward task when you were a student, but can be more complicated for staff of cultural institutions not affiliated with a university.

While it is possible to run all kinds of searches on the Internet, consider a database search as a value-added way to locate information. Universities, libraries, schools, and the Internet contain various databases. Each is like a digital file cabinet full of resources, including publications, conference proceedings, dissertations, book chapters, and other print, image, and video materials. If you are lucky enough to have access to a librarian that can help you navigate database selections, that is an excellent start.

You may have experienced searching for a particular author's work and receiving a message that the article you were looking for is available in various databases. Many databases carry some of the same publications. Databases are subscription services, and their holdings can vary from time to time as librarians remove certain publications and add others from their collections. Some databases cost more than others, and librarians often make difficult decisions regarding how to spend their database dollars. Because database acquisitions are fluid, searchers should be persistent and systematic about searching for publications within databases. With practice and experience, database users tend to develop their favorite go-to choices that offer specific ways to navigate and use them. Still, users should remain open to occasionally checking others.

Open Access Databases

Let's look for a minute at databases available at no cost to the general public. With the growing popularity of massive online open courses, or MOOCs, some databases that were formerly housed in universities and only permitted students and faculty to use them have become available to the general public.[1] Readers should remember that these databases differ from easily accessed Internet sources such as Google or *Wikipedia* because they specialize in housing high-quality peer-reviewed journals and research. Important considerations for using these free Internet databases include whether the publications featured are open access, meaning the author or their institution has paid their publishers a fee to make their work free to the public, or are the type of database that offers a combination of open access and pay-per-view publications. In this case, some publications charge a fee to view materials for a limited duration of time, such as 24–48 hours, or sell a copy of the publication outright. While always subject to change, at the time of this writing, popular free online databases include Google Scholar, CORE, ScienceOpen, Directory of Open Access Journals, and Education Resources Information Center. Each has over a million publications in its collections. JSTOR is a popular database featuring free or reduced-cost full-text arts-related publications from more than five hundred scholarly journals. Universities and museums such as Yale University and the Smithsonian house other arts databases.[2]

Gaining Access to Subscription-Only Resources

What should you do when you've found the articles you need but they are all behind a paywall that exceeds the funds you have available? Your best bet may be to network. While most small and mid-size cultural institutions may not fund employee access to research databases, some larger ones, especially those with libraries, do. Some university libraries also allow in-person access for outside researchers, or offer alumni access to digital resources. Don't be afraid to find the right person and ask. Other options include your local public library, which may have on-site access to the resources you need, or, in a pinch, you can try contacting the author of the article either directly or through programs such as ResearchGate. Many authors are not only willing but eager to share a digital copy of their research. As a bonus, this may be a way to connect with another professional whose work mirrors your own.

Why Quality Matters

As some readers follow this discussion, they may wonder why they can't just "Google" something to find what is needed. While an essential Internet or Google search might get searchers started, they should know how this type of search differs from a database search. In a basic Internet search, the legitimacy of the author or institution providing general information may vary widely. As a basic principle, when searching the Internet, consumers should be aware that the first few results are sponsored or advertised sources, meaning that they have the financial resources to place their information before others. While there is no direct link between the quality of a source and the order in which it appears, searchers should be aware of sponsorship versus quality as a factor in visibility.

Another contrast between Internet versus database sources is the authority of the writer. Anyone can publish their work on the Internet, and peer-reviewing is not required. In this circumstance, consumers must rely on their ability and judgment to evaluate the quality of the information provided, such as making distinctions between a randomized controlled trial and a case study. In a sense, databases do this work for consumers by publishing peer-reviewed work. Either peers in the field or, in some cases, editors will serve as reviewers for potential publications. As part of their faculty duties, professors frequently respond to requests to review work in their area of expertise. Several strategies are usually in place to keep their reviews and opinions about whether a work is worthy of publication unbiased. Examples include preventing reviewers from knowing author names, universities or other affiliated institutions, or locations. This process is known as *blinding* a manuscript for review.

Other differences between Internet and database sources may include how stable the information is. One well-known source from the Internet consists of *Wikipedia*, which is a *wiki*, meaning anyone can edit most pages and articles, although *Wikipedia*, like other Internet information wikis, does have administrators that serve to protect some pages from editing, vandalizing, or adding what is often known as "fake news."[3]

THE POWER AND POINT OF PRESENTATIONS

When you know your program model is functioning well and have done the research to know that it adds something to the field, presenting at a professional conference is a good next step. You may be quite familiar with the professional organizations specific to your discipline. For example, in the world of art museum education, the likely candidates would be the American Alliance of Museums and the National Art Education Association along with their regional or state counterparts. Submitting a proposal to such an organization might be a good fit if you plan to give a solo presentation focused specifically on the work you have done at your institution. You can expand your options for the type of conference that will consider your proposal by connecting with colleagues from different disciplines. The art museum educator used in our example could collaborate on a presentation with staff from a botanical park and a symphony center who offer similar programs for neurodiverse visitors, with an occupational therapist who has worked at cultural venues, or with an educator or administrator whose students have participated in sensory-friendly programs.

Each type of conference will have its own culture and protocols. While some may be geared more toward presenters reading prepared papers, others may encourage active engagement between speaker and audience. Calls for submissions may also be focused on different themes each year. Consider how these factors align with what you want to share and why you want to share it.

Costs and Benefits of Presentations

The monetary costs of presenting at professional conferences can be significant, especially for staff at smaller institutions. In addition to membership dues and conference fees, travel and lodging expenses may strain your budget, particularly when traveling to a city with a high cost of living. When this is the case, a state or regional conference within day-trip distance can be a good place to debut your presentation. You may also want to look into virtual formats, which require no travel and have gained in popularity in recent years.

What makes all the effort worth it is the power of being in a room—whether physical or virtual—with other professionals who care about the same things as you. Sharing your experiences with cultural programming for neurodiverse visitors may connect you with seasoned professionals who can offer advice on refining what you offer as well as those who will hear what you present and use it to build something new or better for their audiences. Even if you encounter a so-called tough crowd, their feedback may help you to discover areas in which your program could be improved.

One drawback of presentations, as opposed to publications, is how long the information will last. While poster presentations, recorded podium talks, and live podium presentations are important, aside from your work finding its way into conference proceedings, it will primarily go unheeded. If longevity is important to you, you might bite the bullet and try your hand at writing for publication.

FINDING THE PUBLICATION THAT'S RIGHT FOR YOU

Writing begins with a match in mind. You can often look for a publication's scope or editorial mission statement within its author guidelines. For example, some publications devote themselves to publishing randomized controlled trials and systematic reviews. There are better places to submit program descriptions or survey results. Other publications clearly state that unless authors have addressed human rights with an institutional board review, they will not be eligible. Also, journals with a high profile may have a meager acceptance rate, which means they receive many more submissions than they can publish.

Be realistic about what you are writing. If it is a program description of one event that hosted 137 children, it may have been vital to you, but might not have the significant national or international impact you hoped to engender. You may also need to consider how your article fits in with the thematic content planned by the publication. Even with published author guidelines, it is difficult to know what a publication has on its calendar for the rest of the year, or how open to new ideas its editors might be.

On occasion, you might be able to determine if an editor is interested in your proposed idea if you write them and ask. If they respond, follow their instructions to the letter. If they don't respond, don't give up. Some editorial boards do not respond to queries as a matter of practice. Try a submission anyway but know it can take weeks or months to determine whether they want to work with you. Know also that it is bad form to submit a manuscript to more than one publication at a time. That's why finding what you believe is the best match for your work is the key to success. If the journal only publishes work every other month, build in a longer wait time. While it is important to let the journal editors and reviewers do their work, it is also reasonable to keep track of time frames related to your submission. Occasionally things do get lost in the shuffle and a query from you is reasonable if you have waited much longer than the published review time. If you find you are waiting longer than you feel is acceptable, you can also remove your submission from consideration and send it elsewhere, but you must remain transparent about this process. Tell the publication you are withdrawing it from consideration and why. The important thing here is to be patient, be confident, and not be discouraged if people reject your work. Keep trying! It's worth the effort and will help others. Co-author Tina Fletcher recalls a situation where she pitched an idea to an editor and had a positive outcome:

> I recently wrote a manuscript and pattern draft about a particular style of weaving I was exploring for a weaving magazine. The editor and I had great rapport and worked well together. After the issue was published, I wrote the editor to thank her for being such a conscientious collaborator and told her that I would love to write a series of health promotion tips for weavers since I am an occupational therapist. A week later she contacted me and asked me to send a formal pitch to her editorial team and provided me the parameters for articles she would be most interested in publishing, such as the number of photos I would use, a sample paragraph, and a list of topics I would like to explore. Soon, I was a regular columnist for the weaving magazine, first writing a series of articles related to healthy weaving habits, followed by a series of articles for weavers experiencing some of the challenges of old age. The editor and I continue to enjoy our working relationship and are both open to new opportunities for collaboration in the future. If I had not been bold enough to make my original pitch, this collaboration would not have happened.

When in Rome: Matching a Publication's Style

While the idea of being a copycat might seem scary and smack of plagiarism, this is not what is meant by making it match. Instead, think of this process as a few technical things to do before the manuscript is sent off for review. First, realize there are many examples of successes related to what the intended publication looks for. A good strategy is to find three to five articles in that journal that are similar to what you intend to publish. For example, it could be on the content of neurodiversity or autism, or it could be on the process of program development. Once you have located some good exemplar articles, it's time to roll up your sleeves and do a deep structure analysis of what the articles look, sound, and read like. After all, these articles made the cut and were published. Your job is to get intimately acquainted with these articles, look for similarities, patterns, and links between them, and align your manuscript so it reflects the same spirit and style.

It's a great idea to study up on style guides, such as APA or Chicago Style, and to determine what style guide the publication uses. Online style guides are helpful, especially if they have sample manuscripts. Many online publications and presentations are available to help writers sound their best—don't be afraid to use them!

After you have tackled the mechanics of writing, such as grammar and punctuation in a similar fashion to authors who were published in the journals you are interested in, it's time to science out the structure of the selected articles. If the format of the article shows word counts of specific portions of articles, good for you. If the articles are printed, get out a trusty ruler and start measuring. First, write the headings of the articles. Usually, there are five or six headings, with additional subheadings. Focus on the main or level one headings first. Determine what percentage of the article fits under each subheading. This can be an eye-opening experience. For example, if roughly 25–35 percent of the selected articles are devoted to literature review and your manuscript doesn't have one, it's time to go back to the drawing board and find a publication that doesn't make such heavy use of literature reviews—or to beef up the one in your manuscript. You may also discover each of the articles has a section that your manuscript does not. If it is an essential piece, such as ensuring ethical standards are met, it might be time to go back to the drawing board. While authors can write a literature review, they won't be able to change up a program design or research study that has already been done. Authors should find another outlet to write for instead. Do the articles have extensive reference lists? Are the references all from a certain time period? Make sure the proposed manuscript matches.

Another consideration for a match is the author's voice. Does the author write in first-person or third-person voice? This often follows along with how formal the style of writing is. Authors who report their work in third-person voice may tend toward more formal language, although this isn't always the case. For example, first-person might read like so, "We passed surveys out to all visitors after the program was over," while third-person might read this way, "The authors passed out surveys to all visitors." While we are at it, let's use the same idea to see how active and passive voices compare. Active: "The authors passed out the survey." Passive: "The survey was passed out by the authors." Always go with active voice.

Hopefully, readers are beginning to appreciate the logic and science of analyzing publications and published articles. There are so many moving parts, but by developing the habit of analyzing them, the process of writing for publication can seem much less intimidating.

GROWING A THICK SKIN

An important thought on writing relates to the art of dealing with rejection. Co-author Tina Fletcher has mentored countless university students working their way through the publication process. Many students are just fine until they receive a rejection or request for major revisions. A good strategy for managing a rejection is to put the work down for a day, revisit it when the initial sting has passed, and thoughtfully read through the editor's information. Editors may offer helpful insights that can strengthen the manuscript for consideration by another publication. Too many excellent manuscripts end up in the bone pile because the authors are disheartened by an initial rejection or critical words.

It is equally important that in the face of a rejection, you suck it up and write the editor a brief thank-you note for their review and suggestions. Remember too, that some reviewers are more polished and professional than others. Ignore the cyberbullies if they reviewed your work and made tacky comments. Know too that your work may go back and forth several times before an editor decides it's good enough to be published. When the nerve-wracking and exhilarating moment of publication occurs, writers can thank their lucky stars if their reviewers were thorough. Co-author Tina Fletcher admits to a record of seven review cycles before one of her manuscripts hit print.

NOTES

1. Meenakshi Agnihotri, "The Use of MOOCS to Change the Teaching of Literature Retrieval," *Integrated Journal for Research in Arts and Humanities* 2, no. 1 (2022): 11–15, https://doi.org/10.55544/ijrah.2.1.8.

2. Terrence E. Young, "Keeping the Arts Alive: Fine Arts Databases," *School Library Journal* 51, no. 2 (February 1, 2005), https://eric.ed.gov/?id=EJ710517.

3. Matthew Wall, "Wikipedia Editing Rules in a Nutshell," BBC News, April 22, 2015, https://www.bbc.com/news/technology-32412121.

A Closing Note

Start Your Own Band

The year is 1982. Francis Chen, co-author of this book, is a young punk rocker living in Austin, Texas. He sports dozens more safety pins in his shirt and slightly more hair than he does today. Francis is out for a riotous night of listening (and moshing) to live punk music at exactly the type of bar where you would never take your parents. As the band finishes their final song, over the buzzing of the guitar amp, the lead singer shouts to the crowd, "Did you like this music? Okay, then start your own band!"

It is with this punk rock spirit that we encourage you to build programs and resources for neurodiverse communities. It may seem that art museums—with their pristine galleries, sport coat–wearing security staff, and long lists of posted rules—couldn't be further away from the grungy and rebellious genre of punk. However, the staff of cultural institutions and punk rockers share a few essential characteristics: a fighting spirit, scrappiness, and a do-it-yourself attitude. Necessity may be the mother of invention, but necessity combined with a lack of resources is the mother of the punk, DIY mind-set.

The necessity to opening your doors to neurodiverse populations should be obvious. For a neurodivergent visitor, the necessity is simple: equitable access to life-enriching experiences and opportunities. For your cultural institution, the necessity is directly linked to its continued existence. To succeed, or even endure, cultural institutions must be relevant and responsive to the needs and desires of their public. You understand the necessity and are fired up to create change. You may even be moshing on the inside. But, as is common in most nonprofits and cultural institutions, you may feel that you do not have the resources you need to be successful.

Did young punk musicians have the backing of big record labels and the resources that accompany them? No. But they had fanzines printed on Xerox copiers, self-recorded promo tapes passed from friend to friend, T-shirts handmade by kids in favor of their favorite band, and underground music venues. And despite the band's lack of polished promotion, did antiestablishment youth turn up in droves to dingy basement bars to hear them? Absolutely. What the punk community had was more valuable than money; they had the power to create their own identity within a network of like-minded individuals.

Does your institution have an excess of staff time or financial resources? Do you consider yourself an expert in neurodiversity? The answer is probably no. Within this book, however, you have witnessed how a resourceful group of passionate people came together to create something larger than themselves. We dug through the recycling bin for materials to create sensory calm-down bottles. We conducted evaluations with posterboard and dot stickers. We built sensory rooms out of refrigerator boxes and ice-fishing tents. We used guerrilla marketing techniques to spread the word about our events. We illustrated our own success stories and communication cards. And most important, we formed our own ragtag band of community members and experts who share a belief in the importance of access to arts and culture. With the advice humbly offered in this book, you too can create something big out of little more than passion combined with a DIY spirit. Do we consider our approach perfectly polished? No. But do neurodiverse communities show up in droves to experience what we have to offer? Absolutely.

Did you like this book? Okay, then start your own band.

Appendix A

Glossary

AASPIRE—The Academic Autism Spectrum Partnership in Research and Education is an international partnership comprising a variety of stakeholders. It focuses on creating guidelines for autism spectrum community research and modifying evaluation tools such as surveys for use by people with autism.

accommodations—Changes to the environment, curriculum, or equipment that helps a person with a disability access required educational content or complete assignments. Accommodations can help students to pursue regular schoolwork, and fall into four categories: presentation, response, setting, and timing and scheduling. Examples: adjusting lighting or reducing noise in an educational setting, pairing written with verbal instructions, and allowing scheduled time for breaks.

accessibility—Quality of a program or environment that allows safe and easy use while maintaining the dignity of a person with a disability. The Americans with Disabilities Act conceptualizes this as related to a site, facility, place of work, service, or program. A classic example is wheelchair use. It must be possible for a person using a wheelchair or other assistive mobility device to have safe and fair access to venues and programs in order for them to be considered accessible.

andragogy—Developed by Malcolm Knowles, it is the method and practice of teaching adult learners, also known as adult education. For more information, see Anne Hartree, "Malcolm Knowles' Theory of Andragogy: A Critique," *International Journal of Lifelong Education* 3, no. 3 (1984): 203–10, DOI: 10.1080/0260137840030304.

Asperger's syndrome—A term formerly used to describe a form of autism spectrum disorder. In 2013, it became part of the diagnosis of autism spectrum disorder and is no longer a separate clinical term or diagnosis.

asynchronous—A program or resource that someone may access at a time of their choosing, rather than at a specific, scheduled time.

autism/autism spectrum disorder (ASD)—Autism spectrum disorder is a developmental disability that often causes difficulties with language, interpersonal communication, and social interaction. People on the autism spectrum may have specific sensory needs or aversions and may exhibit rigid patterns of thought, repetitive movements, and highly focused interest in specific topics or objects. ASD typically emerges by age two to three and does not have a known cause.

biomarker—A wide range of measurable substances in a living organism. Biomarkers can have molecular, histologic (tissue and cell), radiographic (X-ray), or physiologic (body function) characteristics. Common examples of biomarkers are those present when people have allergies or diseases like diabetes. Scientists are looking for autism biomarkers with the idea that autism care can be more personalized and specific if they are identified.

biosketch—Short for a biographical sketch. It documents a person's qualifications and experience for a role in a project. Biosketches usually have specific formats, but in general they contain the person's full name, birth date and place, background information, professional occupation, and major accomplishments, including publications, funded grants, honors, and awards. Biosketches are typically one paragraph long and range from fifty to three hundred words. They are commonly used in grant applications.

co-creation—Being part of an intentional relationship with the idea of making something together. It can be considered a collaboration and is usually to the benefit of both parties, instead of one person doing something for or to another person, such as teaching or treating them.

communication cards—a set of pictures or icons a visitor can use to show what they want, need, or have questions about.

database—In reference to library science, a database is an online collection of information. A database can be searched by library patrons or librarians.

Libraries buy subscriptions to databases to help learners or researchers find useful information.

deep pressure touch—Firm, gentle pressure applied to the body to relax the nervous system and create a feeling of well-being by releasing serotonin and dopamine, also referred to as the feel-good hormones. Examples of successful deep pressure touch include hugs, squeezing, stroking, and holding. The key is that the pressure is not so firm that it feels like restraint or being trapped.

desensitizing—A gradual exposure from the least to the most fear-provoking or noxious situation in order to decrease situational anxiety. Example: to overcome a fear of snakes, start with looking at a drawing, a picture, or a video, and finally going to a petting zoo or other controlled form of direct exposure.

disability—According to the Americans with Disabilities Act (ADA), disability can be thought of as a difference in a person's body or health status that creates problems fully engaging in an important aspect of life. While some definitions of disability are medical, the ADA definition is considered a legal term and differs from those of other agencies, such as the Social Security Administration. For more information, see https://adata.org/faq/what-definition-disability-under-ada.

dysregulation—Being unable to regulate metabolic, physiological, or psychological processes. Common examples related to neurodiversity include experiencing mood swings, having widely fluctuating emotions, and engaging in self-injury such as biting or hitting oneself.

equity—Fair treatment and access to information, education, the arts, health, and other aspects of society for all individuals and groups. Achieving equity often requires eliminating barriers or modifying systems that prevent full participation for some members of society.

exteroception—Perceiving sensations outside of the body, such as temperature and crowding.

fidget—While *fidgeting* is a process of making small movements when restless or nervous, a fidget is an object that can occupy someone's hands, usually in satisfying but purposeless ways, to help them focus, become calm, or regulate their emotions or behavior. They are also known as focus objects and calming toys. Examples include squeeze balls, bubble-popping keyrings, spinners, or twisting cubes.

fine and gross motor skills—*Fine motor* skills enable people to perform detailed functions, such as manipulating a pencil to make a drawing by using the small muscles of their body. *Gross motor* skills enable people to perform large movement functions, such as kicking a ball. Both types of motor skills require a person's ability to stabilize the core muscles of their body.

free appropriate public education (FAPE)—Not to be confused with the Foundation for Art and Preservation in Embassies (https://www.nga.gov/audio-video/audio/foundation-for-art-and-preservation-in-embassies.html), in an academic context, FAPE refers to a free appropriate public education for children ages three through twenty-one who live in the United States, including those with disabilities. This applies to activities that occur during and after school, such as field trips to museums. Under FAPE, the term "appropriate" means a student with unique needs is entitled to an individualized education program (IEP). For more information, see https://sites.ed.gov/idea/regs/b/b/300.101.

identity-first language—See *person-first language.*

Individuals with Disabilities Education Act (IDEA)—States must have procedures to ensure children have access to a least restrictive education environment, or LRE. This means children with disabilities must be educated with their nondisabled peers and should only attend special classes or have supplementary aids when regular education is impossible. For more information, see https://sites.ed.gov/idea/regs/b/b/300.114.

inclusion—Creating opportunities for all individuals or groups to participate in a given situation regardless of age, race, ability, or other factors. Inclusion is achieved when everyone feels welcome and their differences are respected and valued.

interoception—Perceiving sensations inside the body such as heartbeats, feelings of hunger or thirst, or respiration.

learning differences—The unique and individual ways in which students learn. This includes what motivates students, their interests, personal experiences, cultural backgrounds, and individual strengths and needs.

Likert scale—A numerical evaluation scale tool with choices ranging from one extreme to another, such as strongly agree to strongly disagree. Likert scales can be as small as an "agree/disagree" scale, ranging to much larger scales. The most commonly used scales are 4, 5, and 7 points. When the scale uses even numbers, the "neither agree nor disagree" option is removed and the scale is then known as a "forced choice" scale.

low-sensory—Sensory input that is minimized or has a low impact on a person's sensory system such as dimmed lighting, reduced volume, and lowered crowding.

meltdown—An anxiety-based response that comes from an unanticipated change of routine or subversion of expectations, manifesting in an emotional reaction that can include crying, anger, and showing fear.

metrics—Quantitative measures used to gauge the results of an action or progress toward a goal.

microcredentials—Certifications given to participants who complete specific training activities or develop portfolios to show competency in a specific subject.

modifications—Changes in an academic curriculum made for learners with disabilities who would not otherwise be able to understand what an instructor is teaching. Examples: using visual markers such as tape to designate boundaries, or modifying the length and content of assignments.

massive online open course (MOOC)—A free online distance learning program that may be offered in the same format as a university style course or be less structured. MOOCs may be available for credit, obtained with testing center results.

neuroatypical/neurotypical—A *neuroatypical* person is someone who does not meet social/emotional, gross and fine motor, language and communication, social, or cognitive developmental milestones as expected. A *neurotypical* person meets developmental milestones as expected.

neurodisorder—Neurological disorders are brain dysfunctions that impact perception, memory, planning, sensory perception, body use, emotionality, and personality, among others.

neurodiverse/neurodivergent—This term is sourced to Judy Singer, an Australian activist who held that autism is not a disorder but one of many ways that an individual's brain and functioning may develop that is equal to neurotypical people. Persons with attention-deficit/hyperactivity disorder, autism, dyslexia, and other neuro differences may fall under this umbrella term. Neurodivergent should be used to describe an individual, while neurodiverse describes a population or group of people.

neutral warmth—A temperature around 94–98 degrees Fahrenheit, or body temperature. This stimulates thermoreceptors and activates parasympathetic responses, which indicate to a person that they are safe and free from danger, and therefore able to "rest and digest." Usually, experiencing ten to twenty minutes of neutral warmth is enough for most people to relax.

nonverbal communication—The use of facial expressions, gestures of body and body limbs, pointing, and other gestures to supplement verbal communication where words may not be sufficient to express.

person-first language/identity-first language—*Person-first language* uses phrasing that prioritizes the individual rather than a condition that affects them. For example, "a person with autism" rather than "an autistic person." Some individuals may prefer *identity-first language*, which uses phrasing that starts with a condition or disability if they view being autistic as an integral part of who they are rather than as a disorder.

proprioception—A person's awareness of body, space, and movement. Proprioceptors are sensors in tendons that run parallel to muscles. They monitor active and passive joint movement, a sense of the body's position in space, and perceptions of muscle contractions. Having an accurate sense of proprioception contributes to planning and coordinating body movements. Proprioception combined with *vestibular* input helps a person maintain postural control, muscle tone, and body scheme. This results in a person being aware of their body without having to physically monitor it.

sensory-friendly/neuro-friendly—Programs or resources that are designed or adapted to meet the needs of participants who present with sensory processing sensitivities or disorders. This is commonly reported by autistic or neurodivergent people.

sensory modulation dysfunction or disorder—A diminished ability of the central nervous system to consistently respond to sensory stimuli with appropriate intensity and flexibility. May be seen as sensory overresponsivity, also called *sensory avoiding*, or sensory underresponsivity, also called *sensory seeking*.

sensory seeking/sensory avoiding—*Sensory seeking* describes people who seek out an increase in sensory input such as deep pressure in the form of hugs or the use of weighted vests and blankets. *Sensory avoiding* behavior may take the form of negative reactions to noises, bright lights, and avoiding light touches.

sensory processing—The process of interpreting and responding to stimuli after they are registered in sensory receptors. Related terms include sensory detection, sensory discrimination, habituation, sensory gating, neural modulation, stimuli binding, and multisensory integration.

sensory processing disorder (SPD)—Disorder characterized by difficulties organizing and responding typically or accurately to sensory input.

sensory space—A designated quiet room or secluded area where someone may remove themselves from a stressful or sensory-laden situation in order to become calm or self-regulate. Sometimes called a *deescalation space* or *sensory haven*. Sensory spaces emphasize the three "power senses" of deep pressure touch, proprioception, and vestibular stimulation to induce a relaxation response.

sensory slow route—A pathway through a space that provides limited sensory input such as lowered lighting and sound and crowding limits.

somatosensory system—Being able to detect sensations that occur anywhere in the body such as pain, temperature, or pressure. This contrasts with special sensory reception that occurs at one spot only, such as taste and temperature.

special education related services—Related services are used to help a student with a disability benefit from special education as related to a student's individualized education plan. They include speech-language pathology, psychological, physical and occupational therapy, orientation and mobility, and medical services for evaluation and treatment. Other services include health, nursing, social work, and parent counseling and training. These services contrast with medical services. An example includes a school-based occupational therapist who works to help children succeed in educational environments versus one who works to reduce medical challenges to everyday functions. For more information, see https://sites.ed.gov/idea/regs/b/a/300.34.

success story/Social Story—A document with words and/or pictures that walks someone through an experience so that they know what they might encounter and what behaviors are expected. The language used to script these stories is written in the first-person point of view, for example, "When I go to the museum, I know that there are rules about not touching what is on display. I will keep my hands at my sides or behind my back." *Social Stories*™ are trademarked by Carol Gray, who has a specific prescription for writing the stories.

stimming—A form of self-stimulation that may be evidenced as rocking or specific and repetitive movements of digits or limbs. This is typically identified in people diagnosed with autism spectrum disorder. Stimming should not be interpreted as a problematic behavior but as one couched in the context of self-soothing or in expressing excitement or positivity.

supports—Physical or human resources that help individuals with disabilities operate in a variety of contexts.

synchronous—A program or resource that someone must access during a specific, scheduled time, usually facilitated by staff or other instructors.

tip sheet—A short guide offering information in an easily digestible format, such as bullet points, numbered lists, or graphics.

universal design (UD)—The process of designing buildings, products, or environments in a way that makes them accessible to people, regardless of age, disability, or other factors. UD removes common barriers by creating things that can be used by everyone. Examples include curb cuts and wheelchair ramps.

universal design for learning (UDL)—An educational approach that accommodates the needs and abilities of all learners and eliminates unnecessary hurdles in the learning process. The three principles of UDL are to provide multiple means of representation, provide multiple means of action and expression, provide multiple means of engagement.

variant—A form of something differing from other forms of the same thing or from a standard. Examples include the words "colour" and "color," or having extra or different chromosomes, as in the case of Down syndrome.

vestibular system—Comprising sensors in the inner ear, the vestibular system is critical for maintaining posture, balance, equilibrium, and coordinating motor movements, including eye movements. It is involved in maintaining muscle tone and generating and executing motor movements in response to sensory stimuli.

visual-motor integration—Coordination of the visual and motor systems that is essential for paper and pencil tasks and to execute arm, leg, and body movements. Classic examples include producing good handwriting, being successful in sports, and being coordinated. Common difficulties include having difficulty playing sports that require ball-handling skills, being clumsy, and having a poor pencil grip.

wayfinding—The process of finding one's way through an environment or to a destination. Wayfinding materials may include signs, maps, or written directions.

Appendix B

Build Your Library
What's on Our Bookshelves

To learn more about **teaching with technology**:

Bowen, José Antonio. *Teaching Naked Techniques: A Practical Guide to Designing Better Classes.* San Francisco: Jossey-Bass, 2017.

Yes, yes, this is a nasty-sounding book, and the lime green cover doesn't exactly lend itself to being read discreetly, but it will be worth it if you are brave enough to wave it around. This publication is the companion workbook to the wildly popular *Teaching Naked* textbook. Of the two, the *Techniques* book seems to have more practical ideas and hands-on activities. The book has ample activities and is an easy, inspirational read. Readers should have a pad of sticky notes close by because it is worth marking pages for an extra read-through. And I have no idea where the title originated.

For a simple overview of **museum management** policies:

Boylan, Patrick J., ed. *Running a Museum: A Practical Handbook.* France: ICOM–International Council of Museums, 2004. https://icom.museum/wp-content/uploads/2018/07/practical_handbook.pdf

This e-book is described as an elementary manual that trainers and trainees can use in their education, for those who work in museums, and for those who are not directly connected to the museum industry. It is available in a number of languages and contains twelve chapters detailing professional and ethical standards for museums. Included in these are chapters on "Caring for the Visitor" and "Managing People." There are useful appendixes explaining key terms, further information, and the ICOM Code of Professional Ethics.

For a quick read and concise reference and idea book related to **online teaching**, see:

Darby, Flower, with James M. Lang. *Small Teaching Online: Applying Learning Science in Online Classes*. San Francisco: Jossey-Bass, Wiley & Sons, 2019.

This book provides a variety of evidence-based teaching strategies for creating effective online teaching modules. It is especially helpful for making quick adjustments to face-to-face programming resulting in new online versions of the same content. It also offers ideas for educators who want to create hybrid or blended learning opportunities.

To learn more about the **sensory system**:

Dunn, Winnie. *Living Sensationally: Understanding Your Senses*. London: Jessica Kingsley Publishers, 2005.

Dr. Winnie Dunn is an occupational therapist and researcher who explains the complex interactions between sensory processing and behavior. While many people have heard words like *sensory sensitivity* or *avoidance*, Dr. Dunn takes readers deeper into understanding everyday life experiences. This book is for individuals interested in studying their visitors' wants and needs.

To employ a tool that gives visitors the **motivation to follow expectations** such as those in success stories:

Gagnon, Elisa, and Brenda Myles. *The Power Cards Strategy 2.0*. Shawnee, KS: AAPC Publishing, 2016.

The strategy of using Power Cards was developed by Elisa Gagnon. This book ties in high-interest topics as motivators for neurodivergent children with expectations or ways to communicate. Although this is targeted at individual children, cultural institutions may gather what is generally popular with the students at the time they are considering implementing this strategy. In 2022, among the topics that many neurodivergent students prized were Pokémon, dinosaurs, and trains. An institution could tie in the skills of various Pokémon characters to the skills needed to navigate the space and seek help when anxious, among other considered uses.

To develop **skills in writing stories** for neurodivergent visitors:

Gray, Carole. *The New Social Story Book, Revised and Expanded 15th Anniversary Edition: Over 150 Social Stories That Teach Everyday Social Skills to Children and Adults with Autism and Their Peers*. Pearland, TX: Future Horizons, 2015.

If ever there was a DIY book about autism or neurodiversity events to have on the shelf, this is it. This book of Social Stories™ is bursting with helpful information and examples of creating and providing neurodivergent people with written and illustrated communications. Special educator Carole Gray offers a great way to stimulate thinking and jump-start cultural institutions in their program development. It is an easy read and well-designed. You will thumb through this book and turn the corners down for future reference rather than read it from cover to cover. https://carolgraysocialstories.com/.

To understand how **people with autism process information for communication** and develop your own method of communicating clearly to them:

Hadwin, Julie A., Patricia Howlin, and Simon Baron-Cohen. *Teaching Children with Autism to Mind Read*. West Sussex, UK: Wiley-Blackwell, 2013.

The authors discuss using the concept of *theory of mind*—a person's ability to understand someone else's perspective and what they are thinking or feeling—as the basis of helping a neurodivergent person improve their ability to understand and predict another's behavior. The book includes activities about perspective-taking and making judgments of self and others.

To appreciate a firsthand account of **what it is like to be autistic**:

Higashida, Naoki. *The Reason I Jump: The Inner Voice of a Thirteen-Year-Old Boy with Autism*. Toronto: Knopf Canada, 2013.

A Japanese boy with autism wrote this book. The book is small enough to fit in a purse or backpack, and the chapters are short enough to read over a coffee. Because Naoki is nonverbal, his story has extra value in reflecting what he and some counterparts cannot share with spoken words. The book does a beautiful job of humanizing people with autism who have atypical communication styles and provides plenty of food for thought for cultural institutions that seek to understand their audiences.

For strategies useful in **developing appropriate activities** for neurodivergent visitors:

Kranowitz, Carol Stock. *The Out-of-Sync Child: Recognizing and Coping with Sensory Processing Disorder*. New York: A Skylight Press Book/A Perigee Book, 2022.

This book is a gold standard for understanding sensory processing disorders. It's easy to read and has two excellent follow-up books: *The Out-of-Sync Child Grows Up*, and the *Out-of-Sync Child Has Fun*. In addition to helping parents and community members understand what sensory processing disorder is all about, the author provides exciting and entertaining suggestions for activities all children will find fun and engaging. In particular, the *Out-of-Sync Child Has Fun* is bursting with ideas to use in events.

To learn more about how to make **small changes in a learning environment** to improve instruction, see:

Lang, James M. *Small Teaching: Everyday Lessons from the Science of Learning*. San Francisco: Jossey-Bass, 2021.

Dr. Lang offers a series of adjustments and tweaks to content delivery and building a strong learning community using research evidence founded in cognitive theory. He provides relatable examples and teaching techniques that can be used in a variety of educational settings, including those in cultural institutions. The book is small and easy to carry in your bag or pocket.

To discover **why multilayered experiences are important and how to engage the senses, mind, and body of your visitors**:

Levant, Nina, and Alvaro Pascual-Leone. *The Multisensory Museum*. Lanham, MD: Rowman & Littlefield, 2014.

This book has it all—the research references to support why varied learning approaches are desirable, as well as some ways different museums implemented them and the pivotal feedback they received. It's an insightful and impactful compendium of perspectives with over thirty authors contributing.

For guidelines on how to **retool educational materials using universal design for learning (UDL)**:

Meyer, Anne, David H. Rose, and David Gordon. *Universal Design for Learning: Theory and Practice*. Wakefield, MA: CAST Professional Publishing, 2014.

There are tons of books on universal design for learning, but this book comes directly from the source: CAST, or what was once known as the Center for Applied Special Technology. The authors created the concept of UDL, and in this book they provide readers with myriad examples and offer a "dig deeper" section for those interested in getting to the heart of the matter. This book will provide multiple ways for community educators to assess and revamp their school field trip curricula and strategies to design educational materials for camps and other learning experiences. Inherent in the CAST methodology are strategies to provide learners with multiple ways to learn, engage with, and demonstrate their knowledge of content.

CAST design principles can keep this process simple and efficient. https://www.cast.org/.

For a clear picture of **treatment options for children with sensory processing disorders**:

Miller, Lucy Jane. *Sensational Kids: Hope and Help for Children with Sensory Processing Disorder (SPD)*. New York: TarcherPerigee, 2014.

Occupational therapist Dr. Lucy Jane Miller is a researcher who has devoted her career to understanding the four types of sensory processing disorders and gives general information on what it takes to diagnose the condition, select treatment strategies, and work with parents and occupational therapists. While community experiences aren't therapy sessions, this book can be helpful when agencies or institutions write grants. It demystifies sensory processing disorders and helps people use appropriate terminology. Dr. Miller's website is also beneficial. www.sensoryhealth.org.

To learn more about **developing accessible museum programs**:

Pressman, Heather, and Danielle Schulz. *The Art of Access: A Practical Guide for Museum Accessibility*. Lanham, MD: Rowman & Littlefield Publishers, 2021.

This handy book is densely packed with information about policies that drive inclusion movements for museums. The authors explain how to work with leaders in the field and practitioners from other disciplines, and how to evaluate physical and cognitive access in museums. Emphasis is on following tenets of universal design, showing examples of how museums adhere to these standards, and relating examples of museum success stories. This is a good starting point for any cultural institution wishing to understand and develop inclusive programs.

To **better understand the differences and the humanity** of neurodivergent people:

Sacks, Oliver. *An Anthropologist on Mars*. New York: Knopf Doubleday Publishing, 1996.

Oliver Sacks, a neurologist by training and a writer by talent, wrote of his meeting with Temple Grandin in the title essay "An Anthropologist on Mars." Sacks writes a brief summary of the history of autism, how the study and treatments of autism have changed over time, and then shares his time spent with Temple Grandin. Reading this section of *An Anthropologist on Mars* is a definite go-to!

For a comprehensive and engaging **history of autism**:

Silberman, Steve. *Neurotribes: The Legacy of Autism and the Future of Neurodiversity.* New York: Avery, an imprint of Penguin Random House, 2015.

In *Neurotribes*, Steve Silberman gives a caring and humanizing history of society's understanding of and misunderstandings around autism. Silberman goes beyond just explaining past medical misunderstandings to show how society has viewed autism, and how those changing views have impacted autistic people. Meticulously researched and written with great sensitivity, *Neurotribes* is a rallying call to embrace differences and a must-read for anyone looking to deepen their understanding of autism.

For one of the best pocket guides to **teaching strategies** on the market:

Svinicki, Marilla D., and Wilbert James McKeachie. *McKeachie's Teaching Tips: Strategies, Research, and Theory for College and University Teachers.* 14th ed. Belmont, CA: Wadsworth, Cengage Learning, 2014.

This book is a classic in its field, and the good news is that it is an easy read. While the title implies it is a book for college professors, hundreds, if not thousands, of ideas for good teaching are in this little book. One of its best features is the timeline approach they provide—from strategies for preparing for a class months in advance to ways of getting the ball rolling on day one of a class. This book can help community educators prepare for adult learners such as staff or faculty, and can provide ideas for teaching younger learners. Its small size is both a blessing and a curse; it will fit in a purse or backpack, but it might require the reader to put on a pair of cheaters to review the smaller-than-usual print. If the cost seems prohibitive, consider getting an earlier edition.

To better understand and communicate **expected social behaviors** to program participants:

Winner, Michelle Garcia, Pamela Crooke, and Kelly Knopp. *You Are a Social Detective! Explaining Social Thinking to Kids.* Santa Clara, CA: Think Social Publishing, 2016.

This illustrated book is frequently used in classrooms to help students develop social skills. As a museum educator, I found it equally helpful for learning how to effectively communicate expected behaviors in nonjudgmental terms. General rules of the art museum like "do not touch" are fairly easy to communicate, but other rules relating to social behavior like "do not stand directly in front of another person admiring a painting" frequently go unstated. This book will help educators understand the hidden or unstated rules of your institution that may be tricky for neurodivergent visitors and how to convey them in positive terms.

To learn about **conducting focus groups**:

Krueger, R. A. *Focus Groups: A Practical Guide for Applied Research*. Thousand Oaks, CA: Sage Publications, (2014).
    This textbook details the types of focus groups, how to prepare for them, conduct the group, and analyze the data. You'll also find information on telephone and Internet focus groups, along with cross-cultural considerations for multinational and cultural groups. This book will help cultural institutions conduct program evaluations and other more advanced qualitative or mixed-method research designs.

To learn about **aligning accessibility programs with the Americans with Disabilities Act (ADA)**:

National Endowment for the Arts. *Design for Accessibility: A Cultural Administrator's Handbook*. Washington, DC: National Assembly of State Arts Agencies, 2003. https://www.arts.gov/about/publications/design-accessibility -cultural-administrators-handbook.

Index

Page references for figures are italicized.

About the Authors

Emily Wiskera has worked in museum education since 2011, with a focus on accessibility. As interpretation specialist at the Dallas Museum of Art (DMA), Emily develops interpretive materials for collections and exhibitions. She was previously the DMA's senior manager of Access Programs and Resources, developing programs for visitors with dementia, Parkinson's disease, autism, cognitive disabilities, mobility disabilities, and those who are deaf, hard of hearing, blind or low vision. She has written extensively on autism programming and trauma-aware practices in museums. She is passionate about creating dynamic, equitable arts experiences that encourage visitors to create, reflect, share, and connect.

Anna Smith has nearly twenty years of experience in museum education and has been curator of education at Nasher Sculpture Center since 2011. She directs a team that strives to remove barriers to museum experiences for learners with a range of backgrounds and identities. Leading with an emphasis on collaboration, Smith participates directly in programming while upholding administrative aspects of the Education Department and serving on the museum's senior leadership team. Smith holds degrees in art history and museum education and has published and presented on modern and contemporary artists, the role of art in healthcare, and reaching homeschool audiences.

Tina Sue Fletcher is professor emeritus at Texas Woman's University and was a special education therapist in public schools. She has a research doctorate in curriculum design and master's degrees in figurative sculpture and allied health education. She has written over forty publications on autism, social participation, and creativity in occupational therapy, arts, and museum science journals, and book chapters on creativity, action research, and sensorimotor impairment in children. She has worked internationally as an autism program developer and was awarded Academic Educator of the Year by the Texas Occupational Therapy Association. She is an ad hoc reviewer for multiple museum journals.

Lynda Wilbur is manager of Access and Outreach Programs at Nasher Sculpture Center and has been creating meaningful museum experiences for over two decades. She initiated and expanded the museum's accessibility programs for neurodiverse, blind, and vision-impaired visitors, adults with cognitive disabilities, and children with life-threatening medical conditions. Wilbur seeks to foster a person's love of art and sense of belonging, whether at the museum or at a community event. She has published articles and presented at state and national conferences. Wilbur earned MA and MEd degrees and was honored with Southwest Airlines's Hospitality Champion Award for her museum work.

Francis Yong Chen (he/him/his) has been a professional in the field of school psychology since 1999. He works with a neurodiverse population from preschool to adults over eighteen in the school system, including students who are autistic. In this role, Chen works with the students directly and consults with parents and school faculty and staff. He offers parent training to give parents an understanding and working knowledge about neurodivergence. His passion is advocacy. He has co-authored articles in support of transgender and nonbinary youth and was awarded Outstanding School Psychologist of 2020 by the Texas Association of School Psychologists.